Great Streets _____

THE MIT PRESS   CAMBRIDGE, MASSACHUSETTS   LONDON, ENGLAND

THE MIT PRESS   CAMBRIDGE, MASSACHUSETTS   LONDON, ENGLAND

First MIT Press paperback edition, 1995

© 1993 Massachusetts Institute of Technology

This book was set in Bembo by DEKR Corporation and was printed and bound in the United States of America.

Library of Congress Cataloging-in-Publication Data

Jacobs, Allan B.
    Great streets / Allan B. Jacobs.
      p.   cm.
    Includes bibliographical references and index.
    ISBN-13: 978-0-262-10048-9 (HB), 978-0-262-60023-1 (PB)
    ISBN-10: 0-262-10048-7 (HB), 0-262-60023-4 (PB)
    1. Streets—Design.   2. Architecture—Human factors.   3. Urban beautification.   4. Pedestrian areas.   5. City planning.   I. Title.
NA9053.S7J23   1993
711'.41—dc20
                          93-22352
                            CIP

20 19 18 17 16 15 15 14 13 12 11 10

To Janet

To Matthew and Leslie

To Amy and Dominique

To Zachary and Daniel

CONTENTS _____

Acknowledgments   *viii*

An Introduction to Great Streets   *2*

PART ONE _____
Great Streets   *13*

CHAPTER ONE   *The Great Street We Once Lived On*   *15*
Roslyn Place, Pittsburgh

CHAPTER TWO   *Still Great Medieval Streets*   *20*
Via dei Giubbonari, Rome
Strøget, Copenhagen

CHAPTER THREE   *In the Grand Manner*   *35*
Paseo de Gracia, Barcelona
Cours Mirabeau, Aix-en-Provence
Avenue Montaigne, Paris
Boulevard Saint-Michel, Paris

CHAPTER FOUR   *The Grand Canal as a Great Street*   *63*

CHAPTER FIVE   *Once Great Streets*   *75*
Avenue des Champs-Elysées, Paris
Via del Corso, Rome
Market Street, San Francisco

CHAPTER SIX   *The Ramblas, Barcelona*   *93*

CHAPTER SEVEN   *The Great Residential Boulevard*   *100*
Monument Avenue, Richmond, Virginia

CHAPTER EIGHT   *Trees Alone*   *107*
Richards Road at Mills College, Oakland, California
Viale delle Terme di Caracalla, Rome
Beijing Streets

CHAPTER NINE   *Great Street Ensembles*   *115*
Bath
Bologna

PART TWO

A Compendium of Streets: Streets That Teach   *133*

PART THREE

Street and City Patterns: Settings for Streets and People   *201*

PART FOUR

Making Great Streets   *269*

CHAPTER ONE   *Requirements for Great Streets*   *270*

CHAPTER TWO   *Qualities That Contribute*   *293*

CHAPTER THREE   *Conclusion: Great Streets and City Planning*   *311*

Appendix: Pedestrian Volumes on Selected Streets   *316*

Notes   *318*

Index   *326*

On Stegel

Acknowledgments _____

Students have played a major role in my research and writing since the mid-1970s, and it has been the same with this work.

The genesis of this book was a studio course in Spring 1984 at the University of California, Berkeley. The subject was the Van Ness Avenue corridor in San Francisco, from Market Street to the bay. It had always seemed to me, and still does, that Van Ness Avenue could be a wonderful street, a tree-lined strolling street, a street lined with shops, apartments, offices and movies and restaurants. The Civic Center would be a major focus; so would the intersection with California Street, and so would the municipal pier at its end. The intersection with Market Street would be a great beginning. The ornate old auto showrooms on the street would fit right in. There aren't many good strolling streets in San Francisco and Van Ness Avenue was and is one of the few that could be. Our inquiries included a period devoted to finding models that could be used to inform us of what had been tried and had worked well over the years in other cities. We had no problem arriving at a list of streets that might help us, but finding information about them—real information like how wide they were, what was on them, the location and height of their buildings, tree spacing, paving patterns, and much more—was a harder and usually impossible task. Our collective memories and impressions, even sketches, were only modestly helpful, maybe better maybe worse than occasional photographs, usually taken from above. We couldn't put dimensions to our memories. At the same time, the little information that we did find was more than helpful, not to copy but to know what could happen in various-sized streets and to compare our memories and the streets we knew of, even though we might not have seen them, with the situation in which we were working. The students suggested that I ought to assemble such comparative information. That is where the idea of this book started.

Jill Benninghoven, Terry Bottomley, Judith Chess, Pat Eubanks, and Michael Freedman were the members of the studio that began this undertaking, and I thank them. In the years since, there have been many studios and seminars on streets. Some students became research assistants and they have helped in all the ways that colleagues can in an endeavor such as this. Cara Seiderman helped with early literature research and with the first extensive survey of design professionals to gain their thoughts about the best streets. Rajeev Bhatia, Michael Boland, Peter Calogero, Tom Ford, Jodi Ketelsen, Puja Kumar, Carl Maxey, Cheryl Parker, Yodan Rofé, Laura Shabe, and Rick Williams all contributed, particularly on the map and street plan graphics. The hand and thoughts of Bimal Patel are particularly and gratefully remembered. Bimal's involvement was the longest and the most intense. Beyond his intellectual and physical contributions, if there was an early "clerk of the works" on this book, someone to help with and keep track of all the graphics, it was Bimal. Peter Calogero did the same as we came to conclusion. Chris McDonald was an enormous help on the graphics, and I recall fondly the summer of 1991 when, preparing street plans, we thought of ourselves as the "stipple kings."

Beyond those particular students, many others over the years undertook team research papers in a course that I teach with Peter Bosselmann (a course started by Donald Appleyard), and much of that work has been helpful.

My colleague Peter Bosselmann has counseled me and reviewed the research and findings from the start, and I am most thankful. We have worked side by side on many projects over these past years, and this book is better than it would have been without him. Most particularly though, and most pleasant, we undertook interviews and did field research together and, in the doing, learned much about streets.

Jack Kent has reviewed the manuscripts of my previous books and he did so again with this one. Tom Aidala, Donlyn Lyndon, Jay Claiborne, and Peter Hall were all kind enough to do likewise and I am indebted to them. Donlyn and Jay were constant counsels on the work, as was Richard Bender. I have spent hours discussing the best streets with Jaime Lerner, particularly in his city, Curitiba, and his counsel has always been delightfully positive.

Pier Luigi Carci, Jan Gehl, Maurizio Marcelloni, Francesco Rossi, Carl Otto Schmidt, Giuseppi Campos Venuti, and Riccardo Wallach helped me with important information and shared their ideas. Lorenzo Bruno has always been available to advise me on graphics matters.

Kaye Bock has been a constant companion on all the drafts of the manuscript, and over the years has had many suggestions that have helped. Anne MacNeil and Amy Jacobs-Colas helped me mightily with the final drafts.

During the period of the book preparation, I was assisted by grants from the Committee on Research of the University of California at Berkeley, The National Endowment for the Arts, the Fleishhacker Foundation, and the American Academy in Rome, whose hospitality I also enjoyed. The faculty of Berkeley's Department of Landscape Architecture, through the Beatrix Farrend Fund, contributed to the quality of the publication. I thank them all.

Acknowledgments

Great Streets _____

Some streets are better than others: to be on, to do what you came to do. Boulevard Saint-Michel, in Paris, lined with stores, book tables, and cafes in similarly sized buildings covered with dancing light, is a much more pleasant street to be on than is Market Street, in San Francisco, which is somehow uncomfortable as either a walking or a driving street. Princes Street, in Edinburgh, with buildings and stores on one side that look across to a park and to the old city and castle on the hill beyond, is more compelling than Regent Street, in London, regardless of the latter's unified architectural expression and dramatic crescent at Piccadilly Circus. Both were intended to be great streets. Roslyn Place, in Pittsburgh, a short cul-de-sac with large trees and red brick houses, with no pretensions to specialness, is better to be on and certainly to live on than are countless suburban residential streets the world over. The Merritt Parkway, in Connecticut, was always more pleasant to drive along than the Ohio Turnpike, but the old Ohio red brick, tree-lined country highways that crackled as tires moved over the loose but level bricks were better still.

You go back to some streets more often than to others, and not just because the things you do or have to do are more centered on one than another. Maybe you focus a part of your life more on one street for reasons not necessarily economic or functional. Maybe a particular street unlocks memories or offers expectations of something pleasant to be seen or the possibility of meeting someone, known or new; the possibility of an encounter. I would rather drive on local streets to reach my home from downtown than take the freeways. There is more to interest me, to catch my eyes, though the trip is longer. Fifth Avenue, in New York, from Rockefeller Center to Central Park, has more to commend it than does the Avenue of the Americas (Sixth Avenue) over the same distance. Fifth Avenue is not what it once was—the glitz and size of the Trump Tower cannot compare in elegance with the detailed, modest-scaled limestone buildings that once characterized it—but there is a better sense of enclosure and there are more interesting things to see than the set-back monoliths of the Avenue of the Americas and their unwelcoming forecourts. It is possible to recall some streets, what they feel like and look like and the things to do on them, and to anticipate how pleasant it might be to spend time along them.

This book is about great streets, some of the best streets in the world. More particularly, it is about the physical, designable characteristics of these best streets. The book is also about street patterns as the physical contexts for urban living and as the settings for streets, great and otherwise.

A major purpose of this book is to provide comparable information about the physical qualities of the best streets—plans, cross sections, dimensions, details, patterns, urban contexts—for designers and urban decision makers to refer to in their work. Some people will want to decide about the best streets for themselves, and not rely on the experienced judgment of others. What is needed regardless, beyond an understanding of what is likely to be necessary to make a great street, is information about many of them. That information will be more useful if it is in a form that permits comparisons of different streets in terms of their most important physical qualities. In considerable measure this book is directed to that objective, to providing that information so that people might decide for themselves. Beyond presentation and analysis of the best streets, plan and section drawings are provided for many other streets as well, always presented at the same scale to permit comparisons and to facilitate understanding. But the objectives of the book go beyond providing knowledge and understanding, important as these may be. With knowledge at hand, the overriding objective is to help make future great streets—streets where people will want to be.

Roles of Streets in Urban Life _____

In exuberance, after an afternoon on Strøget in Copenhagen (or on the Ramblas in Barcelona, or Monument Avenue in Richmond, or any of a hundred others, preferably close to home), one might exclaim, "Oh, that was a great afternoon! Strøget is a great street!" It is in that sense that the best streets are called "great." Dictionary definitions such as "notably large in size, huge," or "large in number," or "aristocratic, grand," will be discarded here in favor of "eminent, long continued, distinguished, remarkable in . . . degree or effectiveness, remarkably skilled," or "used as a general term of approval." Most particularly, great streets are those that are "markedly superior in character or quality."[1]

Streets are more than public utilities, more than the equivalent of water lines and sewers and electric cables, which, interestingly enough, most often find their homes in streets; more than linear physical spaces that permit people and goods to get from here to there. These may be the primary or only reasons for a few public ways, toll roads, freeways, turnpikes, but only a very few, and we will not be concerned with them here. Communication remains a major purpose of streets, along with unfettered public access to property, and these roles have received abundant attention, particularly in the latter half of the twentieth century. Other roles have not.

Streets moderate the form and structure and comfort of urban communities. Their sizes and arrangements afford or deny light and shade, as anyone who has experienced Phoenix and Philadelphia, Bologna and Barcelona, or Udaipur and Chandigarh will attest. They may have the effect of focusing attention and activities on one or many centers, at the edges, along a line, or they may simply not direct one's attention to anything in particular. The three streets that lead from the Piazza del Popolo in Rome, Via del Corso in the center, give focus to that city as does nothing else. So do Market Street in San Francisco, a hundred Main Streets in small cities across the United States, and Nevsky Prospekt in St. Petersburg.

In a very elemental way, streets allow people to be outside. Barring private gardens, which many urban people do not have or want, or immediate access to countryside or parks, streets are what constitute the outside for many urbanites; places to be when they are not indoors. And streets are places of social and commercial encounter and exchange. They are where you meet people—which is a basic reason to have cities in any case. People who really do not like other people, not even to see them in any numbers, have good reason not to live in cities or to live isolated from city streets. The street is movement: to watch, to pass, movement especially of people: of fleeting faces and forms, changing postures and dress. You see people ahead of you or over your shoulder or not at all, absorbed in whatever has taken hold of you for the moment, but aware and comforted by the presence of others all the same. It is possible to stand in one place or to sit and watch the show. The show is not always pleasant, not always smiles or greetings or lovers hand in hand. There are cripples and beggars and people with abnormalities, and, like the lovers, they can give pause: they are reasons for reflection and thought. Everyone can use the street. Being on the street and seeing people, it is possible to meet them, ones you know or new ones. Knowing the rhythm of a street is to know who may be on it or at a certain place along it during a given period; knowing who can be seen there or avoided. Or the meeting can be by chance and for a split second but immensely satisfying. To be walking on the Via Arenula in Rome, not a particularly fine street, and to hear "Hello, Allan" shouted from a passing bus and to recognize Maurizio and to wave in return to his window-constrained flapping forearm is to feel greeted and welcomed, to be part of something larger than oneself. As well as to see, the street is a place to be seen. Sociability is a large part of why cities exist and streets are a major if not the only *public* place for that sociability to develop. At the same time, the street is a place to be alone, to be private, to wonder what it was once like, or what it could be like. It is a place for the mind to wander, triggered by something there on the street or by something internal, more personal, a place to walk while whatever is inside unfolds, yet again.

Some streets are for exchange of services or goods; places to do business. They are public showcases, meant to exhibit what a society has to offer, and to entice. The entrepreneur offers the goods, displays them, comes out onto the street as much as will be allowed, with wares to be seen. The looker sees, compares, fingers, discusses with a companion, and ultimately decides whether to enter the selling environment or not, whether to leave the anonymity and protection of the public realm and enter into private exchange.

The street is a political space. It's on Elm Street that neighbors discuss zoning or impending national initiatives, and on Main Street, at the Fourth of July parade as well as the antinuclear march, that political celebrations take place. Marshall Berman, speaking of Nevsky Prospekt in his wonderful book *All That Is Solid Melts into Air,* observes, "The government could monitor but it could not generate the actions and interactions that took place here. Hence the Nevsky emerged as a kind of free zone in which social and political forces could spontaneously unfold. . . . For one fleeting moment, Petersburgers had a taste of political confrontation in the city streets. These streets had been political spaces." Later he considers the street as a place where personal and political life flow together.[2] Whether as a meeting ground for the development and exchange of ideas and hopes or as a stage for demonstration and mass expression, the public street is a special political space, most difficult to control, as important in the playing-out of people's most cherished ideals as the piazza or public square. No wonder, if intrigue stories are to be believed, that spies meet on streets (and in parks). It is not terribly easy to pass out nonmainstream ideas in a shopping mall, much less to have a demonstration in one. Lest we minimize the importance of the public street as a political place in favor of more up-to-date electronic methods of communication, recall where the demonstrations and actions and marches of the late 1980s took place in eastern Europe: in public places and most especially in streets.

The people of cities understand the symbolic, ceremonial, social, and political roles of streets, not just those of movement and access. Regularly, if they are aware of what is being planned, they protest widenings as well as new streets, particularly if those improvements will mean dislocation of people or more traffic in their neighborhoods. They object to high volumes of fast traffic on their streets. On the other hand, proposals to improve existing streets, to make them special, "great" places, are common and are regularly approved by voters who tax themselves to achieve this end. Over two-thirds of the voters of San Francisco agreed, in 1967, to spend $24.5 million—a lot of money then—to make Market Street into a great street. It was not to buy or tear down properties or to build buildings, but to make the street beautiful. And it was to be designed to accommodate parades. Time and again, the city has asserted that Market Street should be a great street. Other cities do the same. Chicago, Denver, Minneapolis, Santa Cruz, Sacramento, Toledo, Iowa City are but a few of hundreds of large and small cities that have only recently been concerned with the design of important streets.

There have been times when streets were a primary focus of city building—streets rather than individual buildings. There was an array of reasons for creating the arcaded walks along the streets of Bologna. Over time they have become a hallmark of that city, much beloved and understood to add immensely to its livability. On such streets the facades of most structures are hardly seen, so it is the street, not individual buildings, that prevails. The French preoccupation with making streets the focus of city design during the late nineteenth century, and the rigid building requirements they instituted to insure urban complementarity, are still in evidence. Though the making of those streets may have been achieved in large part by dislocating the poor (this was not always the case), many of the best streets derive from that period. These designers did what they set out to do. By contrast, the last half of the twentieth century has been more concerned with the preciosity or "preciousness" of individual properties, unique signature buildings of their designers and owners, and that, too, shows.

It is not surprising that, given their multiple roles in urban life, streets require and use vast amounts of land. In the United States, from 25 to 35 percent of a city's developed land is likely to be in public rights-of-way, mostly in streets. The percentages may be more varied in European cities, but the amounts are always significant. Streets are almost always public: owned by the public, and when we speak of the public realm we are speaking in large measure of streets. What is more, streets change. They are tinkered with constantly: curbs are changed to make sidewalks narrower or (in fewer cases) wider, they are repaved, lights are changed, the streets are torn up to replace water and sewer lines or cables and again repaved. The buildings along them change and in doing so change the streets. Every change brings with it the opportunity for improvement. If we can develop and design streets so that they are wonderful, fulfilling places to be, community-building places, attractive public places for all people of cities and neighborhoods, then we will have successfully designed about one-third of the city directly and will have had an immense impact on the rest.

A Focus on Physical, Designable Qualities —————————————————————————

Immediately, when searching for the best or most important physical street arrangements in an urban setting, one must contend with the frequent assumption that what is being asserted is that physical design, either alone or primarily, makes the street the great or fine place that it is, and with the reality that such an assertion can hardly be proved. Indeed, some will argue that the physical design of the street, or of almost anything in the urban environment, has little to do with its goodness, and that social and economic characteristics are the crucial variables. That may well be so, but it begs the question. Streets still have to be laid out and designed, and nondesigners at least as much as designers are concerned with their physical as well as their socioeconomic development.

The interplay of human activity with the physical place has an enormous amount to do with the greatness of a street. It is difficult or impossible to separate the two, and few try. Fewer still give descriptions of the actual physical nature of the street upon which human activities—from the most ordinary to the most spectacular—unfold. As Berman promises, Gogol, in "Nevsky Prospekt," magnificently describes the rhythms, activities, illusions, mysteries, enticements, and dangers of that street, but there is little of the physical street itself. Berman helps us by placing the street in the city and giving some important details such as its length, some of the buildings to be found there, the perspectives to be taken from its bridges, and the ever present focal point of the Admiralty Tower. He interprets for us the relationship of the street itself to the larger picture of urban life and of modernism.[3] His analysis is as penetrating as one can find, but we still know too little about the street, how wide it is, how tall the buildings are, whether there are trees, where along its great length there is most intense development, and how these relate, if they do, to the human activities that take place, or to the memories of it being special. Carl Schorske, in his work on the Vienna Ringstrasse, is enlightening in his account of its history in relation to the sociopolitical dynamics of the late nineteenth century, to the expansion of the city from its historic core, to the nature of buildings along it, and particularly to the design of its landmark buildings.[4] The emergence of modernism as expressed in the conflicting ideologies of Sitte and Wagner help explain the nature of what is on the Ringstrasse, but, again, there is little that tries to relate uses and general human activity with the details of street design.

In response to a survey of design professionals aimed at finding out what, in their experience, it takes *physically* to produce the best streets, architect Dolf Schnebli focuses on the difficulty at the same time that he avoids the question. He writes:

The greatest streets are in our mind—the street where I would . . . encounter you in discussion with Socrates, waiting for Pallas Athena to show me the caffe in which I could find Sartre discussing with Corbusier, Melville having a beer with Faulkner, etc., etc.

And he goes on:

A good urban street is always good in a context. Its goodness can change—if Hitler is in charge of the city, all streets are bad. . . . To eat in a beautiful space is nice, but if the food is bad, I prefer good food to an ugly place. I prefer good food in a beautiful place. But bad service may destroy the whole thing. Therefore the best—good food, good space, good service, good company. We could go on.[5]

For Schnebli, then, it would seem that the quality of the space or place is less critical than other factors; the political system, food, service, etc. Fine, but that begs the question. What constitutes the beautiful space where the good or bad food is eaten? Some people might have avoided the Kurfürstendamm in Berlin during the 1930s and 1940s and other streets as well because of their distaste for who might be seen there, but did it sour for all time their memory or enjoyment of the street? To be sure, it is a complicated matter, and political, economic, and social realities, memories, images, desires, whether or not the sun is shining, personal values, and feelings of the moment may be the most telling determinants of the ascendancy of one place over another. Even Schnebli, who, like others, is reluctant at the beginning to say what makes a great street and says, in effect, that "it all depends," ends up by saying that the best—"good food, good service, good company"—includes a component of "good space." It is the good space components, whatever the circumstances, that are of primary interest in this inquiry.

Even assuming that the physical characteristics of the street are not an important criterion for deciding what makes one street better than another, one presumably wants to do one's best to design and arrange the pieces in ways that will be better, that are more likely to please, uplift, attract, or achieve a desired set of values than some other arrangement. It does no good for someone faced with determining the width of a street, the sizes of walks, whether or not there should be trees or benches and where they should be placed, and a host of other possible considerations, to demur and to say that these considerations don't much matter. Even if they didn't much matter, the possibility that they might matter at all raises the question for better or for worse. And how, in the end, does one decide where to put the trees or if there should be any at all? Of course it matters. People frequent and enjoy some streets more than others, for physical reasons as well as for the activities or calm to be found there. We come back to the design of streets.

Criteria for Great Streets _____

Given the difficulty of pinpointing the physical qualities that make certain streets stand out over others, and the fact that different people might come to the question differently, it seems important to be reasonably clear as to what the practical criteria for such streets might be. What is it that a great street should *do*?

First and foremost, a great street should help make community: should facilitate people acting and interacting to achieve in concert what they might not achieve alone. Accordingly, streets that are accessible to all, easy to find and easy to get to, would be better than those that are not. The best streets will be those where it is possible to see other people and to meet them; all kinds of people, not just of one class or color or age. The criterion would work at many geographic scales, from citywide to neighborhood, which opens the possibility of *types* of great streets. Great neighborhood streets would be the foci for people of a smaller geographic area than of a city, conceivably an area as small as the street itself. A great street should be a most desirable place to be, to spend time, to live, to play, to work, at the same time that it markedly contributes to what a city should be. Streets are settings for activities that bring people together.

A great street is physically comfortable and safe. A great street might be cooler, more shady than another street on a hot summer day and therefore more pleasant to be on. There would be no sudden, unexpected gusts of wind off buildings. If there are many people there should not be so many as to make it difficult or uncomfortable to walk; it should not provoke a sense of confinement. Physical safety is another matter, and it can mean many things; but the general concern is relatively straightforward. One shouldn't have to worry about being hit by a car or truck or about tripping on the pavement or about some other physical thing built into the street being unsafe. Lurking human threats to safety? Robbers and muggers? No, that is not the subject here: no recommendations for doing away with trees or permitting only small trees to discourage molesters, no prohibition of set-back entryways that can hide thieves. Light, by all means, to see the way and to see others, and ramps rather than steps where helpful for the comfort and safety of the handicapped and elderly, but no sanitizing of streets to avoid societal misfits.

The best streets encourage participation. People stop to talk or maybe they sit and watch, as passive participants, taking in what the street has to offer. Demonstrations are possible. For over 15 years on the main street of Curitiba, Brazil, a long, long strip of paper has been laid on the pavement every Saturday morning, held down by wooden sticks every meter or so, thereby creating hundreds of individual white paper surfaces. Children that come are offered a brush and paint, and they do pictures as parents and friends watch. Social or economic status is not a requirement for joining in, only desire. Participation in the life of a street involves the ability of people who occupy buildings (including houses and stores) to add something to the street, individually or collectively, to be part of it. That contribution can take the form of signs or flowers or awnings or color, or in altering the buildings themselves. Responsibility, including maintenance, comes with participation.

The best streets are those that can be remembered. They leave strong, long-continuing positive impressions. Thinking of a city, including one's own, one might well think of a particular street and have a desire to be there; such a street is memorable.

Finally, the truly great street is one that is representative: it is the epitome of a type; it can stand for others; it is the best. To have achieved that status, it will have been put together well, artfully.

Determining criteria for the best streets is one thing. Knowing when they are present may be another. Elements of comfort can be objectified more readily than others, although even that task is often difficult. The query, however, is worthwhile. The answer requires a constant search for objectivity, both in the criteria and in the qualities that meet them. It means relying on the judgments and opinions of others, experts and people who use streets, and it includes comparisons of streets, made as objectively as possible. Ultimately, large doses of experience and judgment are involved, and an understanding that the best of the best are likely to involve some magic as well.

Arbitrariness is everywhere in endeavors such as these. People will differ, not only in interpreting hard-to-define criteria, but in setting these criteria from the start and in their personal experiences of any given street. Why should streets rather than plazas or squares be the most important focus of making community? Or, "I was mugged on the Ramblas—why is it great?" Great for what? Great for where? Great when? These are all questions that can make our conclusions somewhat blurred. "Greatest or best for what?" is a frequent response to a question I often ask, "What, for you, is the greatest (or best) street in the world?" One may understand the question however one likes, but it is important to remember that the concern here is with cities and their best streets. Within cities, there are different kinds of streets: for living, for shopping, for working, for walking or driving, for leisure, or for any number of other activities or combinations. It remains to be seen whether or not the physical characteristics that make a great residential street are significantly different from those of a shopping street. As to "when?," exit a concert at the Cancelleria in Rome on a dark, cold, rainy spring Saturday night and proceed along the Via dei Giubbonari, past cars that shouldn't be parked there, through puddles, dodging moving cars that aren't normally encountered on that street, past darkened, grilled-over store windows, and the street is not particularly pleasant and hardly one to be emulated. Please, won't you try it almost any other time, when its shape and its changing directions, its beginnings and endings, and its buildings with their various uses have a chance to work their ways with you, overcoming even darkness and rain?

"But have you ever seen such and such a street?" is the most difficult question, because no one, try as one might, has seen them all. To read Marshall Berman on Nevsky Prospekt and to go back to some of his sources is to want to see it in person. How could someone write so beautifully about a street unless it was great? Knowing friends tell me it is a great street. But getting to it and to all of the others is never really possible. Great streets that I have not yet explored are not in this book.

In the end, some arbitrariness has to be accepted. Long surveys of professionals and of ordinary people on streets, as much field research as possible to test hypotheses, literature examinations, collegial advice, and the assembling of as much information as possible through maps and field visits and measurements all help diminish arbitrariness, but judgment remains.

Settings for Great Streets _____

All streets have settings, in street patterns and blocks and, at a finer scale, amidst buildings and spaces. Maybe it is the contrast of one street with surrounding ones, in size or direction or shape, or in the nature and size of the buildings that are found on it, that sets the one street apart and makes it special. Perhaps a unique location is the critical ingredient to some best streets. It is well, then, to be familiar with the settings of the streets that are of interest. We will find, as well, that these settings are important in themselves. They are enormously different one from another, in their patterns, the sizes and shapes of their blocks, the amount of space that they consume, and in their relative complexity. Like individual streets, these settings change, too, over time. Boston's downtown street pattern in the late 1900s is strikingly different from what it was in the late 1800s. The changed pattern of buildings and spaces over the area is equally dramatic. Urban settings, both at the scale of streets and blocks and of buildings and spaces, are also the settings of people's lives. As much as individual streets, they contribute to the making or nonmaking of community, to the relative ease with which people may have contact with each other, to accessibility and focus. So discussion of urban physical settings makes up a significant part of this book. As with individual streets, street and block patterns are more or less measurable urban makers and changers; designers and tinkerers should know them, as the settings for great streets and in their relations to each other.

There is magic to great streets. We are attracted to the best of them not because we have to go there but because we want to be there. The best are as joyful as they are utilitarian. They are entertaining and they are open to all. They permit anonymity at the same time as individual recognition. They are symbols of a community and of its history; they represent a public memory. They are places for escape and for romance, places to act and to dream. On a great street we are allowed to dream; to remember things that may never have happened and to look forward to things that, maybe, never will.

The search here is for those physical elements most likely to make urban streets places where the magic can happen. In that search, we will look first, in Part One, at some particularly great streets, the finest of their types, and will try to understand what it is that makes them so. Along the way we will digress to consider some no-longer-great streets and to explore why their status has changed. Next, understanding that a handful of streets cannot in themselves embody all the information that students and professionals or lay designers want at their fingertips when they make or change streets, a compendium of streets will be presented and discussed in Part Two. The plans and cross sections of all these streets are drawn at the same scale, to enable visual comparisons. Field notes and as much comparable data as possible for these streets are included. Part Three presents street and block patterns in the form of square mile maps as well as plans of urban buildings and space arrangements, each at scales that permit comparisons. In Part Four we will see that some answers are possible: from the study of both great and not-so-great streets and from the street and block patterns, what can we say about physical, designable things that are most likely to produce great streets? Finally, a designer will know and understand that there is an open end: magic.

PART ONE   *Great Streets*

Roslyn Place

A.B.J. '91

Roslyn Place, Pittsburgh

Step into Roslyn Place and you are likely to sense, immediately, that you are indeed in a *place,* a special place, a handsome place, a safe place, a welcoming place, a place where you might wish to live. First though, you have to see it, to know that it is there, which will happen easily if you are moving along Ellsworth Avenue, just east of Van Aiken Boulevard. Your eyes will be drawn into the street. It is different from other streets, enough so that you will want to pause, to step in, to see what it is like. People do that. At times, on a Saturday or Sunday afternoon, a strolling couple is likely to ring a doorbell and tell whoever answers that they were just passing, were attracted to the street and houses, and wish to know if the houses are as nice inside as they seem from the walk ("we like them" comes the answer), if they are privately owned ("yes"), if there are any for sale ("not just now"), if they often come on the market ("occasionally"), and if it would be possible to be contacted if ever one does?

Roslyn Place is small, and buildings and landscape are arranged so that there is enclosure, a space. From Ellsworth, at its start, past the metal gate posts that you might or might not notice, to the four two-and-one-half-story, red brick, wood trim, pitched-roofed townhouses that end it, Roslyn Place is about 250 feet long. There are fourteen more dwellings in the other nine tightly grouped buildings that line the narrow street and sidewalks. Each dwelling has a small front yard. The space created can be likened to an out-door room some 65 feet by 250 feet. The walls of the room are the brick houses. The ceiling is made from the branches of the large sycamores in front of each house, and from the sky. And in this analogy the small spaces between buildings that lead to rear yards are the windows and doors. The houses are of the same height, and though they may look alike at first glance, there are in fact five architectural variations.

Roslyn Place is a well-defined, intimately scaled street of solidly built structures similar in appearance. But it is more than that. It is physically comfortable. The best images are of the spring, summer, and fall when the full-leaved sycamores give shade and are dappled with sun. The street is cool when you most want it to be. In winter, if sun is to be had, it will get to the street for at least part of every day, through the leafless branches.

Narrowness and enclosure and intimacy bring a feeling of safety to Roslyn Place. There are no garages and cars have to park on the street, on both sides, leaving only one narrow traffic lane in the center. One doesn't drive fast on a street like that. A kid, even a young kid, goes outside to the street

Roslyn Place, Pittsburgh: plan and section

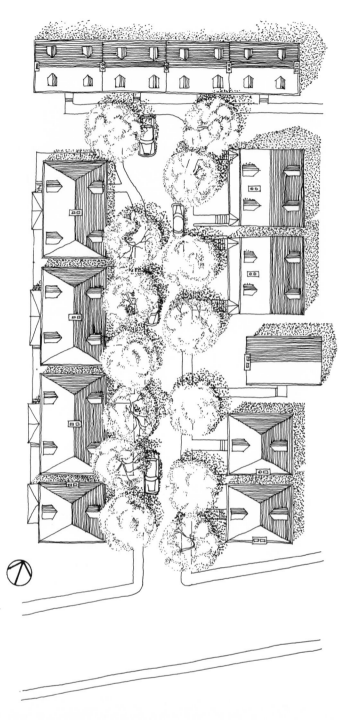

Approximate scale: 1″ = 50′ or 1:600

to play or to meet another kid and a parent can feel safe, as much as a parent ever can. "Stay on our street" is all the kids have to know. On a winter weekend morning, early, before parents would like to get up, sure, it's okay for Amy, age six, to try sledding with neighbor Susie in the center of the street. And then there are all those windows facing the street, and even if all the blinds are drawn one knows someone is behind them, not far away, present.

When it is easy to see people, when you almost can't avoid it, then it can be easy to know them. Here all of the distances are short. It is only 45 feet from a house window or door to the sidewalk across the street, and from the center house of the street to each end is about 120 feet; these are distances that permit recognition of faces. Looking from one end of the street, a person's form and shape and body movements are recognizable, even if facial features are indistinct. More important, in a small space, there are 18 doors that people walk into and out of, so people pass each other and each knows where the other lives. They say "hello" at least, and often more. And there are windows to attract attention, especially if someone is moving inside. Most walks, to rear yards, are shared walks, so at the very least one must deal with a neighbor. Parking is tight, so you have to deal with neighbors over that, too. Recognition, discussion, communication, community are encouraged by the nature of the street.

On a Saturday morning in the spring, Izzy Cohen, chemist, scientist, is screaming at the retired butcher who parked last night where Izzy usually parks and who did it in such a way as to take up two spaces. The butcher responds; together they move up and down the street between their houses. From the house stoops, raised above the street, there's a good view. Violence is threatened, if not now, surely next time—if there is one. The shouting will end and, later, more intimate discussions of what went on and why will take place in small knots of two or three neighbors. Surely Izzy will want to explain to each group what happened. The butcher doesn't speak. He is a quiet man. Solitude, if you want it, is also possible, but it is more difficult to find than social intercourse. In the morning someone will sweep a walk, others will garden, people will come and go. Maybe a date will be made for coffee later or for dessert after dinner. At some point, maybe in the late morning, certainly in the afternoon, some of Curly Steiner's kids, maybe Curly himself, will work on the big, black, old family Cadillac, like they have been working regularly for the last three years. A mystery, for on most days the car itself is usable.

Roslyn Place can be quiet in the afternoons. Some kids may be playing or talking, but parents are more likely to be inside or in the privacy of small rear yards. On a weekday there is some activity. Maybe some shooting the breeze late in the afternoon when people come home from work, but then, in the evening, there is quiet.

It would be hard to build another Roslyn Place today. Rules and officialdom wouldn't permit it. There's no off-street parking, the street is too narrow (how would you get a fire truck to the end?), and the houses are too close together (side walls only three to four feet apart), so the side windows are too close, no privacy, to name only three transgressions to efficiency, safety, and a reasonable quality of life. But those problems are really positive attributes. No off-street parking means no curb breaks or driveways to interrupt the street and walk, and no blank garage doors to deaden the houses. It means keeping the car out of the house and, in this particular way, activating the street, but quietly, even complicating it a bit. That's what the narrow street does, too. No one need be afraid of cars or speed on Roslyn Place. A fire truck can go down the center, and if it couldn't the street is short enough for fire hoses to reach as far as necessary. As for the closeness of the build-

Roslyn Place Houses

A.B.J. '91

ings, the narrow walk between them does what it is supposed to do, even more: it gets you from the front to the rear without passing through the house, giving access as well for the rubbish man. There are windows on those side walls, to be sure, but neighbors understand about privacy and rarely look from one to another, and those windows provide cross ventilation in rooms that otherwise wouldn't have it (less need for air conditioning).

All the smallness and closeness—but closeness with enough room for healthy, even gracious living—makes for a density that is greater than would be permitted for the same types of housing (remember, these are single-family houses) in most of the urban United States: some 14 dwellings per gross acre (including the street). That density means there are a lot of people around. It means that public transit can be supported; it means that small stores within walking distance are likely to survive, and they do, on Walnut Street, a block away; and that schools, too, can be close. It means, in short, community, or at least the chance of community.

There is something else that's special about Roslyn Place. The street is paved with wood blocks, not exactly a modern street material. Wood block can be slippery in the winter and, over the years, becomes uneven. From time to time, people in some office downtown, thinking to do public service, decide to repave the street. Residents successfully resist: people know a great street when they live on it.

Over time, say 25 or 30 years, the physical nature of Roslyn Place has changed remarkably little, though some of the people may have changed. The houses look the same. Some of the front porches on one side have been integrated into the houses; not much else. Curly Steiner is older and looks it. He says there are no kids any more. Birdy, his wife, says that they couldn't have the same kind of block party down at the end of the street that they once had. Curly, who doesn't have curly hair and never did, says that Izzy thinks he's the mayor of the street, acts like it. In his house, Izzy remembers everything and everyone who lived in each house and when. Charlotte, Izzy's wife, returns from an errand. She recalls how the residents got the city to repave the street with wood blocks about five years ago and to declare the street a landmark. The telling point, she says, is when they reminded the city people that this was the first time it had been repaved in 75 years. Up the street, in front of where the Jacobs used to live, a young couple, not of the street, walk, pause, look, talk to each other, project themselves into living here and think how nice a prospect that would be.

Via dei Giubbonari, Rome

Strøget, Copenhagen

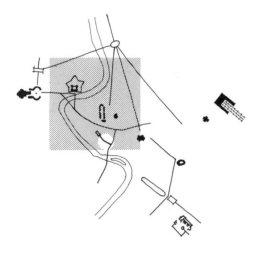

Via dei Giubbonari:
street and building context

Via dei Giubbonari in Rome has existed since ancient times. Early, the street was known as a center for the making and sale of vests; doublets. Today, most of the stores sell clothes, though no doublets, and there are other things to buy as well. At each end, funnel-shaped widenings draw you in, help you to choose this street rather than another. It is not a long street, less than 1,000 feet (300 meters), but you would not know that when you start because it bends and becomes ever narrower toward the center so that it is not possible to see one end from the other. The shape of the street itself does not tell you where it is going, but you are drawn in all the same. The sky plane, a clear, curving arrow, reflecting the street plan and at the same time angling downward with the receding perspective, takes you on your way, beyond what is visible on the ground.

Strøget, in Copenhagen, is ancient as well. A lineal collection of four streets, it is considerably longer than the Via dei Giubbonari, some 3,500 feet (1,000-plus meters), and is centrally located in the city. Indeed it may be said to be the main central street of Copenhagen, but is similar in many physical characteristics to the Via dei Giubbonari.

Approximate scale: 1″ = 400′ or 1:4,800

Strøget: street and building context

Approximate scale: 1″ = 400′ or 1:4,800

These two streets represent the very best of a type: the old, long-continuing medieval street that usually winds at least a little, is relatively narrow, and has about it a certain sense of mystery, determined largely as a result of its tightness, its relatively tall buildings, and an inability to see from one end to another. What is there beyond where you can see? There are hundreds of streets like this, mostly in Europe, though they once were plentiful in Boston and other cities in the eastern United States as well; but these two can stand for the best.

Once on Via dei Giubbonari, attracted by one of the funnel-shaped widenings at either end, you want to see where it leads, even if you already know, and you want to experience what is more immediately around you as well. There are many buildings, even more doorways, and almost continuous store windows at the street level. Buildings here have solid masonry bearing walls, not thin skin surfaces hanging between structural columns. Wall thickness and building solidity are made clearly evident by their visible contrast with the glass panes in them. Buildings and other stores as well are deep, and the windows show this. How deep are they? What is in there? There is a bit of inviting mystery; something to be explored. Above, there are more windows, shuttered or open depending on the time of day and where the sun may be. The buildings on both streets are, for the most part, unremarkable, but they make their presence felt: sturdy, solid structures of three to five tall stories that define the pathway. Heights may vary but there are few abrupt changes, and because buildings are higher than the street is wide, especially

Still Great Medieval Streets

Along Via dei Giubbonari

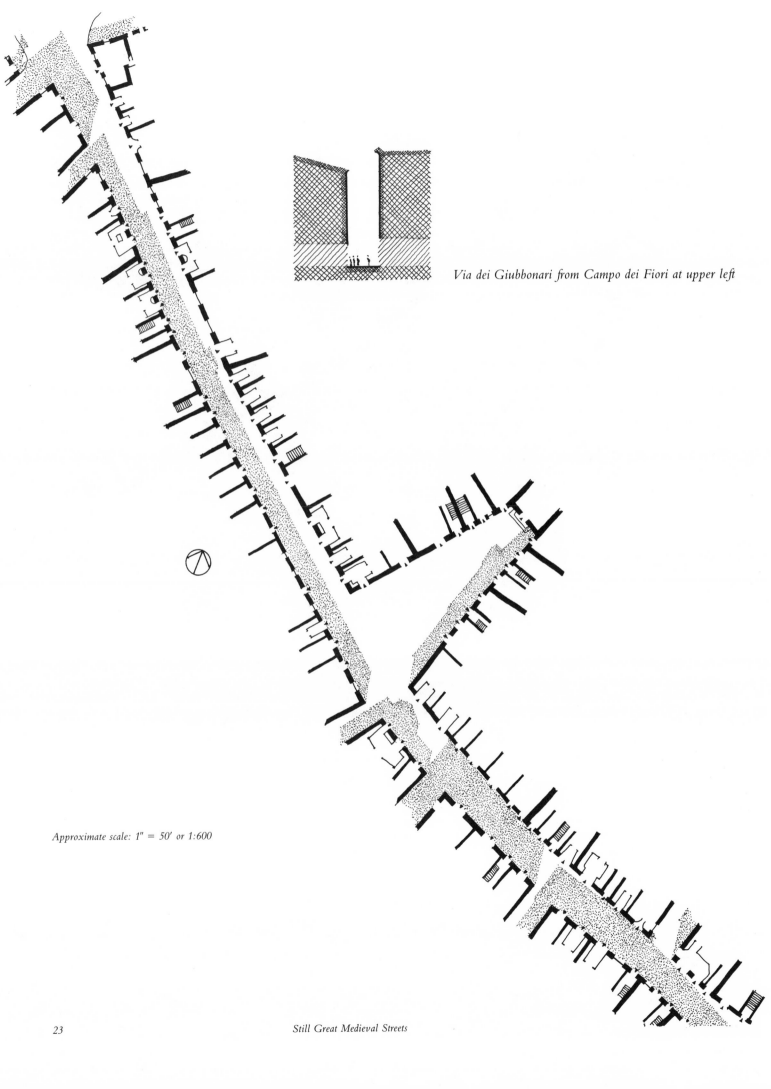

Via dei Giubbonari from Campo dei Fiori at upper left

Approximate scale: 1″ = 50′ or 1:600

Still Great Medieval Streets

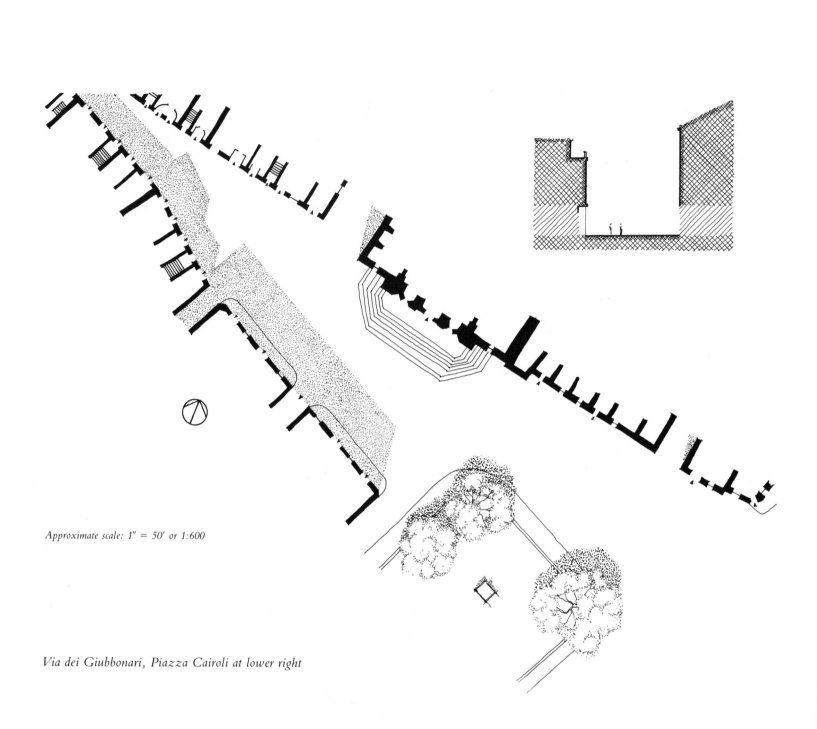

Approximate scale: 1″ = 50′ or 1:600

Via dei Giubbonari, Piazza Cairoli at lower right

Via dei Giubbonari from Campo dei Fiori

Largo del Libari on Via dei Giubbonari

toward the center where they can be 60 feet compared to a street width of 16 feet, there is a strong sense of verticality, a sense reinforced by the vertical lines that occur where one building stops and another starts. A typical building front on Via dei Giubbonari is 62 feet long (19 meters) and there is a doorway every 15 feet (4.8 meters). On the Strøget, buildings average 47 feet in length and doorways are almost as frequent as on Via dei Giubbonari.

Though architecturally undistinguished, building facades on the two streets are richly detailed: shutters, sills, cornices, frames, signs, lights, downspouts, shutter fasteners, and more. Light passes over these details and surfaces, so there is constant change of brightness and of shadows.

Doorway – Via dei Giubbonari

Near the center of Via dei Giubbonari, there is a small piazza lined with more small shops and entrances to upper-floor apartments, and there is a very small church, appropriate to the size of the space. From this point, where the street approaches its most narrow dimension, both of its ends can be seen, Campo dei Fiori at one end and Piazza Cairoli at the other.

Strøget, too, has open stopping places, squares or *pladser* along its longer route, each marking the start or end of one of the four old streets, and they are more important than the single space on the shorter Via dei Giubbonari. They are places to stop, to sit, places where there is more light and where there are breaks on the narrow path. People do gather at them, local people, not just visitors. The *pladser* are the settings for formal and informal entertainments that last long hours. Each is different from the next, but there are always restaurants or coffee shops on a square, as well as food stalls and other attractions. The funnel-shaped Højbro Plads is a major focal point of the city and seems to have people in it always. On Strøget, at the side yard of the Helligåndskirke, there is a fence that provides more places to sit, face to the street, back to the fence. Behind the fence is a line of old trees whose branches overhang the street. Along the line of benches chess players vie with each other or, in a good-natured way, con an unsuspecting passerby into a low-stakes contest. It is also a good place to play a guitar or flute. There is more relaxed socializing on Strøget than on Via dei Giubbonari. Then, too, there are a series of wonderfully playful spires along Strøget to focus upon, if only for a moment, as you walk the street.

Both of these streets are comfortable. Their narrowness and the nature of the buildings along them protect them from wind. Via dei Giubbonari is particularly comfortable on hot summer days. Both would be more pleasant in winter if they could have more winter sun.

Both streets are for everyone and both are accustomed to crowds of people, though certainly not all the time. They bring people together, all kinds of people. They both act as spines, central structural elements to the area around them, and both have strong beginnings and endings. Because Strøget is longer, serves a much larger area, and is more central to the whole city—it leads from the City Hall to the Kongens Nytorv at the Nyhavn Canal—it is especially impressive in terms of the variety of people it attracts. There seems to be a gradation of stores (and maybe even of people) from west to east, from less expensive offerings near City Hall to high style, high prices nearer the canal. People mix physically, and even if they choose not to socially, they can't help seeing each other, being with each other, at least in part.

Days have a pace and rhythm on these streets. On the Via dei Giubbonari, in the early morning, say 6:30 or 7:00 A.M., the first sounds and activities are generated by the market at the Campo dei Fiori. The opening noises are from the market stalls that are set up every morning, from some carts going to it, and from the first shoppers. Window shutters are opened and some few

Still Great Medieval Streets

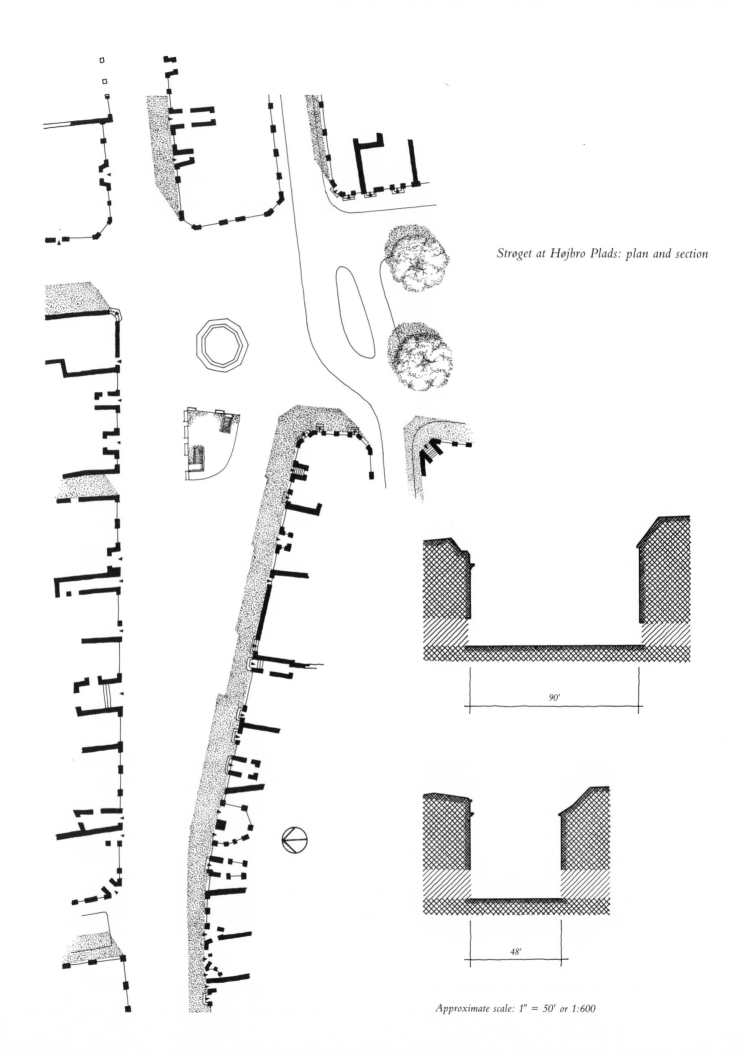

Strøget at Højbro Plads: plan and section

90'

48'

Approximate scale: 1" = 50' or 1:600

Strøget at Højbro Plads

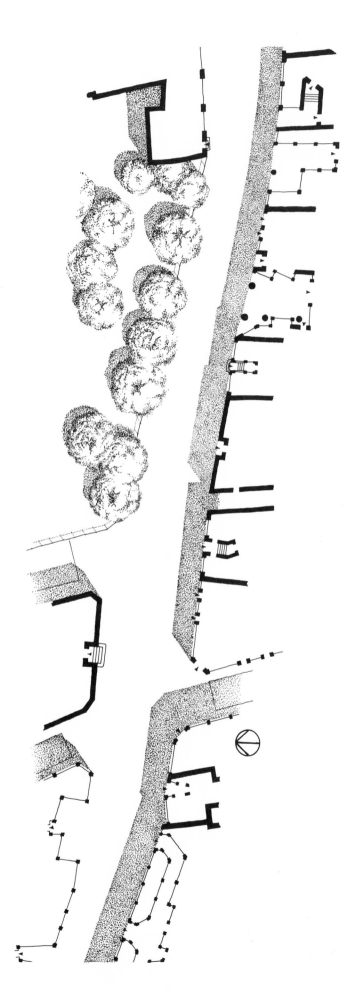

Strøget at Helligåndskirke: plan and section

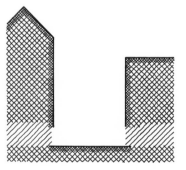

Approximate scale: 1″ = 50′ or 1:600

Strøget at Helligåndskirke

Still Great Medieval Streets

Along Strøget

doors and window grates, mostly metal, are opened at the bars or at the *alimentari*. There are not many people. Some walk toward the bus routes on Via Arenula, some to the market, some to morning coffee. This is the time of day when a car might try its luck on the street, though no driver seriously trying to get from one place to another would think of using it regularly. Like Strøget, it has no curbs to separate pedestrians from cars. It is all one cobblestone surface. The floor of Strøget is mainly concrete pavers. On Strøget the bakeries and coffee shops are the first to open and regulars stop into them to start their days. Outside, on the street, small delivery trucks bring goods to the stores and food for the stands that will open later.

By midmorning the Via dei Giubbonari is crowded. All the stores have opened, over 60 of them. The funnel opening at Via Arenula is jammed with parked cars, and people weave through them on their way into or out of the street. Though it is crowded, people can walk at almost any pace, except really fast. An occasional motorbike is an intrusion. Some people read the newspapers posted outside the political headquarters midway along the street. Passing acquaintances see each other, stop, talk for a few moments. There are many young people, and tourists. Older women head toward or return from the market which is at its peak. There are more women than men. Sounds bounce off of the buildings, mostly from people talking. Upper-floor shutters are likely to be open and a woman may appear, momentarily, to look down.

After one o'clock in the afternoon, people leave and the stores close. Again there are the sounds of shutters and door grates, this time rolling down. The street almost empties. Past one-thirty, someone heads quickly for the market to catch a still open stall (the butchers seem always to be the last to close). An occasional couple walks through, during and after the lunch period. The bars remain open, but after two aren't very busy. The market is closed; the stalls are taken down and packed on carts, and some of them are moved along the street, pushed by their keepers to storage for the night. A cleaning crew attacks the Campo. On Strøget there is no slowing at midday. If anything, there is more activity and it continues until later.

Later in the afternoon on Via dei Giubbonari, there is a second opening of stores and a second crowd, a much larger crowd now. People often rub shoulders at the narrowest section of the street. Here it is only 16 feet wide and the crowds are as great as on the Strøget, but in a more confined space. They walk slowly, couldn't walk fast if they wanted to. The sounds are of many people talking. This is the late afternoon–early evening stroll. If you stand in one place long enough, you may see the same people pass two or three times; shopping, to be sure, but also meeting friends, talking, strolling. A car, in grave error, inches its way toward Via Arenula. At the other end, at the Campo dei Fiori, people meet and talk in small groups. Some children are kicking a football. There are families. After seven-thirty there is another closing, and much later, after the restaurants and gelateria and the small cinema on the square and the bars on the street close, Via dei Giubbonari is still. Far to the north, in Copenhagen, Strøget is more likely to have people on it until much later, especially in summer. They may gather in knots, to talk or to watch a street entertainer who knows there will be people there at Højbro Plads.

Late at night there may be no one on Via dei Giubbonari. Shutters are closed. It is dark. There are shades only of dark gray and black. Only the physical form is left; receding vertical planes curving toward a closing, a hint of light from the piazza to let you know where you are. There is the occasional sound of heels on cobble, a couple or a single person. Once or twice the abrasive sound of a motorbike may blast through. It is still a pleasant place to be, though not as nice as in the light, where details keep you moving. On such a street, maybe this same street, four centuries ago Benvenuto Cellini, hurrying home or in escape, might have taken a wide berth at corners for safety. There is no need to do that now, but, as on Strøget, the center is still the best place to walk.

CHAPTER THREE

In the Grand Manner ————————————————— —

Paseo de Gracia, Barcelona

**Cours Mirabeau,
Aix-en-Provence**

Avenue Montaigne, Paris

Boulevard Saint-Michel, Paris

In the building and rebuilding of cities, there seem to have been relatively few times when the major concentration of design efforts has been on streets: not on the citywide pattern of streets or the laying out of whole areas, but on the functional-sensual arrangement of the streets themselves—their sizes, the detailed design of all their parts, and their embellishments in the contexts of their particular city. Freeway design in the mid- and late twentieth century does not constitute such a period, concerned as it is with the rapid movement of vehicles and therefore with a roadway removed, even walled off from its surrounding urban fabric. By contrast, the latter half of the nineteenth century and into the twentieth, particularly in France, was such a period. Here the detailed design focus was on streets as much as or more than on the buildings that lined them. A major objective was to beautify the city, to assert during an era of rampant laissez-faire capitalism the historic primacy of the public role in city building—of the public realm, with the streets its major component—over private interests and private development. There were other major objectives: to move people and goods through medieval street systems that had become impossibly congested, to improve communications, to add sanitation lines and other infrastructure systems, and to open up crowded *quartiers,* including those where social unrest was fermenting. Boulevard streets, albeit with earlier precedents, are the keynote of that period, and it is not surprising that many of the great streets were designed and built then or soon after. Design attention was rewarded with achievement.

A boulevard is more than a wide street. Boulevard streets evoke images of size and formality, with an emphasis on grandeur. An American urban planner's definition, in 1927, was "A broad avenue decoratively laid out in a formal manner, especially with park space in the center."[1] Webster calls a boulevard "a broad, landscaped thoroughfare."[2] François Loyer is more focused and helpful, explaining that these wide streets were conceived "not as a single unit, but as three distinct routes—the two sidewalks and the roadway itself—separated from each other by rows of trees."[3] Countless variations in design are possible. Among their most important functions was that of giving structure and comprehension to the whole city, often as large monumental ways that linked important destinations manifested in the form of large buildings. The models of sixteenth-century Rome were adopted and greatly enlarged upon. Boulevards, more often marking the boundaries than the centers of districts and neighborhoods, were also intended as, and have become, major destinations in their own right, first as residential and then as business addresses, as shopping streets, and always as special places of promenade. Their roots are long in time and place, from intensely urban Rome during the papacy of Julius II (Via Giulia and Via di Ripetta) to the urban-rural boundaries and the elimination of the defensive ramparts in Paris.[4] The Champs-Elysées, a grandfather of grand boulevards, dates from 1667.

The very idea of grand boulevards as exuberant, community-building projects, particularly as realized in Paris, is anathema to some people. How could places so connected with the tearing down of where people lived, their homes and their neighborhoods, however spatially and hygienically mean they were and regardless of their physical disrepair, be considered positively? Moreover, there are strong connections—of ideas and programs of massive governmental intervention in city change, of economic boosterism, of huge publicly aided real estate ventures for private profit, of public works projects, and of architect-conceived city design and improvement concepts dependent on such programs—between the rebuilding programs of late nineteenth-century Paris through the City Beautiful movement of the early 1900s to the post–World War II redevelopment programs in the United States and, with them, the renewed displacement of urban poor. Nonetheless, neither the idea nor the reality of boulevards is dependent upon governmental programs that obliterate earlier urban fabrics and drive out the people that live in them. Neither Haussmann's clearance programs nor those urban redevelopment projects in the United States produced most or perhaps even the best boulevards. It is not a requirement of boulevards that they be associated with social injustice, although they do imply hierarchy, and therefore produce a measure of imbalance between areas.

Boulevards have much to teach, not only about the design of a particular type of street but about streets in general. They are first and foremost public, and their design purpose, beyond that of movement of vehicles and goods, is for people. They may well serve as boundaries of districts or as connections between areas or for the city as a whole, but they are most intimately experienced in small segments, as part of daily urban life or as special destinations: as places for the enjoyment of the city, as promenades, and as comfortable places for walking.

There is no one boulevard that, once described and explained, can stand for all. It is not so easy. The Champs-Elysées, without question the best-known of the grand boulevards, perhaps the best-known street in the world, is no longer, in the early 1990s, the great street it once was. In any case it is only one of a type, and there are many types. Each of the four choices that follow represents a different type, and each has distinct physical characteristics and a different cross section from the others. Each has something different to teach. Undoubtedly some important boulevards are left out, but the four that follow are without question great streets in a grand manner.

Paseo de Gracia ⎯⎯⎯⎯⎯⎯⎯⎯

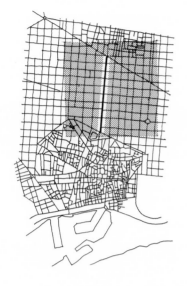

Within an approximately 200-foot (61-meter) cross section, which is only about 30 feet less than that of the Champs-Elysées, and roughly one mile (1.6 kilometers) of length, from the Plaça de Catalunya to just beyond the Avenida do Diagonal, the Paseo de Gracia in Barcelona has everything one would want on a grand boulevard and does everything one would want a great street to do. Its design reflects and promotes the Mediterranean tradition of strolling in public, especially at night, just as the Ramblas did, earlier in the city's long history.

To start, the Paseo de Gracia is centrally located and it seems clear that it was meant to be the main street of a growing city, a major city addition that would surround but not destroy the ancient Gothic Quarter. Sloping gently upward toward the hills in a southeast-northwest direction, it has a clear but not overly pronounced beginning and end: the central Barcelona square at the Plaça de Catalunya, and a narrower and less grand cross section just beyond the Avenido do Diagonal at which there is a monument. There is a clear connection to the older city, via the square that provides a transition to the older main street, the Ramblas, and, to the northwest, along a visual and physical continuation of the boulevard itself to the post–World War II city expansion beyond. Ultimately it is the distant hills and mountains that terminate the view outward from the Paseo de Gracia. The six traffic lanes at the center (five in one direction and the sixth for buses in the opposite direction), some 58 to 60 feet wide (17.6 to 18.3 meters), move large amounts of traffic at a rapid pace through the city to major destinations both within the central area and beyond. The metro rapid transit passes under this boulevard, emphasizing its central linearity in the city. For auto users there are levels of linear parking under the Paseo de Gracia. Block lengths are relatively short, 360 to 380 feet (110 to 116 meters), and because their corners run diagonally to the streets, like all corners in the late nineteenth-century city development pattern,[5] each intersection presents a welcoming opening to streets and neighborhoods on either side. Over its one-mile course the Paseo de Gracia intersects with two major cross streets (not counting the Diagonal) and these, too, provide focal points along the way.

The 70 feet on each side of the central auto roadway is where the intricacy and the richness lie. There is a step-by-step slowing down of pace from the fast-moving central way to the broad 36-foot-wide (10.9-meter) sidewalks and their abutting buildings. First there is a 16-foot-wide (4.8-meter) median strip, planted with large plane trees about 24 feet apart and reaching heights of from four to five tall stories. The trees are close to the central roadway. Next to the median there is an 18-foot-wide (5.5-meter) access road for local, slow traffic and for parking. The access road and the median act as one, a slow zone for autos and people with a variety of designs and plans to meet changing needs and to respond to changing opportunities: diagonal or parallel parking, subway entrances, ramps to and from underground parking, landscape, lighting, and sitting possibilities. Only the line of trees, including their spacing, the locations of lights (also near the central curb), and the curb at the sidewalk are inviolate.

In the Grand Manner

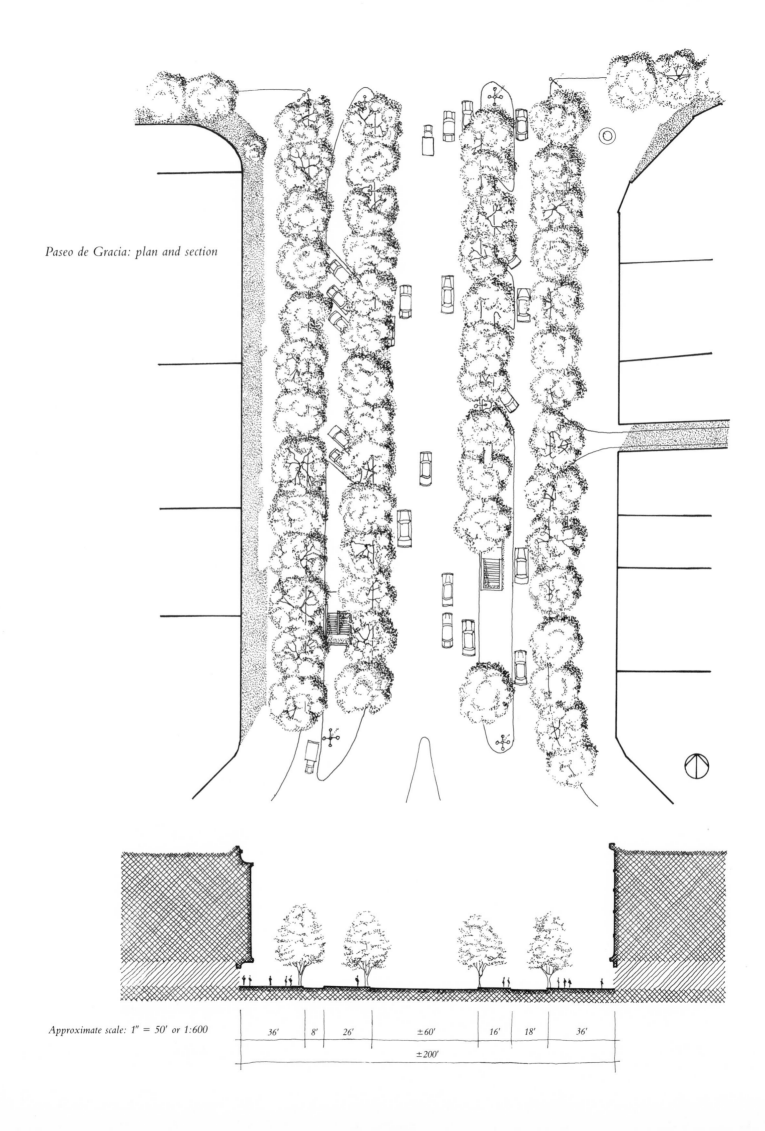

Paseo de Gracia: plan and section

Approximate scale: 1″ = 50′ or 1:600

| 36′ | 8′ | 26′ | ±60′ | 16′ | 18′ | 36′ |

±200′

Along Paseo de Gracia

Paseo de Gracia

Paving tiles by Gaudi

The sidewalks start out simply enough. Thirty-six feet is broad, so they can accommodate a lot of people with ease. Along the curb there is another line of plane trees, these planted a bit further apart than the ones in the median, about 27 feet center to center. Their branches start to spread at about 15 feet and, at their highest, can almost form a continuous canopy with those in the median. In total there are four lines of large trees planted along the street. They come as close as possible to intersecting streets. The paving of the walks is exquisite, one of the few walk surfaces anywhere that truly makes a difference to a street design. It consists of six-sided Gaudí-designed tiles, each of an intricate three-dimensional design of a helix and plant-leaf forms that together create a larger design. The color is a soft blue-gray that shines and sparkles and looks blue-green when wet. It is a delight, even a privilege to walk upon it. There are details to be added to the sidewalk and to the access road–median before we can move on to the buildings themselves. There are at least four kinds of lights. The first is a high, contemporary, almost universal "cobra head" type fixture on a thin pole; these are painted an olive green to help them recede from sight. Mostly they are for the central roadway, and the less said of them the better. Then there is an older, classic, single, moderately ornate light fixture atop a shaped wrought iron standard that stands about 12 to 14 feet high. Their spacing varies; they are often 60 feet apart (but they can also be as close together as 33 feet). They are located to the sidewalk side of the trees, providing a low light that takes you along the way at night. To mark each corner, four to an intersection, in the median, are grander, five-lamp fixtures, of an ornate turn-of-the-century design. At night, looking up the street, with a sprinkling of shop lights and headlights or tail lights of moving cars and the dark shapes of trees, it is these five-lamped corner fixtures that stand out most and mark the way. The last of the lights are the playful, swirling, leafed, intricate iron-steel Gaudí-designed lights intermittently placed along the street at the center curb. They have both a high light that pretends to serve the auto and a low one for people. They are set in sensuously shaped tile benches. There are often benches, too, along the walks, placed to face the walk and the promenade. And finally, many of the corners along the walks have circular Gaudí benches with trees coming out of their centers and with flowers as well. The public way has been very richly provided for.

The buildings with their stores that line and define the Paseo de Gracia are as one with the street: there are many of them, they tend to be complex and richly detailed, they are diverse in design, yet generally respecting of each other and the street, and for the most part they are done well. The buildings are of similar, if not the same, heights. Older ones, five to seven floors high, are similar to newer ones with eight stories. Corner buildings, especially at the two major crossings, may be higher. Six buildings to a block face is normal, with lengths ranging from 30 feet to 129 feet (9 to 36.5 meters), but with 40 to 60 feet (12 to 18.3 meters) seeming most common. Most of them are extremely well designed, and often—but certainly not always—art nou-veau in style. Antonio Gaudí is most nobly represented by the Casa Milá and the Batlló House. The Casa Amatller, by Puig i Cadafalch, is there as well. Notably, very many of the buildings have large bay windows at the upper floors that can overhang the walks by as much as 5 feet (1.5 meters). Richly detailed, their large windows are like eyes on the street. It is possible to imagine oneself in one, looking down upon and along the street.

Bay windows on Paseo de Gracia

At sidewalk level, beyond all that is in the public way, the stores and what is in them become a part of the street. The windows to these establishments, which sell a variety of goods and services but are perhaps mostly clothing stores and restaurants, are kept sparkling clean and attract the window shoppers' eyes into the ground floor, making it a part of the public way. There are also major destinations for large numbers of people on the street, notably movie houses. Stores are often not large, one to two to a building, and doorways, both to stores and to private entrances, are typically less than 25 feet apart.

The wide sidewalks and the improvements along them were designed for people to walk and to stroll and to sit. People do, in large numbers. At the same time, they are wide enough so that a line of temporary stands can be placed along them, from one end of the street to the other, for a special purpose, such as a book fair, and still leave room for many people to walk in comfort. Normally, or during special events, the Paseo de Gracia is a won-

Casa Milà

derful place to walk, to be, to meet friends. The street is wide. Standing in the middle of one sidewalk one may not be able to recognize a face on the far sidewalk, a distance of some 170 feet, though it would be possible if the person were in the median. But it is nonetheless one single street, not two or three separate strips running side by side. The central location in Barcelona, the four lines of trees, the lights, the benches, the paving, the buildings of similar height, the memory that one side is like the other, and the elegant execution of it all unify the Paseo de Gracia and make it a single and special place.

Cours Mirabeau _____

Residents and visitors alike of Aix-en-Provence, France, remember and can agree about the Cours Mirabeau. It is the largest public presence of the city, and it is a great street.

The Cours Mirabeau is a relatively flat east-west street that is almost one-quarter of a mile long (approximately 430 meters). Its start is marked by a grand circle, officially named the Place Général de Gaulle but generally known and referred to as the Place de la Rotonde, in the center of which is a major monument-fountain, and it ends at Place Forbin, with the much more modest and more compelling Fontaine du Roi René. Gateway statues to the street itself, at the circle, are dated 1883, but the street is much older, having been decreed in 1649. It is at the southern edge of what was the medieval city; the quarter was rebuilt in the nineteenth century according to the medi-

Cours Mirabeau

In the Grand Manner

eval street plan and is composed of a wonderful labyrinth of climbing, winding streets. On the other side it borders a not uninteresting, more modern section of the city: a grid of streets covering an area perhaps half that of the old city. Size and design alone would account for the street's singular presence in Aix. A straight quarter mile may not be very long in most cities, but it is here. The width of the street, approximately 150 feet (close to 48 meters), is truly spacious in such a small city. It stands in contrast to anything else in Aix. At the same time, it is difficult to say that the Cours Mirabeau really goes anywhere, at least not in the sense in which boulevards were conceived as major traffic movers, to get from one major city destination to another or to get around the city. Rather, just past the Place Forbin it peters out in different directions, then connects again with circumferential boulevards. No, it seems that the Cours Mirabeau was built for its own sake, a large attractive and attracting presence in its own right, as much so as any plaza, square, park, or public building.

The street section is some 150 feet wide if measured somewhere near the second of the small fountains that mark its path. Actually, the section varies, from approximately 135 feet (41 meters) at its start at the Place de la Rotonde to 153 feet (46 meters) at the statue of Roi René. Gradually the central roadway and the walks on either side become wider (or narrower), the walks moving into (or out of) the street. It is not entirely clear whether this gradual change in width makes the street seem equally wide in perspective looking into it, or whether the opening at the large circle is more dramatic because of the closing down at that end. Greater width at the end may well compensate for the tighter city fabric that is to be found there. The variable width of the central cartway, from 45 to 57 feet (13.7 to 17.4 meters), accommodates four traffic lanes comfortably. Traffic moves slowly; the distance is short and there are the two small fountains along the way, in the center of the street. Symmetrical sidewalks on either side of the street account for the rest of the right-of-way. At one time there appear to have been marginal access roadways, 18 feet wide, closer to the buildings—one remains for a block on one side and curbs and different paving patterns reveal their earlier presence on the other—but they are not significant design elements

Cours Mirabeau: section

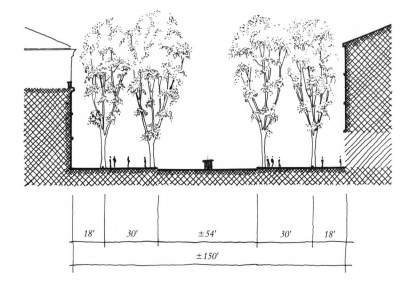

| 18' | 30' | ±54' | 30' | 18' |

±150'

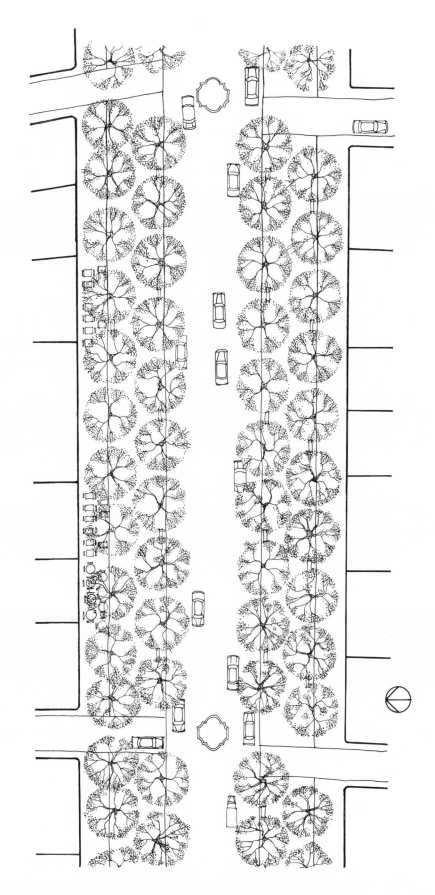

Cours Mirabeau: plan

Approximate scale: 1″ = 50′ or 1:600

In the Grand Manner

now. Buildings line and define the right-of-way. Most are four or five stories tall, from about 48 to 60 feet, though some are only three stories. The Grand Hotel is the highest at about 70 feet. Buildings vary in size and design, but are complementary to each other. Mansions date from the seventeenth century. A light tan, buff stone, or stucco stand out as the prevailing building materials and color. Streetlights at varying distances from each other, from about 50 to about 90 feet apart, stand near the curb. And then there are the trees. More than anything else, it is the trees that make the Cours Mirabeau the street that it is.

Each side of the Cours Mirabeau is marked by two lines of plane trees, one at the street edge and one at about 18 feet from the building line. They are set in planting areas that are about 2 meters square. Along the street they are 30 to 33 feet apart, in a diagonal pattern. The two rows are about 27 feet apart. The trees are big, as tall as and taller than the buildings, 50 and 60 feet and maybe 70 feet high (15 to 21 meters). They are trimmed so that major branches do not intertwine but leaves probably join overhead in the summer. Branching starts high, often well above 20 feet. What they do for the street and for light patterns is wonderful to behold. Large moving patches and patterns of shadow, of leaves, and of tree trunks and branches fall over the walks and the street. Vertical surfaces of buildings and tree trunks show the same uneven tracery of dark and light, shadow and bright sun. When a tree dies, it is replaced with a serious one, a baby by Cours Mirabeau standards perhaps but an adult for other less noble streets.

Walking along the Cours Mirabeau, even in the springtime after the trees have been pruned, is to walk in large patches of sun and shade. People appear and disappear, as do cars in the center traffic lanes. The tree trunks are like columns, and to walk among them is to be in a tall, lace-ceilinged arcade. The north side is lined with restaurants, bookstores, shops, and a department store. Typically building facades are 35 to 60 feet long. There are three to four store entrances or private entryways to a building. Restaurants have outdoor table areas that extend to the first line of trees, some a bit beyond. There are five small streets from the older part of the city that intersect with the Cours Mirabeau but they are hardly noticed: nothing is made of them. Even the small fountains at intersections call momentary attention to themselves and the main street, not to the crossing ones. One may stop, to look into windows, to buy a book or card. The reason may not be a need for anything but just a reluctance to reach the end. Moving east, the street becomes somewhat darker, more enclosed at the modest statue of the king. Returning, on the shady south side, there are fewer stores and many ground floors with no public-serving commercial enterprises at all. Banks and a few small, pretentious, stylish clothing stores are more likely on this side (although there is one patisserie de luxe). There are benches between the trees. Without knowing for sure, you have a sense that if you bring your own food or buy food to take with you from the other side, or from elsewhere, or if you just want to sit and relax without the necessity or cost of sitting at a

Cours Mirabeau

In the Grand Manner

table, then you do it on the south side. Nearing the beginning of the street, at the entry sculptures and the circle, it gets lighter again. The walk hasn't taken long. One searches and easily finds reasons to do it all over again.

Avenue Montaigne ————————

The Avenue Montaigne is not a street for everyone, far from it. Its buildings and uses reflect privileged wealth, power, high fashion, moneyed elegance: the most expensive hotels, boutiques with famous designer names, offices of foreign governments (not third world), and chauffeurs. It was not always that way. A country path in 1672, it was designed in approximately its current form in 1770 and had an early history as a meeting place, the location of "Bals." It was a dark street, the effect of double rows of elm trees.[6] There is a lot to be learned from this short grand boulevard, and it has little to do with wealth or power. Rather, the Avenue Montaigne shows us how very much can be placed in a relatively small width of public right-of-way to create a wonderful street that serves many purposes. These are lessons that can be applied anywhere.

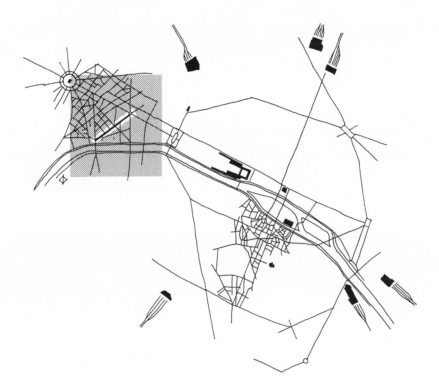

Avenue Montaigne starts at the Champs-Elysées, at the Rond-Point, and it ends at Avenue George V and the river, a distance of about 2,000 feet (615 meters). Only four streets on one side and two on the other (one is common to both) intersect with it in that distance. In cross section it is like a miniature version of the Champs-Elysées or, better, the Paseo de Gracia, with all of their most important parts. It is about one-half of the total width of the Paseo de Gracia. In total, the public right-of-way width is approximately 104

In the Grand Manner

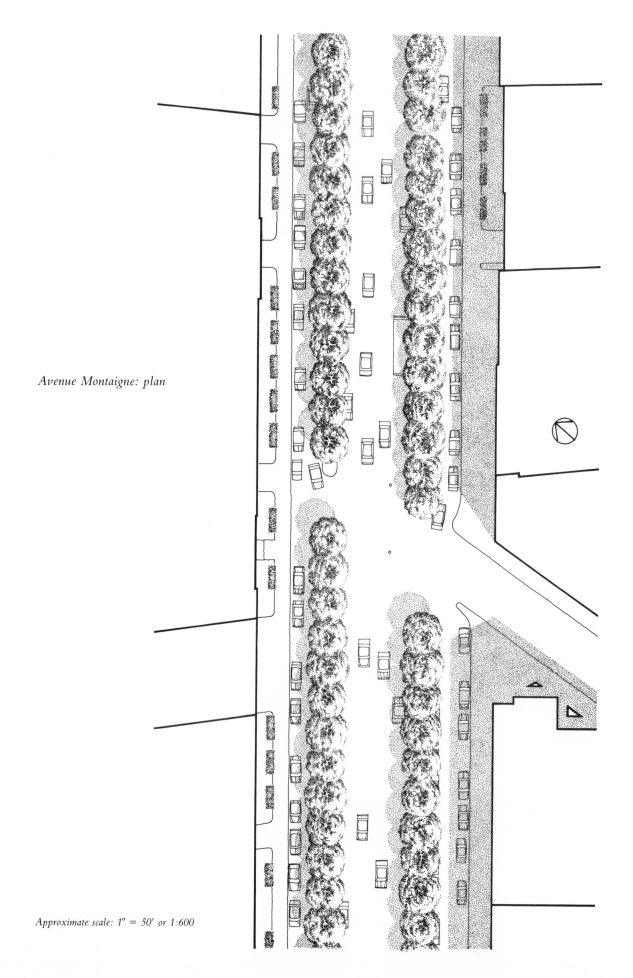

Avenue Montaigne: plan

Approximate scale: 1″ = 50′ or 1:600

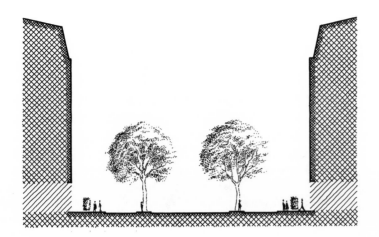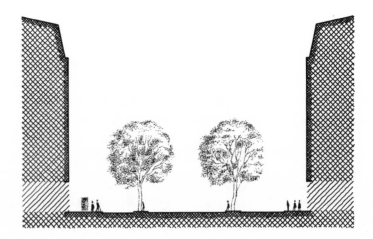

Avenue Montaigne: section

feet (32 meters). There is another 7-foot (2.1-meter) building setback on both sides, in front of the building line. The buildings are of the same height. Within that space, the center traffic lane is only 42 feet (12.8 meters) wide, yet accommodates four lanes of traffic, three in one direction and one for buses and taxis going the other way. Then comes a planting strip, only 6 or 7 feet wide, that accommodates chestnut trees closely planted at approximately 18 to 20 feet (6 meters) between centers, as well as occasional benches and bus stops. The space is very narrow, yet everything seems to work. Most importantly, the closely spaced trees, whose branches meet overhead, set up a transparent yet real picket fence of living columns that separates the pedestrian-dominated area from the vehicular roadway. This is not to say that the auto is excluded from the remaining public way: the next 14 feet (4.3 meters) is a narrow access road; one moving and one parking lane. But fast movement is impossible. Autos and pedestrians mix. It is as much a place to walk the dog as it is to search for a parking space or to pick up a friend. It has a pedestrian pace. Another 10 feet (3 meters) is for sidewalks and then there are low hedges that mark a 7-foot planting strip or front paved area in front of the buildings. Along one of the blocks the access road has two parking lanes and the 7-foot setback is used as the walkway. In either case, but mostly where the access road is narrower, it is a wonderfully tight boulevard—almost a contradiction in terms—that is at once intimate, symmetrical, and gracious. Its physical qualities have nothing to do with wealth or station, but with the designable, buildable environment.

The intersections, like those on the Paseo de Gracia and most boulevards with this basic design, deserve attention. These streets were conceived and built either before the automobile or when there were relatively few of them on the roads. Many may have been designed by engineers, but not by traffic engineers. Terms like "turning movements," "weaving distances," "lane ca-

In the Grand Manner

Along Avenue Montaigne

pacities," "conflict points," or "levels of service" had not been invented, let alone developed into what some think of as a science. No one understood that these kinds of intersections, with so many possible turning movements coming out of or onto the boulevard, could be dangerous, slow, and congestion-producing: too many drivers trying to do too many things at a given location and therefore getting in each other's way, to say nothing of the pedestrians'. Today, traffic people shudder at the thought of such places, won't permit them, and try to do away with those that exist. Then why do such intersections remain on the Avenue Montaigne, the Paseo de Gracia, and on many other boulevards; more importantly, why do they work?[7]

It pays to stand at one of these intersections for an hour or two and observe them. One can see all sorts of driver and pedestrian behavior. First, it helps if the main line of traffic, in the center, is in one direction, as on the Avenue Montaigne. Fewer movements are possible. Then there are other rules and regulations and timed lights that can minimize conflicts. Most importantly, however, there is behavior. Drivers and pedestrians are not fools. They know when they come to the intersections that there are many possibilities, that others are trying to get in when they are trying to get out, that still others are likely to turn when they want to go straight, that a pedestrian is likely to want to cross as they want to turn, that someone will even back up in order to correct a mistake or to make an illegal turn, and, knowing these things, they act accordingly: they proceed cautiously, slowly. In short, they adapt, and everything works out. To be sure, traffic can at times move slowly, always more slowly on the access streets, particularly at the intersections. There can be what engineers and laymen alike refer to as congestion. But so what? It is not necessary or even desirable to move fast on these side roads or at most intersections. There, the pace should be more deliberate. There can be enough speed in the center lane: not a freeway pace, but fast enough. If the design is well thought out, well executed, and well maintained, all of which seem to be the case on the Avenue Montaigne, then why would one want to be in a hurry to leave? It is an extremely pleasant, intensely urbane place to be.

Boulevard Saint-Michel —————

What makes the Boulevard Saint-Michel, in Paris, special is the light and the stores and cafes. The mixture of natural light that filters through the trees and the welcoming transparency of the ground-floor windows of commercial uses invites the passerby and calls attention to the goods displayed on racks or tables along the sidewalks. At the same time, even on a bright sunny morning, the shops and cafes are lit with incandescent and neon light that contrasts markedly with the deep shadows and shade cast by those same trees. It is not so much the monumental apartment houses that line the boulevard, especially at the Place Saint-Michel, for there are long months when these can hardly be seen, blocked from view by the trees. Nor is it the Bernini-inspired wall fountain at its start, which rarely gets sun, nor the wonderful opening out at the Luxembourg Gardens, as impressive as that space is. Rather, it is the light and the shops.

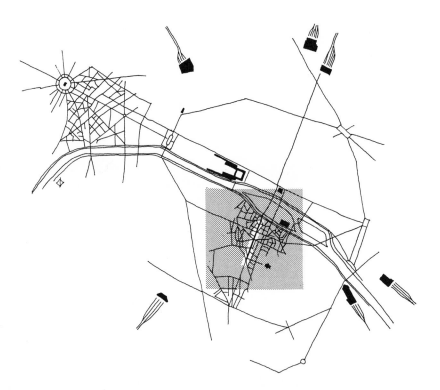

The Boulevard Saint-Michel is about 100 feet (30 meters) wide and runs in a north-south direction. Its most inviting stretch runs from the Place Saint-Michel, at the Seine, to the Luxembourg Gardens, a distance of about 2,500 feet (about half a kilometer). It is similar in width to the Boulevard Sébastopol of 1852 and to others of the period.[8] The central automobile cartway, with three and sometimes four lanes in one direction and one—a bus lane—in the other, is about 50 feet (14 meters) wide. The walks, generous in width, are close to 25 feet (7.6 meters). The light-colored buildings are uniformly five floors (including the ground floor) plus an attic story.

The sidewalks need every bit of space and, given what is on them, could use more. They are crowded with public and less public paraphernalia: kiosks,

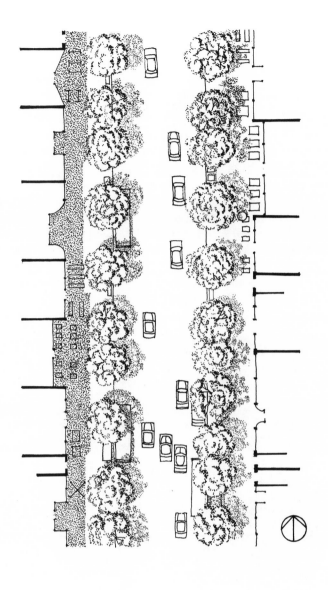

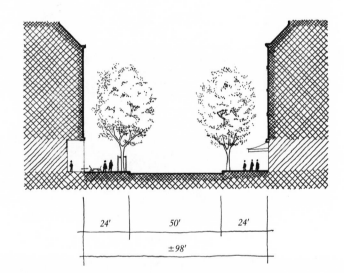

24'   50'   24'

±98'

Approximate scale: 1" = 50' or 1:600

benches, bus shelters, clothes racks and book tables, tables and chairs at cafes, light poles, trees, many, many people, and, for long stretches, not-so-portable metal crowd control fences, presumably there to keep people from spilling over into the street or crossing where that may not be the thing to do.

Start with the trees. The ubiquitous London plane trees are regularly spaced at about 30 feet (9.5 meters) apart and they are large and full-leafed. They might not start branching from a central trunk until about 17 feet high, and then, overhead, the foliage takes over. The canopy creates large patches of dark, moving shadows that contrast sharply with a brilliant light, perhaps made all the more so by reflections from the light-colored building facades. The darks seem very dark and the sunny spots are brilliant. One is aware of

Boulevard Saint-Michel

Great Streets

Along Boulevard Saint-Michel

the lighting inside stores during morning and early afternoon hours. It is not the kind of lighting one expects to see during daylight hours, and its sharp contrast with areas of deep shadow probably accounts for its prominence. Outdoor electric and neon shop signs are turned on as well, and there is a day-night feel about the street that is remarkable.

Stretches of the sidewalks are a bit like an attractive obstacle course. At any pace you choose to walk, there are people to get around, or tables and chairs at a cafe, or an old or new kiosk. Attractions are at least as plentiful as obstacles: books on tables in front of stores, shoes, sweaters, jackets, dresses, shirts on sale on racks or on those same tables and chairs. They all attract, slow the pace, make you want to look, browse, consider, remember and compare prices, perhaps buy. In the daylight hours it is hard to walk fast on the Boulevard Saint-Michel. The attraction is to the street. The corners can go by unnoticed or almost so. The Boulevard Saint-Germain, with a large cafe at the corner, is less compelling than is the continuation of Boulevard Saint-Michel.

In the Grand Manner

Walking gently up toward the Luxembourg Gardens, on the right side, one passes a wall of an old university building, a part of the Sorbonne. A closed door seems to have been that way for a long time. High, large, iron-grated windows have a gray, unwashed air about them. The building walls, light in color, nonetheless seem heavy. It is the kind of wall that can have a quickly deadening impact on an otherwise fine street, the kind of silent darkness that accompanies institutional buildings along the southern side of the Boulevard Saint-Germain, not favored by the sun. Here, though, at least for a good part of the day, there is sunlight and the sharp, moving patterns of light and shade work their magic. An otherwise mundane, even deadening facade comes alive.

There is less sunshine during the winter months: fewer hours and a lower sun angle cause the buildings to block the light more easily from the street. But the trees have lost their leaves, inviting whatever light is to be had. The branches cast their tracery against the sky. The street is not as light, not as dramatic. Slogging along in the rain or slush, however, there are the lighted stores and, weather permitting, the racks and stands of things to buy. Boulevard Saint-Michel remains a fine place to be and in any case, especially in Paris, spring is just around the corner.

CHAPTER FOUR

The Grand Canal as a Great Street _____

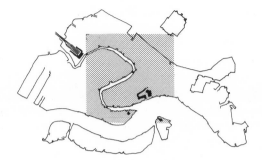

Once the Grand Canal is perceived as a street it follows easily that it is also a great street. As much as any street in the world, it stands for a whole city. It is as much Venice as is the Piazza San Marco. Say the words "Grand Canal" and you can imagine yourself on it and in Venice. The canal evokes a time-lessness that one can imagine inhabiting; of quiet water and land, of sea power, of gondolas, of mystery, of romance, costumes, theater, make-believe, decadence, narrow winding passages and geraniums on balconies, of nostalgia and reveries and sadness, and of reflections. Even if you have never been there you may know it through Canaletto or Guardi or Turner or Whistler or Sargent or countless other painters and poets, to say nothing of films. Naysayers will tell you that the city and its Grand Canal are dying, economically and physically (as the waters rise and the land sinks), but to know Venice at all is to know that it will survive.

Most of all the Grand Canal is a public passageway, a way to get from place to place. Its width varies from about 150 feet (45 meters) at its narrowest, such as at the Rialto Bridge, to as wide as 452 feet (138 meters) at its start, near the Dogana. Mostly it is about 190 to 200 feet wide. Part of a water-land composition, it connects buildings, neighborhoods, and settlements of Venice with each other. It is the main street of Venice. There are other water streets—canals—of course, in Amsterdam, Copenhagen, Bangkok, St. Petersburg, and most abundantly in Venice itself, but none are as compelling as the Grand Canal.

It is the physical qualities of the Grand Canal that make it such a great street and so fitting a subject for study. It is not the people you see that make the Grand Canal a place you want to be; except in five small sections from the railway station to the Piazza San Marco, there is no place to walk. Nor is it the stores or meeting places that front the canal; again, they are few and far between. Nor is it economic activity, or a continuation of the public realm into the ground floors of abutting buildings, as on the Boulevard Saint-Michel. No, it is the physical qualities of the canal itself that are so compelling. On the Grand Canal variables such as people or economic activities may be less important than on other streets simply because they are less present, and so it is easier to concentrate on what has been designed and built. Overwhelmingly, in the end, it is movement and light that teach the most about this great street, and by extension about others. First, though, it is well to travel the Grand Canal to see how it is made.

The more you look and see, the more you learn. The clear perceptions of
the fresh eye can become clouded, less clear with time and familiarity. With
time, subtleties make early conclusions less certain. Awareness about the
physical qualities of a place comes in layers, one layer often contradicting an
earlier one. Initial understandings may be discarded, others modified, others
built upon. It is that way on the Grand Canal.

The water is calm, mostly a light olive green mixed with cerulean blue. In
the early morning it may be a mixture of blues and greens and yellows that
can be indistinguishable from the sky, so that one hardly knows where one
stops and the other starts. In Venice, in the early morning, an artist might
paint the air, permitting shapes of buildings to emerge at times not all that
different in color from the air itself, only darker, maybe with some pinks. At
these times there is a faint horizontal line in the water, a clue to where the
buildings emerge. Generally the buildings are light-colored and richly detailed, as becomes apparent as soon as the sun burns off the morning haze.
At first impression, they seem to be of similar if not the same height along
the water's edge. Each has a separate entryway, often simple; a stone landing
in front of a door, with steps into the water and poles to tie onto and presumably to keep boats from hitting each other and the building itself. The
windows and balconies are often complicated. At water level, aside from
window-type openings there may be other breaks in facades, perhaps for a
boat to enter, perhaps an old secondary entrance now closed. The large,
gently sloping roofs are invariably of tile, a pink-red. The buildings, one
after another, define the canal, they are its edge; they grow out of the water.

Except in a few locations, the activity along the Grand Canal is of boats, not of people. People are in them, but it is the boats themselves that provide the activity and its pace. The largest and most visually prominent are for people, the *vaporetti* or water buses, but they are not the most frequent. Rather, the canal seems mostly to be a service street, with boats carrying goods, food, supplies, waste. The boats are moving slowly, generally in lines but not always so. Speed is not permitted. The wakes are mild: they don't beat against the buildings, the tied-up gondolas, or themselves. The *vaporetti* move from stop to stop, and that means from one side of the canal to the other; care is required. From time to time a *traghetto,* a local gondola ferry, moves across the canal, perpendicular to it, with one or two gondoliers and passengers standing huddled in the center; here, too, care is required. The pace is slow, even, rhythmic.

One side of the canal is almost always in sun and, especially in the winter, eyes are drawn to that sunny side, whichever one it is. There are times when the shade is compelling, particularly on hot days, but more often our eyes move to the sunny facades. If nothing else makes us aware of major directional shifts, moving along the canal, perhaps the sun does, first on one side and then on another. Each one of the five main reaches of the canal from the Piazza San Marco to the railway station is in a different direction from the others and so the buildings are always oriented differently; a different side, a different angle. We are aware of change and understandably there can be confusion as to direction. To know, from a map, that the canal snakes its way through Venice in an inverted S is not to experience it that way. Except at the Rialto Bridge, and at the canal Rio della Frescada, the curves are experienced slowly and therefore may seem less abrupt than they really are. We need landmarks to help us and thankfully there are plenty.

Eyes return to buildings. One, whose whole facade is a tile mosaic, stands out, but it is only one. What stands out more are the complicated Venetian windows and balconies in the otherwise flat facades. The windows themselves have mystery. There are circles and arcs and pointed arches and double

The Grand Canal as a Great Street

curves and thin, delicate columns traced in stone—usually white, sometimes pink, with streaks of gray or black. Walls appear to be made of thin layers and more layers of delicate stonework. There are more openings than there are windows. The numbers of surfaces and minute changes in surface direction seem countless, much more than on a Renaissance facade in Florence or Rome. Then, there is a layer of shutters, in one way or another integrated with the window opening. They, too, can be complicated, keeping out or letting in or otherwise modifying the light. And, maybe finally, maybe not, there are the windows, often of small, pained, leaded, uneven, colored Venetian glass in wood frames. Somewhere in all this there may be a layer of cloth, drapes that roll down or move from side to side. Add to the openings balconies, balustrades, cornices, chimneys, and countless richly detailed facades that are almost all different, and see that as many are Renaissance and baroque in style as are earlier Venetian Gothic or Byzantine, and you have a street facade that is very compelling, especially in the changing light.

Toward Salute from Accademia

The canal's buildings are old, and it is not so easy to maintain them, especially the high-ceilinged palaces. Many are empty or seem to be nearly so. There is a sense of forlornness about them and on stretches of the canal itself. There is little sense that many people are behind those windows, or if they are, that they often look at the canal. Nor are the buildings or their entrances particularly welcoming. These are indeed fronts and front doors, most of them in a formal sense. Berenson wrote of Venetian buildings that those on the narrow canals were as finely considered and as richly executed on the exterior as those that could be seen and appreciated from a distance, from the more grand canals and public ways. He explained that he thought this to be a simple consequence of the generally held values of the time. Owners, and designers, he thought, simply didn't know how to do things differently, that doing something less architecturally complete because it would be less visible would not have occurred to them, that "there were no architects, builders, carvers who could do less well."[9] Be that as it may, the fronts of *these* buildings are different from the rears (where there are rears), and these fronts can be on the intimidating side. You wouldn't just come up and ring the bell unannounced. You would more likely have business there. The prospect of standing alone on the stone water-surrounded entryway, especially if one's welcome is not assured, is not particularly inviting. Perhaps one tells the gondolier to wait until entry is gained. Nor can you just go on to the next palazzo if you want to do that. Getting into and out of small boats, however gracefully one may learn to do that, is not the most pleasant part of any trip. Rear entrances may be more easily navigated, though on foot, especially if one knows one's way around, but a rear entrance is a rear entrance after all and the fronts, whether because of condition or design, can be a bit forbidding.

If individual palaces along the canal are not enough to serve as landmarks, there are plenty of others. There are three bridges, each different from the next, each noteworthy in its own right. And there are major destinations: the car park and bus terminal at the Piazzale Roma (the least pleasing landmark), the quiet, calm, modern train station (Santa Lucia), the central market, famous (Santa Maria della Salute) and less-famous churches (San Geremia, which marks the entrance to Canale di Cannaregio), the customs house (Dogana), and of course the urban living room at Piazza San Marco. These landmarks take you along your way; you can place them in space and time. Beyond the receding, curving plane of the canal's facade, occasional towers also mark the path.

Four way stations stand out—at San Marco, at the Accademia, at the Rialto, and at the railroad station. All are places where there is great activity, where the pace quickens, where there are more people. San Marco is the great focal point of Venice. Everything seems to start and stop here. Symbolically at least, this is where the sea voyage ends and land life begins. And it is where the Grand Canal begins. The Piazza and Piazzetta, measured against other major urban squares, are smaller than is generally recognized, made large by contrast with the tightness and smallness of their surroundings and with the whole of Venice. The wide promenade that runs the length of the Bacino di San Marco ends just beyond the Piazzetta, where the Grand Canal begins, a crowded ending-beginning point with views toward the sea and the urban mystery of the canal and its city. The latter three way stations, because they stand along the canal itself, are of greater interest. At all three there are bridges and the canal narrows. Perhaps there is no more activity than elsewhere on the canal—no more boats—but at each of these locations everything takes place in a more constricted space and there are more stops, more service boats and gondolas at rest. In short, there is some congestion

Piazza San Marco: building context

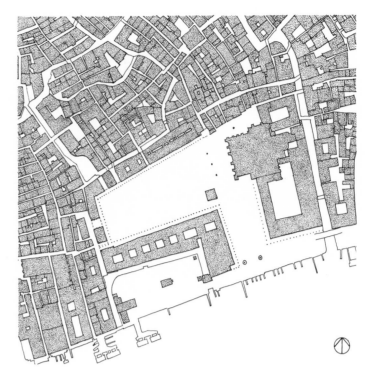

Approximate scale: 1″ = 400′ or 1:4,800

and more excitement, all the more so at the Accademia and at the Rialto, because, at least in one direction, the canal bends just beyond the bridges, giving a greater sense of enclosure within which the activity takes place. Movement may be slower at these locations, but the senses and reflexes are more acute.

One can walk along the Grand Canal only at the railway station area, for a small stretch east of the Ponte degli Scalzi, at both sides of the Rialto, and at the Piazza San Marco: very little as compared to the entire 2-mile length (3.2 kilometers). There are many other places along the canal to stand, where the public can come to the water's edge. They are meeting places and transfer locations and they command one's memory, however small they may be.

Grand Canal at Rialto Bridge: section

Great Streets

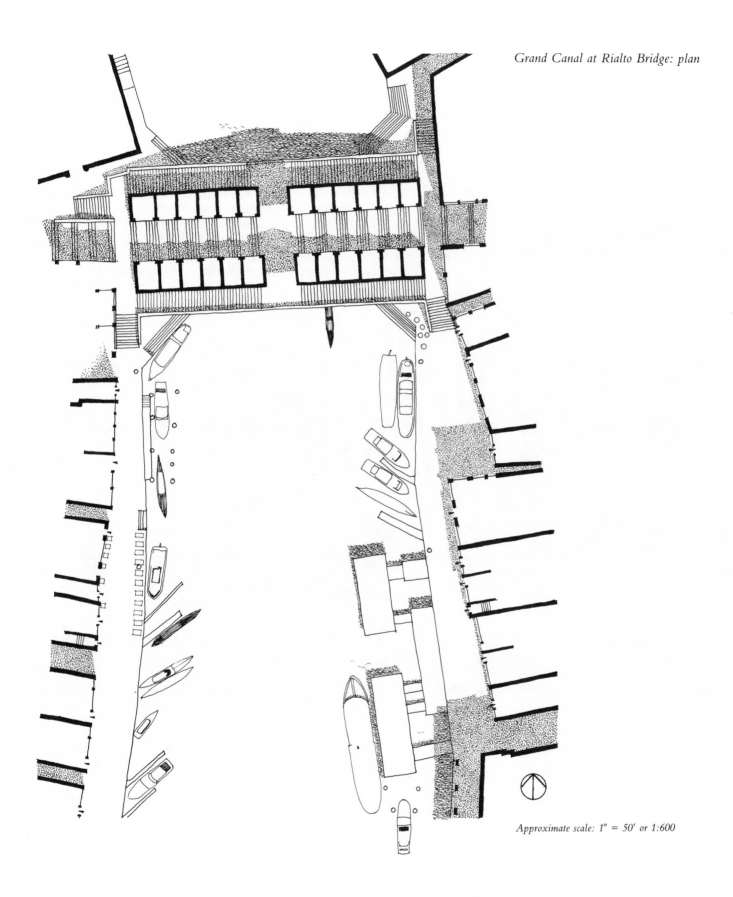

Approximate scale: 1″ = 50′ or 1:600

Toward Rialto

Where it is possible to walk along the canal, the views are rarely open or uninterrupted, not even views of the water. Rather, sight is always through or around something: poles, boats, gondolas, water taxis, *vaporetti*, ticket stations and shelters, kiosks, stands, always something. Many of the small shelters and kiosks have an impermanent look about them but have been there for years and will continue to be. And there are people. The eyes work around them all except for the one object or person you want to find. Later, remembering Venice and the canal from a distant time or place, we may edit out the visual memory of all the intrusions and recall only the water, the line of buildings, the bridges and the peopled walk itself.

Back on the canal, we sense its largeness, perhaps not in relation to other streets we know, for such spatial comparisons are often difficult to make, but in relation to the other canals and walkways around us and to Venice itself. In contrast to everything else, it is very, very large—truly the main street. Canals and walks that lead from it are often narrow and dark: with the promise of quiet coolness in the summer, they intrigue, they invite. What might they be like? A splash of sunlight somewhere along a narrow canal or at an intersection with another canal or pathway maybe 200 feet away where it is possible to see passing people, the Strada Nuova, or the Ruga Ravano, for example, is all the more inviting. It is not unlike being on a great river, being invited by each tributary to explore what might be upstream, especially beyond the first turn, where they go out of sight. The main river, the canal, is not so abrupt as its tributaries, but is long and gently turning by comparison. If for no other reason, the Grand Canal would stand out because of its contrast with its surroundings, its width and its long sweeping path through the center of Venice.

We look at the buildings again. There may well be a sense of their being of a similar if not the same height and even a rhythm of widths, part of a gently curving street facade. Closer inspection indicates otherwise. Building heights, one next to another, can vary by 40 feet or more. Some are narrow, some are wide. They are not all palaces, far from it. Some are only two stories, with simple flat facades and box-shaped windows, not unlike modest houses on nearby Murano. Nor are the buildings of one period. The canal buildings have been built and rebuilt over time, so there is great physical variety. Yet the impression persists of buildings of similar height and of a physical wholeness. Perhaps it is because there is a dominant median height of about four stories, often topped by a strong cornice line and certainly by ever-present, gently sloping tile roofs. The pink-red roofs are a common background. Trying to draw them, it may be difficult to know for sure where one leaves off and another starts. Or perhaps the impression of a similar height derives from the gentle curves of the canal and from long longitudinal views along it rather than acute, angled views across it. Looking along the canal, not directly across it, the sides of the taller buildings are visible. They are likely to have windows and may be of a similar color to the shorter buildings next to

Toward Rialto from Accademia

them. Except in the most extreme cases, and then only when the tallest buildings are close, the sides tend to fill in the differences in height. It is the view of the whole that is most memorable.

All of those different sizes suggest social and economic differences as well as physical diversity. Smaller buildings and rooms, more modest floor to ceiling heights, lesser materials, simpler detailing, all required less money than their larger, grander counterparts. It does not seem that all of the inhabitants of the canal could have been of the same economic status. The Grand Canal may not have been a street for everyone to live along, but it was not for only one class either, and if you could not live there, you could and can certainly go there. The canal calls you to it; it calls everyone. It is the main public street.

The Grand Canal is significantly different from other great streets we have studied. The most attracting, winding medieval streets are narrow and have about them a sense of mystery. The Grand Canal winds but is wide and sweeping in scale and scope. Other great streets have about them an indication, even a public invitation to what is behind the wall or window or door, especially at the ground floor. That is often not so on the Grand Canal, where there are few public entrances and it is not until the upper floors that one begins to have a sense of what is inside. The building heights on the canal, though they may be recalled as similar, exhibit great diversity. There are few opportunities to encounter people on the Grand Canal. Still, it is special for the truly significant way in which it is different.

12 March @ Rialto.

The Grand Canal as a Great Street

It is the details and it is the light and the water.

The Grand Canal is lined with first-rate buildings. They attract attention. It's not for nothing that so many are historic monuments. Overwhelmingly, they are richly detailed and in small or large ways they are different from each other and worthy of study. But it is more than that. The whole physical setting attracts the eyes and helps the eyes do what the eyes want to do, what they must do, that is, to move. Everything is moving; the light, the shape of the canal in its sweeps and turns, the boats and the people, and the water. The light, as the sun moves (even if the viewer is stationary), is always changing as it passes over all of those surfaces and their minute variations in shape and surface direction. And since each building is different from the next, and since there are significant variations on any given facade, monotony or sameness never occurs and the eyes are always on the move, attracted by and following the light. The buildings are indeed a feast for the eyes. But, obviously, that's not all. Unlike on almost any other street, here the street surface itself is alive. Shapes of every size and color endlessly appear and lose themselves in the water. The variety is without end. The eyes dance in response. Only in the black late hours of a moonless night do the reflections cease, though never entirely, and then, when there is little light and only dark shapes, the canal can be an ominous, even closed-in space. Then, one is doubly attracted to any light and its reflection on the water. In the light, the changing light, the fluidity of the horizontal water shapes combines with vertical arcs and curves of the building details and at times they are one.

CHAPTER FIVE

Once Great Streets _____

**Avenue des Champs-Elysées,
Paris**

Via del Corso, Rome

Market Street, San Francisco

Arguably, the Avenue des Champs-Elysées is the most famous street in the world.[10] It is the epitome of a grand boulevard, the one most thought of as preeminent; it was a model for others. Many people would also agree, including officials responsible for its design and maintenance, that by the 1990s it was no longer what it once was and that it needed change.

The Avenue des Champs-Elysées is a formidable presence in Paris, running in a straight 230-foot-wide (70-meter) line some 1.25 miles (2 kilometers) from the Place de la Concorde to the Place de l'Etoile, focusing there on the Arc de Triomphe. In plan, nothing in all of Paris except the River Seine can match it in scale. Its two main sections are vastly different: the first, from the Place de la Concorde to the Rond-Point, is two wonderfully landscaped promenades divided by a river of fast-moving traffic; the intensely developed second section runs from the Rond-Point to the Place de l'Etoile. It is this latter half that is of greatest interest here. On the ground, it is held together as one grand avenue not so much by the width of its right-of-way as by its beginning and ending foci, by the uniform width of its central, ten-lane cartway, about 87 feet (26.5 meters), and by the large, severely pruned London plane trees that line it. The distinct rise in topography approaching the Arc de Triomphe dramatizes and focuses. The views from the Arc are impressive, particularly so to the southeast, back down the Avenue des Champs-Elysées. The Arc de Triomphe, however, is not a real presence until it is close at hand. For pedestrians walking toward the Arc, trees block the view.

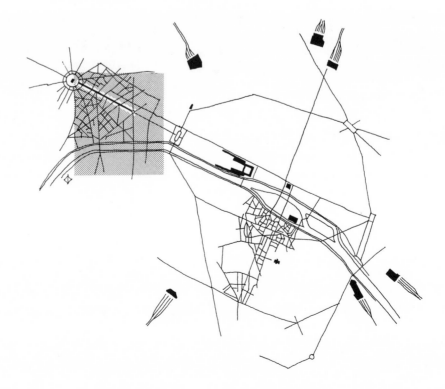

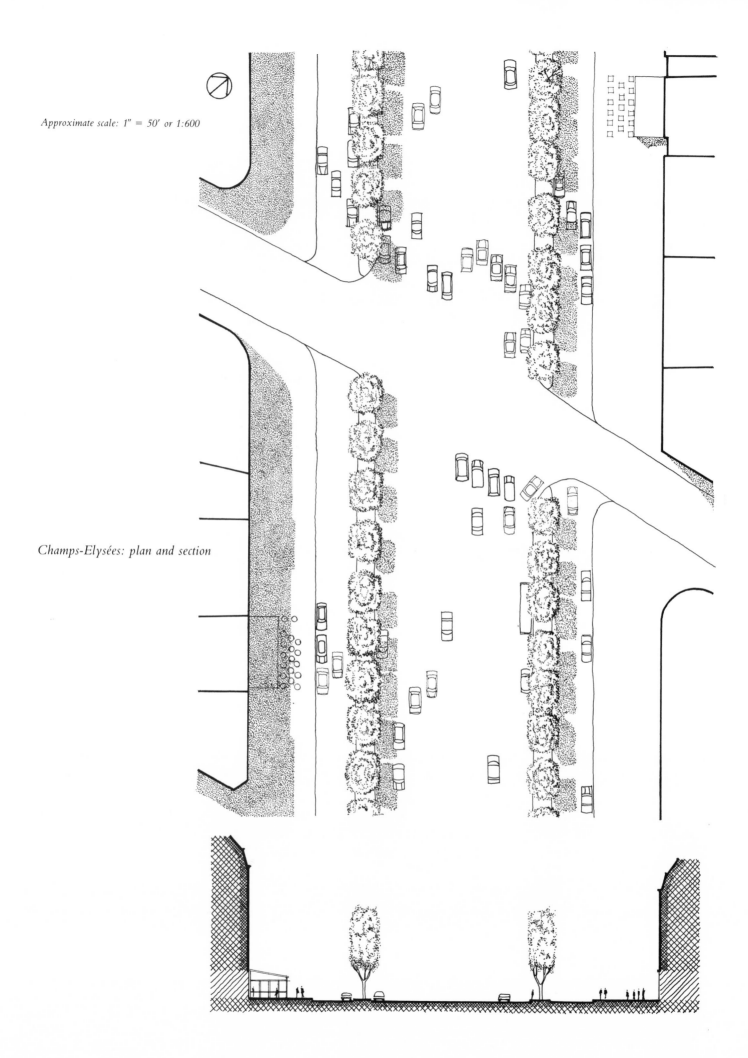

Champs-Elysées: plan and section

Boxed trees and access street -Champs- Elysées

The problem with the avenue, what keeps it from being a great street, lies in both what exists and what is absent from the right-of-way itself, not in the buildings that line it. The buildings, generally the same height, about 75 to 80 feet (22.8 to 24 meters), are visually interesting even if not all are outstanding. There are many windows, many doors and cornice lines to cast shadows; there are balconies, generally light-reflective materials and colors, and eye-catching details. Large ground floors offer a cacophony of signs, windows, and entrances that entice. Nor is it the uses themselves that have caused the avenue to deteriorate, though some would hold them to be a major detraction. There is no inherent reason why fast food restaurants, auto showroom windows, movie theaters, entrances to shopping malls, or airline ticket offices need be incompatible with a great street; perhaps a far cry from high style or what used to be, but hardly a problem for a major public way. There are not many elegant uses on the Boulevard Saint-Michel and yet it is a great street. In any case, there remain on the Champs-Elysées more than a handful of known restaurants, cafes, stores, and other destinations. The large spaces on either side of the central roadway, some 70 feet (21.3 meters) on either side, are often barren. Moreover, what exists in them is often wrong.

Once Great Streets

Cafe, Champs-Elysées

The trees, to be sure, are large and are reasonably spaced at about 30 feet (9-plus meters). But they are strangely pruned in a box hedge–like manner, high above ground level with barely a 10-foot (3-meter) span of foliage on either side of the trunks. Their form may be fine for the long vista up and down the avenue, especially when there is a parade, but they do no good whatsoever for the street user: they provide no shade, no visual protection from the center ten lanes of traffic, no immediate positive presence. They might as well not be there. Another row, closer together and pruned to afford shade, would help. The trees are in a strip about 10 feet wide that houses large kiosks, portable fences haphazardly placed for crowd control, and streetlights.

There once were and sometimes still are generous access roads, about 22 feet wide (6 to 7 meters). This space is now sometimes used for auto access and parking, sometimes not. When it is used for parking, it is as often as not a crowded metallic hodgepodge that exists in that 70-foot space between the too sparse trees and the buildings: a not-too-well-ordered parking lot. Where the parking has been removed, the space has become part of a vast no-man's land, except for the parking of motorcycles. Sidewalks along the buildings, a generous space of almost 40 feet, are interrupted by "temporary" structures that house cafes. They can protrude as much as 16 feet (5 meters) with another 13 feet for tables and umbrellas, a total of close to 30 feet. The tables and umbrellas are not the problem, rather it is the abrupt one-story "temporary" restaurants that create dead spots, backwater eddylike spaces between one and another, and force pedestrians away from the building line, away from stores, into the barren, wide-paved areas. In short, because of unthoughtful additions or subtractions to the wide walkway–access road areas, they are unpleasant places to be.

Damage has not been done to the stretch of the Champs-Elysées from the Rond-Point to the Place de la Concorde. Each side of the central roadway is wider, some 112 feet (34 meters), but each is full, mostly of trees. Approximately 55 feet (17 meters) from the curb begin four rows (three rows on one side) of closely planted elm trees, some 16 feet (5 meters) apart. This dense linear bosc, in such contrast to the open walk and ever-present London plane trees that line the roadway, is an extraordinarily pleasant place to walk a long distance, pausing at benches along the way if desired, in deep shade. The way is marked by outstandingly executed rain shelters, refreshment stands, lavatories, lights, and benches. The trees come as close as possible to the few intersecting streets. Buildings are really not a part of this street-park.

Physical design issues along the Champs-Elysées, beyond the Rond-Point, have not gone unrecognized. Design plans seem to be drawn up at regular intervals;[11] they include underground parking, more trees, new street furniture, new paving, elimination of the access roads, pushing back the restaurants, and the like. Merchants, it seems, are hard to convince. They want access and auto parking as close to their entrances as possible. Trees could take away the views of their businesses. Never mind that there are hundreds of examples of fine successful commercial streets without significant parking and heavily planted with trees. Never mind that new, special paving rarely makes a significant difference. World-wide, merchants seem to see the problems and proposed solutions similarly. There are successful models, if one wants to use them, in Paris and on streets in cities the world over. The Avenue des Champs-Elysées needs more content, mostly linearly disposed, to create more human-scaled subspaces, an urban allee, within its very wide right-of-way. That should not be too hard to do.

Via del Corso _____

Goethe wrote admiringly of the Via del Corso in the eighteenth century.[12] It was, for him, a special street, worthy of his attention. He measured it, approximately 3,500 paces by his count, slightly more than one mile or about 1,625 meters by ours; he made observations about its width relative to its length and the height of buildings—"The width bears no proportion . . ."— and about the grand buildings that lined its length, about its fine year-round maintenance; and most of all he observed its use, most keenly on Sundays and feast days and during the period of Carnival with its nightly horse races. The writing is most alive when he describes the street's use on Sundays by wealthy Romans in their carriages and the protocol used in that narrow

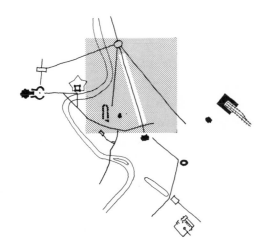

Via del Corso at Piazza del Popolo:
street and building context

Approximate scale: 1″ = 400′ or 1:4,800

space, and the rush of costumed participants, spectators, horses, pageantry, and general festivities of Carnival. There was an enormous amount of action in a very narrow space.

The Via del Corso has not changed much in physical terms during the 200 years since Goethe wrote so admiringly of it. For some of its length it is at least as active and full of people as it was then, including on Sunday afternoons. Toward the end of the twentieth century, however, it would be difficult to call the Via del Corso a great street. Why? It presents a more perplexing problem than does the Champs-Elysées.

Via del Corso is in the heart of the city and is straighter, longer, and even wider than most streets. Together with the Via di Ripetta, Via del Babuino, Piazza del Popolo, and Piazza Venezia, it marks and orients the city. The Piazza del Popolo, its beginning, and the Piazza Venezia, its end, are as known as the street itself, and were designed in part to emphasize the street just as the Via del Corso was designed to be a special, memorable, public way. The Via Condotti, perhaps equally known for its view to the Piazza di Spagna and its fashionable shops, starts from this street. The Piazza Colonna is the most notable of the public squares along its path. Many buildings of similar height (four to six stories, ranging from 65 to 75 feet) define the Via del Corso, which for the most part is 36 feet wide (about 11 meters). The buildings may not be old by Roman standards, but most were there when Goethe wrote. It is a long-continuing street with a famous history. Beyond the Piazza Colonna northward, there are many stores, windows, and en-

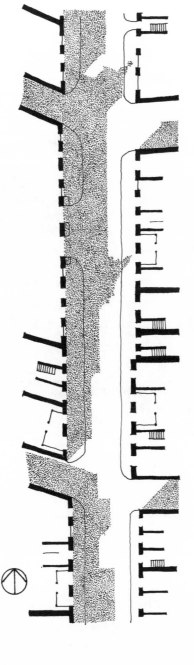

Via del Corso near Piazza del Popolo: plan and section

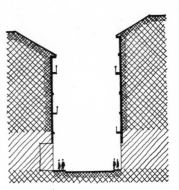

Approximate scale: 1" = 50' or 1:600

trances. The shops are of all types, but most sell clothes.[13] The street, especially where the stores are most concentrated, is crowded with people: 850 to 1,000 can pass a given point during a five-minute period on a shopping afternoon. On Sunday afternoons, when stores are closed and as many window and door shutters are drawn as are up, people of Rome, especially young people, come to this area and to this street to stroll, to see and be seen. Location and history have a great deal to do with its use. It is as central as any street can be in Rome. Shops leading from the Via del Corso or the Via Condotti and others as well are among the most fashionable to be found anywhere in a style-conscious city. People come to shop in them and to window-shop. The stores along the Via del Corso cater to a wide variety of

From Piazza del Popolo

age and income groups, not only to the wealthy. If it is not *the* main downtown shopping street of Rome, it is one of them. Crowds can easily get to this area, perhaps more easily than to many others. A main station of the Metropolitana, Rome's Subway, is located at the Piazza di Spagna and in recent years an extension of the line has given access to large housing developments at the city's periphery. Residents of these not-too-well-developed outer areas, particularly the young looking for activities and interesting places to go, find this area easy to reach. The Via del Corso, then, has many characteristics of a great street: location in the city, a long straight form amid an irregular street pattern; definition; a strong beginning and end; open spaces along its way; stores, activity, and people. What keeps it, then, from being a great street?

Given its regular narrow width relative to the height of buildings along it, the Via del Corso seems long and unrelenting. The slight bend at the Via di Caravita makes the ends difficult to see from some points, depending on which side of the street one is walking on. Nor are those ends overly compelling, especially from a distance: from near the Piazza del Popolo the wedding cake Altare della Patria at the Piazza Venezia is too distant and too white. From the other end and much deeper into the street, the obelisk that marks the Piazza del Popolo, a light beige-pink, melds with the gateway behind it and is difficult to see. No complaint, however, can be registered of the famous, framed, funneled entry from the Piazza del Popolo onto the Via del Corso.

Under certain conditions, the height of buildings along a street, in relation to the street width, can become oppressive, and that situation seems to exist along much of the Via del Corso. For what seem like long sections of the street it is dark and the heavy, tall buildings seem to weigh on the street, especially if there is little or no sun or light reflected from windows or buildings. It may not be so much a matter of proportions as it is of actual dimensions. The width-to-height proportions where the street is 36 feet wide vary from 1:1.66 to about 1:2. Many fine streets are similarly proportioned. The narrow Via dei Greci, off the Via del Corso, has a width of about 15 feet (4.5 meters) and building heights of about 48 feet (14.6 meters) giving a ratio of 1:3.2, and it is a compelling street. But the Via dei Greci is short, there is an arched passover toward its end, and in absolute terms a height of 48 feet is considerably less than 66 or 72 feet. For large sections of Via del Corso, most notably toward the Piazza Venezia, the buildings themselves do not help. Past the Via Condotti the buildings tend to get larger, longer, heavier in detailing and with much less transparency at ground level. It is an area of banks and institutions. Building mass, at the upper floors, is rhythmic but

Heavy facades, via del Corso

Once Great Streets

uninteresting. Where the street is wider, as at the Via delle Convertite where it is 63 feet wide (19.2 meters), it is easier to look at the street and see what's there: the buildings, the stores, people sitting or walking. It is not so much the proportions as it is the changed, more open perspective that is afforded. At the Via di Caravita, walking south, the street narrows again to about 33 feet, and the large, long buildings are experienced in tight perspective over a considerable distance once again. When those buildings are dark in color, because they have not been cleaned or painted in a long while or because the building material is dark, and when the facade is of heavy stone with high, large, grated, unwelcoming windows, then the street is not a pleasant place to be. Painting and cleaning help but are not enough. Noise, a crush of large buses and their exhausts, and narrow sidewalks all add to the discomfort. People's pace quickens; they seem to want to get out. The openness of the Piazza Venezia becomes more inviting.

There are street widenings or *piazze* along the Via del Corso, breaks in the relentlessness of the narrow way, places that permit more sunlight and a better perspective of the street: the Largo dei Lombardi, Largo San Carlo al Corso, Largo Carlo Goldoni at the Via Condotti, and the Piazza Colonna are the most notable. By and large, though, none of them is outstanding in design treatment, though the shops and proportions of the latter two are inviting. They don't help the street as they might, nor does the street make them better places.

Decisions that affect the use and looks of the Via del Corso seem at logger-heads with each other and with the street itself. Regulations as to how it can be used change with location and with time of day. To a casual user, without precise knowledge of what the regulations are, what can and cannot be done on the street seems ambiguous. Toward the south, it is for buses and taxis, some private cars (it seems), speeding police cars, and motorcycles, and for pedestrians on much too narrow walks, 4 to 6 feet wide. Toward the Piazza del Popolo, the street seems to be mostly for pedestrians, but then why do we occasionally experience more police cars and what appear to be official cars? Walking in the center of the street, at its northern end, is not overly comfortable just because the curbs are there, to the right and left, resulting in a feeling of uneasiness, as if one were being tolerated on the automobile's turf. No one, it seems, has quite decided what the street should be.

Physically, the Via del Corso is not all that different from when Goethe wrote of it. The shops and their windows may make it better, while the lack of people living in the upper stories, and the deadening ground-floor banks, where they occur, may make it worse. The Via del Corso could be improved, not least by firm decisions on the use of the street itself, by doing more with the *piazze* and widenings along the way, and by making it a more comfortable place to walk. Perhaps, however, the most significant difference between the Via del Corso now and in Goethe's time is simply that a lot of time has passed. In the late 1700s there weren't many streets like Via del Corso, and now there are many, and better.

Market Street _____

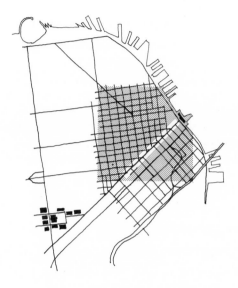

Sometimes, after school, I used to go to my father's office in the Underwood Building on Market Street, on the south side, a half block east of New Montgomery Street. That was during the 1930s and it was a big thing to do. I loved going downtown and Market Street was the best part of it. It had everything you could want: offices, stores, the big Palace Hotel, places to eat, streetcars, lots of people—all different kinds of people—movies, a little bit of everything. The big movie houses were on Market: Pantages, the Warfield, the Golden Gate, the St. Francis, the Paramount, the Fox. Some of them had big orchestras, or an organ, and some also had vaudeville shows. All the buildings crowded right to the street and there were stores in them—not like the Zellerbach Building that was built in the sixties with gardens around it and which left a big hole along Market. That was an insult to the street. My grandfather had his shirt-making workshop and sales office on the second floor at 25 Kearney, near Market Street. Up at Eighth and Ninth was where the honky-tonk was. There were sideshows and drunks. Market Street had lots of places to eat: cafeterias, like Clinton's, for quick meals. There were bars and grills, like the Palm Garden Grille that had a seafood bar outside. I think they're almost all gone now. Fire engines used Market Street too; when you heard the sirens, everyone stopped and watched, especially for the long hook and ladder truck.

Most of all, though, there were people and streetcars and so many different activities, and I loved it. To a kid—I was a young teenager then—it seemed big and grown-up and sophisticated, especially toward evening on a gray, rainy day. There were rush hours three times a day: in the morning, at lunch when office workers and shoppers strolled and went to the cafeterias and restaurants, and in the late afternoon, when people waited for their neighborhood streetcars to go home. Most of the transportation system focused on Market. Streetcars, big, heavy iron monsters, full of people, went clanging down to the Ferry Building and the big turnaround loop. At times there would be four streetcars abreast at the same place on the street, two going east and two heading west. The turnaround at the Ferry Building, maybe not unlike the transportation turnaround at the square in front of the train station in Amsterdam, was a very busy place. Ferries, big ones, disgorged workers from the East Bay who either picked up a streetcar or took the pedestrian overpass above the Embarcadero to the foot of Market and then walked up the street. Other streetcars and trolleys and cable cars stopped at or went past the Ferry Building, too. The streetcars ran close to each other, the outside ones run by the Municipal Railway and the inner ones by the Market Street Railway. They were only two feet apart and people waiting in the street for the inside cars crowded into that space, with cars running on both sides of them. Sometimes the streetcars raced each other up the street—real competition.

Market Street was for big events. On parade days my dad could get us into a fifth-floor vacant room looking down at the street. We'd watch the marches, especially the big Army-Navy Day Parade with all that music and noise and the flags, and the Labor Day Parade spectacle with the different unions represented, each it seemed with its own band. Politicians marched. The sidewalks were jammed.

I remember going home after being at my dad's office. We'd come onto the street at about 5:05 and cross over at Second Street and wait at the Muni island. The street was jammed with people, people coming out of buildings, walking to the Ferry Building, all kinds of people. We'd get on a crowded streetcar, and I'd look at all the sights

Market Street at California Street – 1937

Drawing from a photo by Paul Ward in Paul C. Johnson and Richard Reinhardt, San Francisco As It Is, As It Was *(Garden City, N.Y.: Doubleday and Co., Inc., 1979).*

Market Street at California Street – 1992

and the changes as we headed west toward Twin Peaks and the tunnel. We got off at Vicente, just past the three-mile-long tunnel, on the edge of our neighborhood, St. Francis Wood, and then we were home.[14]

Market Street, in San Francisco, was once a great street. If San Francisco had a Grand Avenue, a Broadway, or a Main Street, Market Street was it. Sooner or later, people who write about San Francisco get to Market Street; how it was, the major buildings, especially the grand hotels, how much of the city and its people were focused there, its development and landmarks before the earthquake and fire of 1906 and the major buildings along its length that were lost as the fire progressed, the street's rebirth after the fire, the street-cars, the parades, the grandeur, and the honky-tonks.[15] Old-timers talk about Market Street as being great once, but not now. "Once" seems to have ended a few years after World War II. For sailors, soldiers, and marines passing through the city during and just after the war, Market symbolized San Francisco's vitality, friendliness, and America's hopes for the future. But it is not a great street now, despite major efforts to make it so. The city has changed, and Market Street has changed.

Location has had a lot to do with Market Street's eminence. It is a true spine of the city, like no other San Francisco street, leading from the Ferry Building at the bay to the foot of Twin Peaks, three miles to the southwest. It is at the break point or seam between two different gridiron street patterns, the diagonal edge of the historic North of Market downtown area and the large rectangular blocks to the south. Streets and views focus on Market Street, especially from the north side. From Twin Peaks the most compelling view to the northeast is straight down Market Street, to the Ferry Building. It is wider than streets around it and it is long and is located where it can be and is noticed—a major presence. It was meant to be a major street.

Location and size and contrast haven't changed, but other things have. Focus is one of them. Places like the Ferry Building, the Palace Hotel, Lucky Baldwin's, the Case Building, the major stores and the movie houses were not only major destinations, they were also memorable buildings. They were something to see. More important, it wasn't just the well-to-do who came to Market Street, but everyone, rich and poor, resident and visitor alike. The streetcars responded to and helped create and strengthen those destinations. If only in relative terms, there are fewer major places to go on Market Street now, at the turn of the twenty-first century. In population San Francisco is not that different from what it was at the close of World War II, but in the 1990s there are many more locations where major things happen. To be sure, some important stores remain on Market, and there is even a new one, in a large building at Hallidie Plaza. There is more life and focus there, where the stores are and where the Powell Street cable car ends, than anywhere else on the street. But Market Street as a whole doesn't have the liveliness and attraction that it once had. Even the most visually prominent focus of all, the Ferry Building at the foot of Market, was largely obliterated by a freeway in the 1950s, only to be regained in 1991 with the freeway's demolition.

Those double sets of transit lines and the streetcars on them did more than bring people to the street. They were a major physical presence themselves, one that dictated the pace and scale of Market. The cars were large. Picture two or three or four abreast, moderately spaced behind each other, rolling up and down the street, never so fast that a young man wouldn't assume he could catch up with one at the next stop if he had just missed the one he wanted. You couldn't not notice them. Their pace was more that of pedestrians than that of autos. They stopped regularly, putting off and picking up people along the street. The physical consequences were a lot different from what results when most of the transit vehicles and the people are underground and when there are but four stops, as there are now under Market, rather than many on the street.

Not only has time brought larger and fewer buildings, it has changed the way they address the street and are seen by people. Until at least the late 1940s, a pedestrian walking on Market Street saw stores. Regardless of what was going on above, the street level had stores, with windows and doors and signs. One could and did look in them. Access to upper-story offices might be through simple rather than elaborate entrances. For the walker, it was a procession of shops and each one was a bit different from the next. Above all it was busy, eye-catching. Contemporary office buildings are more likely to have entrance lobbies or banks or other large, nonpublic space along the sidewalk. There is less to catch the eye and less of interest.

Above the street level, the change is at least as striking, maybe more so. While once the view might have been of stone or stucco or tiled buildings with individual windows and individual blinds, and of individual people or their implied individual presence, today's views are largely of anonymous patterns, usually of vertical or horizontal bands that may make identification of individual floors difficult, to say nothing of the windows or of what or who might be behind them. In short, it seems that the most severe changes, the ones that have made the difference between a great street and a less great one, are those that have lessened community focus on Market Street while at the same time diminishing individuality and interest.

It isn't as if people don't know that the street is not what it once was and don't care; they do. More than two-thirds of the voters, in 1967, voted to spend almost $25 million to help make it a great street once again. That was when the subway was being built. Wider sidewalks, trees, refurbished lights, new wide paving and large granite curbs, a new family of street signs and benches and specially designed trash bins and other new details, and three large new plazas and more small ones were carefully designed and built. They make a positive difference, but not as much as one would have thought. After 20 years the trees are still not a major presence. They are not big enough and don't look robust. Brick crosswalks, as continuations of the sidewalks, have been replaced with some hard-to-describe reddish-pinkish

Section of Market Street: plan, 1990

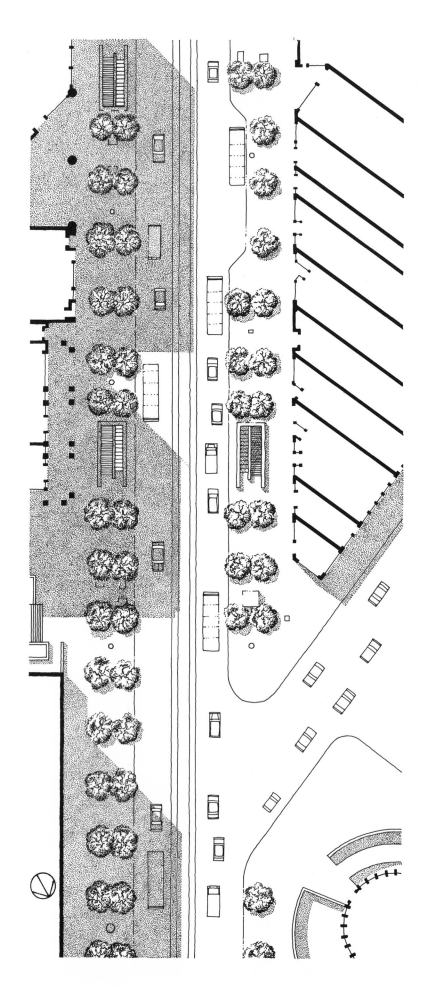

Approximate scale: 1" = 50' or 1:600

Cross section of Market Street, 1990

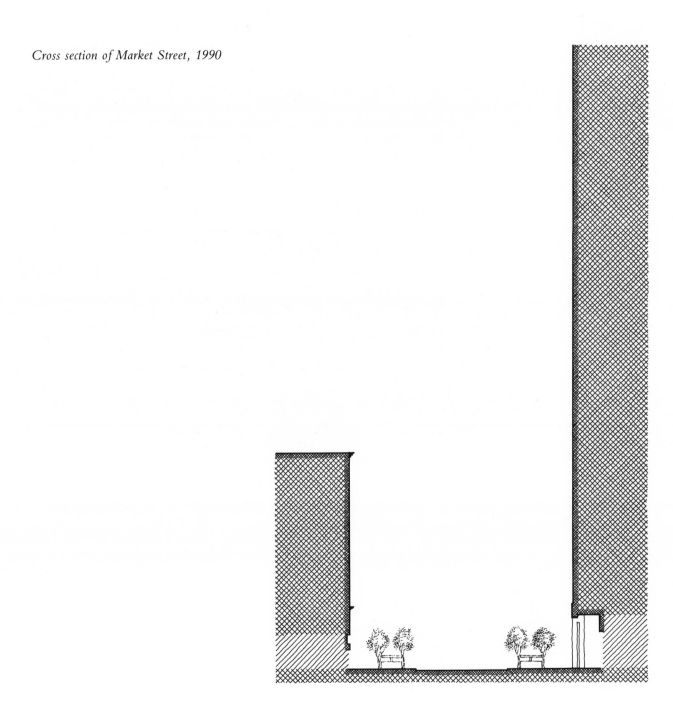

Once Great Streets

aggregate material. Asphalt seems to creep over the special paving materials. There is a difference between cleanliness (and the street *is* kept clean) and maintenance (such as of trees and sidewalks) that seems to go unrecognized.

Of the public open spaces, only Hallidie Plaza at the foot of Powell Street and the small Mechanics Monument area at Battery Street seem to work well. The foot of Market, where the streetcars turned around, is the barren, asymmetric Justin Herman Plaza wasteland. Civic Center Plaza, marking the intersection of the "city beautiful" axis of City Hall and its attendant civic buildings with Market Street, is large and windblown, with a strange, off-axis fountain that wants to be in Oregon, the home of the idea that generated it. Hallidie Plaza, though, is a well-defined, sunny, comfortable space, with a focus of activities that calls attention to Market Street and enlivens it for a block or so in both directions.

There is little, save new buildings to replace the not-so-old buildings, that might overcome the anonymity of so much of the architecture that now lines Market Street. And it is unlikely that the street surface will soon see the kind of public transit activity that once helped to make it a great street. But, over time, the ground floors of buildings could be changed to be more inviting to people and the two large, uninviting public spaces could be redesigned and rebuilt. Indeed, as the freeways that cross Market Street in front of the Ferry Building and west of the Civic Center come down there is renewed interest in a major new plaza at the foot of Market Street, one that shows an understanding of what was lost. Finally, those trees can still be cared for and allowed to grow. If they ever become large, they would be a real presence and might just hide some of the buildings on the street.

CHAPTER SIX

The Ramblas, Barcelona _____

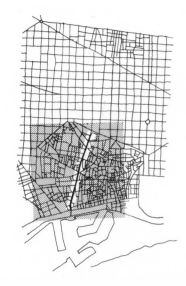

In a city with perhaps the best streets in the world, the Ramblas in Barcelona stands out. Its placement in the city and in the Gothic Quarter, its grand scale in relation to its narrow, winding surroundings, the people-welcoming nature of its design, and the quality of the buildings that line its edges make it a street for everyone to come to and know. It responds and caters to a centuries-old strolling tradition. The Ramblas, really three successive Ramblas leading in a long, not quite straight line from the Columbus statue at the port gradually upward to the Plaça de Catalunya that marks the start of the nineteenth-century city, is a very strong presence. It is a street clearly designed for people to be on, to walk, to meet, to talk. And it succeeds. The wide, central, tree-lined and canopied promenade, a focus for walking, with cartways for automobiles pushed to the sides in grand reversal of the norm, is a stroke of genius that establishes the social orientations of the street. It cannot be ignored, nor would anyone want to. It is hard to conceive that anyone—old, young, man, woman, resident, visitor—who knows Barcelona would not know of the Ramblas and remember it with affection.

Central Promenade, Ramblas

Along the Ramblas

To be sure, many of the physical things that go to make it the Ramblas can also be found on other fine streets. Though long, it has a distinct beginning and end; one knows where it starts and stops. Many buildings of reasonably similar height (five to seven stories) line the street and define it. Stores below with windows above give the street a sense of transparency, a view or feeling of what is inside. There are many entrances, as many as one every 13 feet. The building facades are generally complex in terms of surface and detail, and while they certainly are not all the same, they do get along with each other just fine. There are many buildings, not just many entrances and windows. Some can be as narrow as 15 feet wide. There are significant destina-

Along the Ramblas

tions along the street—a major theater and public market—as well as
intersecting streets. There is a subway stop near the theater. As if the stores
and restaurants that line each side were not enough, there are, in discrete
sections along the central walk, stalls that sell birds and flowers, larger stalls
for magazines, and umbrella-covered tables for drink and food served from
bars across the narrow auto cartways. There are places to sit. Attention has
been paid to streetlights (though there are some recent unfortunate additions), particularly at street crossings. And there are trees, large London
plane trees with branches that start some 15 to 20 feet from the ground,
creating an interweaving canopy high above and green, dappled light below.

Door detail, Ramblas

The Ramblas was designed for walking, and it succeeds so well that it would stand out anywhere. Moreover, its size, length, and regularity, in such arresting contrast to the winding dense passageways of the Gothic Quarter it bisects, cannot help giving orientation and order to this oldest section of the city and to the whole of Barcelona. The Ramblas, today, evolved from its origins as a seasonal drainage swale that established the limit and position of the medieval town wall. As landscape architect Laurie Olin has noted:

Most appropriately in Spain (as in southern California), sycamores, the genetic parents of plane trees, are found naturally lining these normally dry, sandy stream beds. Even today, as one walks from the Plaça de Catalunya down the gently curving route between the planes and buildings on each side (pressing like banks of a stream), one can feel the ghost of the old watercourse.[16]

The central walkway, the grand passage, varies in width from approximately 36 feet (11 meters) at its narrowest to over 80 feet (24 meters) at the Plaça de Catalunya. Mostly, though, it is about 60 feet wide. The trees, not as regularly spaced as they at first appear, but most often less than 20 feet apart, are set about 2 feet in from the curb. Those closely spaced trees, like a row of columns, give protection from the one-way traffic on either side. The two automobile cartways vary in width from 15 to 33 feet (4.5 to 10 meters), usually with two driving lanes and a parking lane. The sidewalks along the buildings can be as little as 3 feet wide and as much as 20 feet (6 meters), but are usually less than 10 feet. What all of this means is that the natural place to walk is in the center, not on the narrower walks along the stores, and it means that people are constantly crossing those two bordering streets, humanizing them, giving some pause to motorists. In short, pedestrians are given the preferred section of the right-of-way, the center, so they set the pace and tone for the whole. Distances are short enough so that a person in the center can recognize people on the side walks or make out what is in stores even if it is not possible to appraise the goods in the windows. The design assures comfort: shade in the summer and sun in the winter, thanks to the deciduous London plane trees and the building heights permitting sun for at least parts of the day during the winter. It is an uncomplicated design and it is amazingly effective.

The street is particularly appropriate to its location. The surrounding city pattern has winding streets that may be less than 10 feet wide, lined with buildings up to six stories high. It is a tight though not unpleasant street pattern, but streets can wind and turn, making orientation difficult and providing a bit of mystery. There was and still is high density (though less so now than in years past): many people and activities in a relatively small space. So the Ramblas exists in contrast to its surroundings; it is spacious, perhaps as much so as is the Grand Canal relative to surrounding Venice. When you come to the Ramblas, you know where you are. Or, if while walking in the old Gothic Quarter you happen to wonder where you are, it is possible and likely that your reference point will be the Ramblas. Its presence is always felt. It can be thought of as a long, linear urban park, a bright

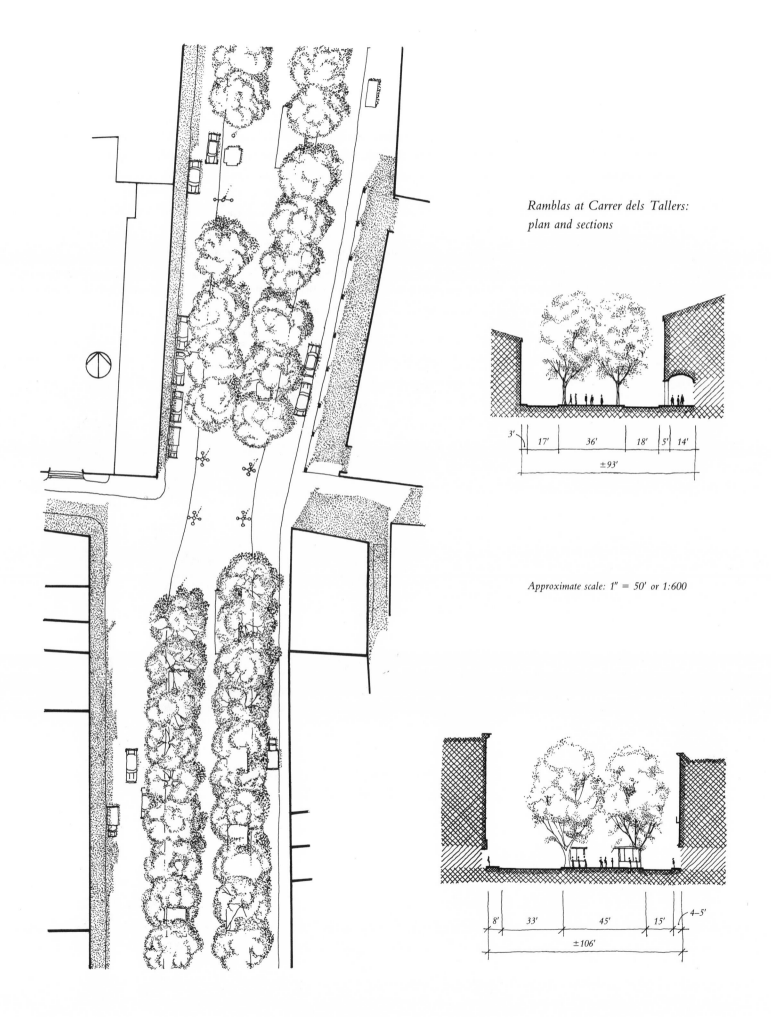

Ramblas at Carrer dels Tallers:
plan and sections

3' 17' 36' 18' 5' 14'

±93'

Approximate scale: 1″ = 50′ or 1:600

8' 33' 45' 15' 4–5'

±106'

breathing space amidst the dense, often dark, always shady urban fabric that it marks so well.

Not everything is as a perfectionist might wish on the Ramblas. Some buildings, vacant or partially so, are not maintained as well as they might be, so at some points there is grayness or a bit of grubbiness that can be disconcerting. Near the Columbus column-statue there are some newish buildings that seem not to belong because they are not on the building line, and the trees in front of them have been left out—a mistake. The paving design, muted colors in striped concrete, is uninspired. And there are new and not-so-new leftovers from continuous attention and efforts to improve a changing street, most notably a set of high streetlights with strange reflectors and a rather recent electronic information and advertising signboard.

The blemishes are minor. The strong basic design overcomes them all. Late in the evening, maybe at eleven, the older streetlights have been turned on and they mark the passageway with a yellow-gold sparkling line. At night, as in the day, the Ramblas is informal and comfortable. It is still possible to stop for a drink, even on a cool drizzly evening, when there remain many strolling people. It is a great place to be.

CHAPTER SEVEN

The Great Residential Boulevard _____

**Monument Avenue,
Richmond, Virginia**

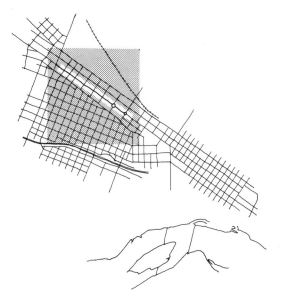

The residential boulevard may be a unique North American contribution to world streets. Generally wide, such streets are invariably tree-lined, they often have graceful curves, they are shaded and cool in the summer, and they are quiet. They come with or without a planted median (through which a trolley may once have run) and they are long. Lined with large homes, spaced at some distance from each other and well set back from the street on cared-for lawns, these streets bespeak a sense of well-being. They are supposed to. Often they were the centerpiece of land development promotions and were finely built in advance of the homes that were to line them, to give a sense of what was to come, to tell the prospective well-to-do owner-builder that this would be just the place for him and his family. Roots of these streets may be in French boulevards or English villages and in the residential sections of earlier American small towns, with elm-shaded main streets. They are often associated with suburban development, not as often with central urban environments. The various parkways that connect the lakes and that are part of the park system of Minneapolis are such streets, and so is Massachusetts Avenue in Washington, D.C., Shaker Boulevard in Shaker Heights, Ohio, and Fairmount Boulevard or Euclid Heights Boulevard in Cleveland Heights, immediately east of Cleveland. Still others are St. Charles Avenue in New Orleans (an urban example) and Orange Grove Boulevard in Pasadena, California. Monument Avenue is urban and it is not far from the city center. Nor is it necessary to be well-to-do to live along it. But its physical design is compelling.

Monument Avenue is a main street in Richmond, Virginia. It starts with a different name, Franklin Street, at Capitol Square in the downtown area, one and one-half miles away, and becomes Monument Avenue at Stuart Square, marked by a statue of Jeb Stuart. It then proceeds straight in a northwesterly direction for many miles to the end of the city. At its officially named beginning, Monument Avenue is part of the Fan District, two blocks in from this area's northern edge.

The Fan District is one of tight urban streets lined with mostly brick townhouses that share common walls, and with one-, two-, and four-family dwelling structures and apartment buildings set close to each other and narrowly set back from the sidewalks. The grid street pattern is created largely by square blocks, approximately 350 to 380 feet on a side. The lots are small, often 20 feet wide and less, particularly closer to the city center, nearest the point of the Fan. Greater size seems to come with greater distance. Some of the closer-in streets have a character not unlike those in Philadelphia; streets

Monument Avenue: plan and section

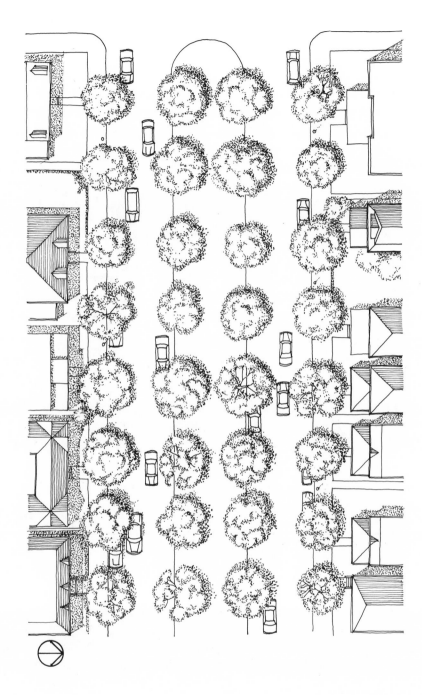

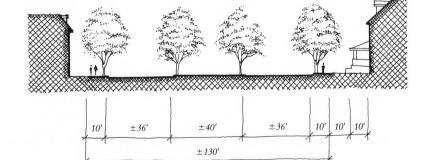

Approximate scale: 1″ = 50′ or 1:600

10′   ±36′   ±40′   ±36′   10′   10′   10′

±130′

     The Great Residential Boulevard

Monument Avenue, near Boulevard

of narrow brick rowhouses. Along some streets, there is a sense of elegance and of early wealth. Just to the east of the Fan District lies the Richmond campus of the University of Virginia; many new buildings mixed with old ones, students, growth, activity, some spilling over into the Fan. It is the kind of area that, during the 1950s and 1960s, was characterized as "inner city blight" and subjected to federally sponsored urban redevelopment. Black people might have been displaced to areas further out, perhaps into the Fan. Into the 1990s, many other cities still have large, sparsely settled "gray areas"; Richmond has the university. Attention and care has been paid to the Fan District by people who saw the potential of the location, the urban streets, and the housing. There has been much restoration, often, it seems, by young people. Not all of the Fan District is in the best condition, and if there was wealth then some of it seems gone now, but the elegance and the urbanity remain.

We are interested in the stretch of Monument Avenue running from Stuart Circle to North Boulevard, a distance of eight blocks covering close to one mile (1.6 kilometers). This is the section that is a great street: an urban residential boulevard close to the city center; a grand remembrance to a lost cause, the Civil War. It is a positive achievement of physical design that is a social achievement as well.

Monument Avenue, Richmond

Monument Avenue's street section is deceptively simple. A 40-foot (12-meter) central median is flanked by two 36-foot roadways which in turn are bounded by 10-foot sidewalks. Houses and small apartment blocks are set back 20 feet from the walks, except that porches, when they exist, are only 10 feet back. Buildings are two and one-half to three and one-half stories high. Just inside the curbs, along the two walks and in the median, are pin oaks and sugar maples, mostly the latter. They vary in height from 30 to 50 feet and they form four straight lines.

The linearity of extremely well-executed parts—the trees, the median, the streetlights, details of the curbs and street paving itself, and the houses—

The Great Residential Boulevard

Monument Avenue; large, single family house

punctuated by four monuments along the way, accounts for the special physical character of the street. The tree spacing is uniform, 36 to 40 feet apart, and the trees line up across the street. Trees come as close as possible to intersections. Linearly, their crowns often join together, reinforcing the four lines. There are two streetlight designs (the most elegant is an acorn globe on a dark green, fluted pole); their spacing varies from 80 to 115 feet, but they, too, create lines along the sidewalks. The two automobile cartways are paved with a gray asphalt brick, bordered on each side by 3-foot-wide concrete strips. The 36-foot-wide cartways each permit two parking lanes and two moving lanes, more (by one parking lane) than what is permitted on a street of that width designed in the early 1990s. Since there are no breaks in the curbs, the linearity is again emphasized. Finally, there are the buildings. Though they are different one from another in design and in materials (though many are brick), they are of similar height, so they, too, form lines along the street. They are close enough to each other that, walking or driving along the street, one does not normally see rear yards between them.

All is not linearity on Monument Avenue. In addition to the focal points that start and end the street, monuments of Stuart at the start and of Stonewall Jackson at North Boulevard, there is the grandly scaled Lee Monument and the one at Stuart Circle as well. Each is a focal point, each a reason to pause

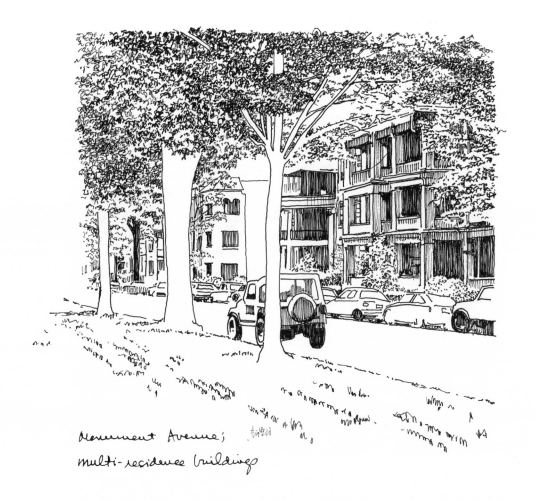

Monument Avenue;
multi-residence buildings

if not to stop. In the length of a mile, these special moments are important as reminders that we are on a marked, special path and that when we have passed the last one we are no longer on it. Traffic on this section of Monument Avenue moves purposefully but not with great speed. For reasons not altogether understood—perhaps the monuments and the five other intersections, perhaps just the pleasantness of the drive and the not overly wide cartway—drivers seem to proceed reasonably, not speeding.

The special character of the buildings along Monument Avenue lies more in their diversity than in the qualities of their individual designs. Some are outstanding and all are pleasant. They are all domestic-scaled, they all have doors that face the street; all have many windows, usually with fine panes, many have porches that permit people to inhabit the street without actually being on it. Bricks are in a wide variety of earth tones. The 10 or 20 feet of front yard, a transition between public and private realms, permit a variety of landscape designs, including more trees and flowering plants. Every bit as noteworthy are the various types and sizes of the residential buildings: various-sized single-family homes, and a range of others that house from two families to perhaps six and more in apartment units. People of different incomes and with different family characteristics need and use and can afford different types and sizes of space. Economic and social diversity follow.

Monument Avenue, then, is not a street for one class of people but for elderly as well as for young and middle-aged people and for the well-to-do as well as the less well-to-do, if not for the lowest-income people. There are not too many well-designed residential boulevards that can respond to the housing needs of a diverse population.

On a Sunday morning in spring, the trees have already bloomed. It is quiet, but there are people using Monument Avenue: churchgoers, joggers, cyclists, walkers. What look like university students enter and leave apartment units. Older women, at windows, watch a passerby. At various corners there are some small notices, and maybe a balloon or two. It seems that this is a route for a charity walk of some kind today. In small groups of ten to twenty, people are walking on this part of Monument Avenue, having come off of one or two of the intersecting streets. In time it becomes noticeable that groups are walking in both directions. There are people of all ages, blacks as well as whites in the same group. They pass along for several hours. There must have been reasons to choose Monument Avenue as a part of the route. Without knowing for sure, one would like to think that it represents to the larger community a special street, a most pleasant street on which to be.

CHAPTER EIGHT

Trees Alone _____

**Richards Road at Mills College,
Oakland, California**

**Viale delle Terme di Caracalla,
Rome**

Beijing Streets

Drive along a country highway almost anywhere in the world, not a freeway or an *autostrada* but a country road, and at some point you are likely to see a tree-lined lane or street leading from the road you are on, back to some often unseen destination. Two lines of trees, one on either side, draw your attention. One single line usually won't do. The single line may mark the boundary of a field, rather than a purposeful pathway. The trees mark the route. They make the drive or lane or roadway special. The prospect of being on that pathway is an inviting one. You may wonder what is at the end, perhaps a house. You can picture yourself on that lane, almost experience it in anticipation. If you know it, then you also look forward to being on it because it is pleasant, comforting. You have arrived. Even if the roadway you have been traveling along has had its own trees, the intersecting road is different, special. The trees are likely to be more closely spaced than on the main road. You will move more slowly.

There are urban counterparts to the rural, tree-lined roadways where trees alone make great streets. Three are Richards Road, the entry street of Mills College, in Oakland, California; the Viale delle Terme di Caracalla in Rome; and one of the tree-lined streets in Beijing, China.

Richards Road _____

There is no advance warning of a special street that starts just beyond the open entry portal of Mills College for Women. Once there, however, driving or walking, the street takes over, creates its own welcoming, compelling environment; overwhelmingly, it is the trees that make the street what it is. To be sure, Richards Road is not a public street: it does not meet the criterion of always being open to all, although anyone is free to use it. Its greatness lies in a design that invites people to it and that helps to make community for the college.

The automobile cartway is rather narrow, about 30 feet (9 meters), and the street is relatively short, only 1,200 feet (less than 400 meters), ending at an open plaza that is flanked on two sides by an auditorium and a library building. There are other buildings along the street, the Spanish-style music building, a chapel, gymnasia, and the smallish but elegant Victorian home of the college president. There is a small pond off one side at the end of the street. All of these are pleasant enough. They are all well set back and, to be sure, they are all present. But it is the trees that make the difference.

Close to either side of the narrow 4-foot walks that parallel the auto cartway there are good-sized London planes in an alternating pattern, first on one side

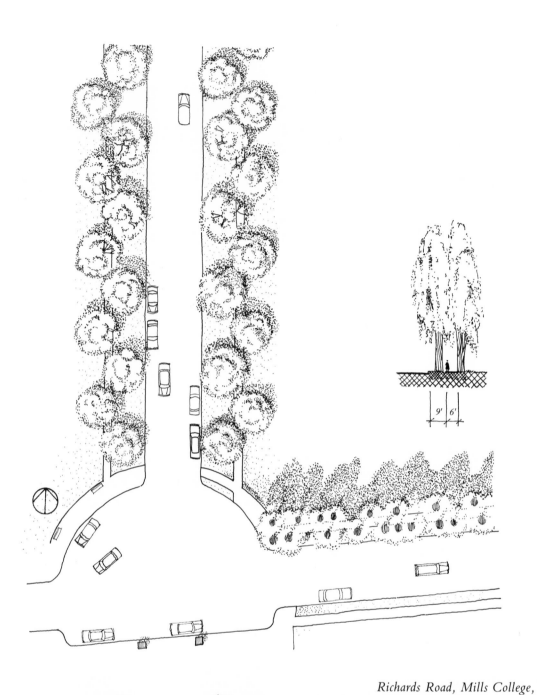

Richards Road, Mills College,
Oakland: plan and sections

9' 6'

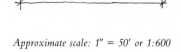

4–5' | 18' | 30' | 18' | 4–5'
±76'

Approximate scale: 1″ = 50′ or 1:600

Richards Road

of the walk and then on the other. At about 8 or 9 feet from the ground their trunks divide, usually into three main branches, and these divide again upward and outward until neighboring branches meet overhead, though branches of trees on either side of the street do not meet. The trees rise from a grass lawn. The two double lines of trees contain the whole space while at the same time each walk is itself tree-lined. The asphalt of the auto cartway is a relatively small part of the overall green floor, walls, and ceiling of this lineal space. Walking, there is no major focal point, only this pleasantly enclosed green room.

At the end of the street, at the plaza, where Richards Road intersects with a lesser street that runs perpendicular to it, there are also two tree-lined walks, but the trees are different and so is the scale. Along this second street, the walks are 4 to 5 feet wide. Immediately against this narrow walkway are giant eucalyptus trees with trunk diameters of up to 5 feet. Spacing between

Trees Alone

trees can be less than 3 feet. To walk here in this narrow, tall, brown, blue, silver, olive vertical space, with side openings that are like Gothic windows, and surrounded by the unmistakable eucalyptus smell, is to put oneself consciously into an overtly sensuous place, albeit one that is not long. People come to walk on this narrow path and then return to the cool green leaf-defined openness of Richards Road, and back out to the gate and the main passing roadway.

Mills College for Women is a small, almost isolated community, and once within it there are well thought out arrangements of old and new buildings that bring people together in pleasant ways, that help them to be aware of each other and to enter into exchange. Richards Road is in this tradition and says to the visitor, as she or he comes in or goes out, that this is a special, welcoming place.

Viale delle Terme di Caracalla

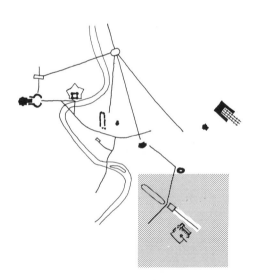

Mostly it is the physical design qualities of the Viale delle Terme di Caracalla in Rome, between the Circo Massimo and the Piazzale Numa Pompilio, that make it stand out as a great street. It's not the Obelisco di Axum that marks its beginning nor the Piazzale at the Baths of Caracalla that marks its turning point, nor any buildings that line its way, for there are none, nor the park setting through which it runs, nor even the Baths of Caracalla themselves, but the strong design of the street itself.

The Viale delle Terme di Caracalla is wide, about 150 feet (45 meters) from outside curb to outside curb. It runs straight for about 3,000 feet (700 meters). Its central artery, approximately 50 feet wide, is marked for two lanes in each direction but, in the Italian style, is perfectly capable of handling three or even four high-volume, fast lanes to and from central Rome, as needed or desired. Between the central roadway and each of the two 25-foot-wide access roads on either side, there are tree-planted medians, each with two species of trees in double lines: tall, stately Roman pines alternating with low *Quercus ilex*. The ground surface is packed earth mixed with pebbles, pine needles, and sometimes grass. There are street lamps to light the central roadway. It is the trees, again, that make the difference.

The pines, two abreast, close to the curbs, are about 30 feet (9 meters) apart. Between them are the *ilex*. There are major trees, then, every 15 feet (4.5 meters) along the street and less than 25 feet (7.6 meters) apart across the medians. The trees in one median line up with those in the other. At the outward extremes there are only walkways, beyond which are rolling lawns with scattered trees and informal paths. The pines present a procession of red, tan, brown, and sienna columns topped at a height of maybe 50 feet with the solid-centered, lacy-edged, oval mass of light olive to almost green-black needled foliage. High above the ground the almost horizontal branches of adjacent trees and the breathing foliage they carry come together in two long ceilings, one over each median. The pines alone give the street presence.

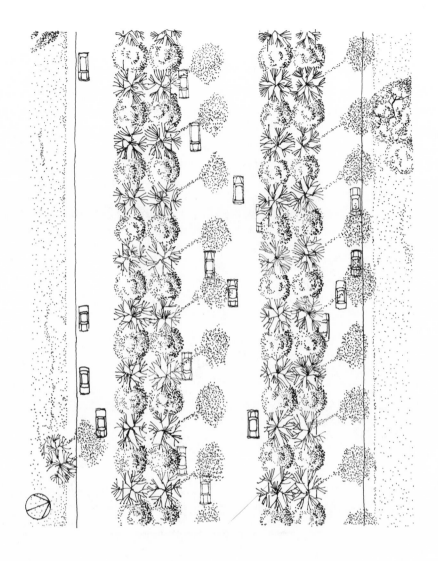

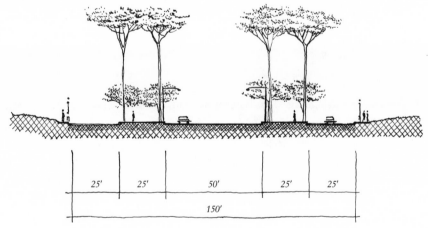

Viale delle Terme di Caracalla:
plan and section

Approximate scale: 1″ = 50′ or 1:600

| 25′ | 25′ | 50′ | 25′ | 25′ |

150′

Trees Alone

Viale delle Terme di Caracalla

Their height and linearity can be seen from a distance. In a city full of stone landmarks, these rows of pines are yet another way to understand the city and one's location in it. Below, closer to the ground, there is another ceiling made of the dark, spreading *Quercus ilex*. Some of their branches meet, others do not, so there is both light and shade, mostly the latter. Against the bright, hot Roman sun and in welcome contrast to the undefined large spaces at the street's beginning at the Obelisco di Axum and the Circo Massimo beyond, the tree-covered medians attract walkers with a promise of coolness. Even the fast-moving traffic in the central lane is no deterrent. During the winter months, when there is less sun, it is pleasant to walk on the side paths. If the design of the Viale delle Terme di Caracalla was meant to attract walkers from central Rome, perhaps a bit tired from journeys to historical sites already navigated, to the Baths of Caracalla another half mile or so distant, then these dark, cool, tree-lined paths are the way to do it.

Beijing Street

Beijing Streets ────────────── There are great streets in Beijing, China, made only of trees. There are many of them, of many different widths and designs, but the one that stands out most clearly is the one that passes in front of the Friendship Hotel compound, on its way to and from the center of the city.

Consider streets lined with closely planted trees of different ages and species—two rows of species A, 30 years old, alongside of which are rows of species B trees, maybe 10 or 15 years old, and then still other rows of species C trees, maybe only recently planted. As each tree species becomes mature or is otherwise needed, the long lines of that species that run the length of the street are harvested.

As you travel along roads and streets in and around Beijing, in country or city, it is the trees that take you along the way. It isn't buildings which, increasingly, are set back from the street, and it is not usually some focal point to fix the eyes. It is the trees and the tree trunks. People and more people use the streets, not in automobiles but on foot, on bicycles, and in buses. Trucks keep them company. The streets may or may not be used for strolling and visiting, but mostly it seems they are used simply to get from one place to another. What a fine way to travel, amid linear boscs of trees, shaded from the sun in the summer, with an ever-changing light. The sound, overwhelmingly, is the sound of bicycle bells. People move at a moderate

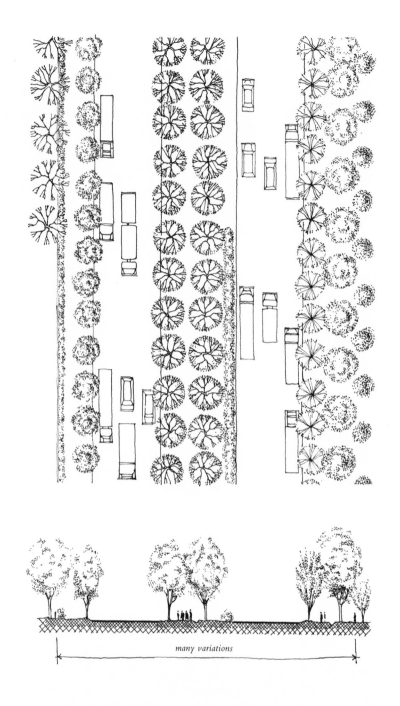

A Beijing street: plan and section

Approximate scale: 1″ = 50′ or 1:600

many variations

pace; they can see each other's forms and physical characteristics. They may choose to talk. At least they have the opportunity to do so. Within an overall design framework, each street changes over time as in their turn lines of trees are replaced by others. Here, trees are for utilitarian purposes, to grow wood for use, while at the same time providing a comfortable, pleasant, and it seems community-building physical environment for travel.

CHAPTER NINE

Great Street Ensembles

Bath

Bologna

Individual great streets are our primary concern. For a street to be special, it should be the street itself that counts, not particular historic buildings (though they may contribute), nor a plaza nor a discrete event on the street. Nor is our search for particularly finely designed urban areas or neighborhoods. It is for individual streets. And yet, in certain cities, though no single street stands out as best, either in relation to other great streets elsewhere or for that particular community, there may be an assemblage of streets of a particular type that is memorable and upon which we focus. It is more the Garden District than St. Charles Avenue in New Orleans, more the French Quarter than Bourbon Street. It is easier to think of the views, hills, light quality, and Victorian houses of San Francisco than of any one street. The system of canals is more the focus in Amsterdam than is one canal, and it is the medieval quarters of Italian hill cities more than any one street that are most remembered. It is the assembly of particular types of streets in Bologna, the arcaded streets or "streets with porches" as they are referred to locally, and of a particular scale of street in Bath that are so memorable, and to which we now turn.

There are some 25 miles (40 kilometers) of covered walks along streets in the city of Bologna. None of the streets stands out individually as a great one, but together they are unique. In Bath, England, much is made of the Circus and Royal Crescent and the Lansdown Crescent, but it is the array of lesser streets, diminutively scaled, both commercial and residential, that creates a special environment for the community. In both cities it is the overall physical quality of many streets taken together as a single experience that stands out as memorable, not the qualities of any one or two streets. Nor is it the outstanding pattern of streets in these cities that stands out, as in Savannah or in Amsterdam (each of which has its own fine streets), but the physical qualities of many similar but different streets that demand attention. Bologna-style streets are found elsewhere, notably in Bern and Vicenza, and other cities from time to time try to emulate them, usually without commitment or staying power. As a type, they are a singular expression of what a street can be, like no other model. The streets of Bath are triumphs of comfortable, human scale, combined with a distinctive color and architectural style. They have been emulated elsewhere, even parodied; Main Street in Disneyland may owe more to Bath than to small town North American namesakes. In Bologna, the portico streets are said to make community, and that may be so of the Bath streets as well.

Bath _____

The streets of Bath, commercial as well as residential ones, are characterized by domesticity. Streets and most buildings are small, homelike, familiar, intimate. Distances within the city are small and much of Bath fits into less than one square mile. The city as a whole falls easily and with relative compactness into its larger, rolling country setting. For the most part, everything is done well, particularly the streets. They are narrow. Regularly, public rights-of-way are less than 35 feet (10.6 meters) wide, with 4- or 5-foot sidewalks and auto cartways that vary from 15 to 22 feet. Commercial streets, like Westgate Street or Cheap Street, are no wider than residential streets, and since the latter often have small setbacks, behind iron fences, to accommodate light wells for basement entries and windows, the actual building-to-building distances on the residential streets are larger than on the commercial ones. The streets themselves are models of utilitarianism, comprised of two narrow sidewalks, curbs, the auto cartway, streetlight poles, no driveways, no trees.

An area of Bath:
street and building context

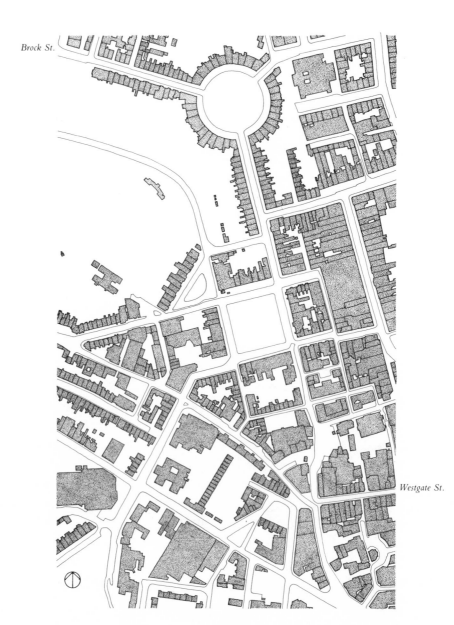

Approximate scale: 1" = 400' or 1:4,800

Great Streets

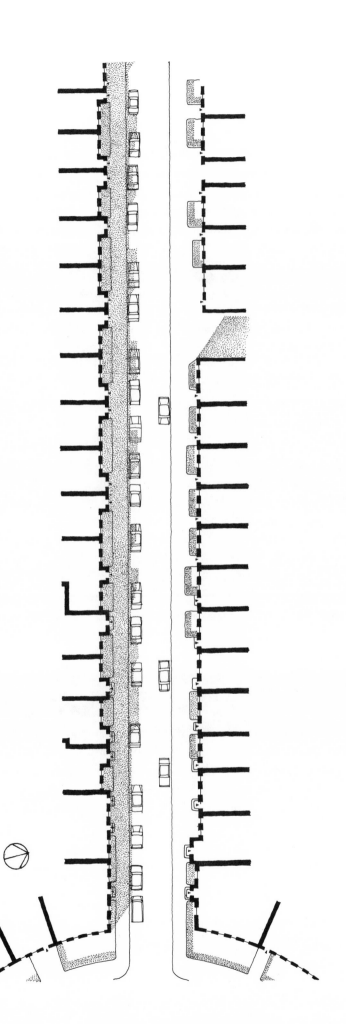

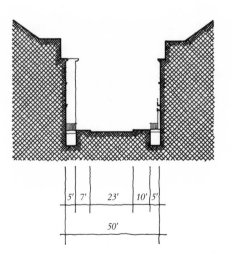

Brock Street, Bath: plan and section

5'	7'	23'	10'	5'
		50'		

Approximate scale: 1" = 50' or 1:600

Great Street Ensembles

Aside from a loose grid in the city center, there is no special pattern to the streets. Generally they follow the topography. Streets end more than they continue, so that there are visual closings or openings, the former by buildings at intersecting streets, or by trees, and the latter by views out, toward distant hillsides and country. One is continually aware of the nearby green countryside. Intersections are frequent and can be focal points, such as at Kingsmead Square or where New Bond Street meets Northgate Street, or at Bridge Street, and there are openings and sometimes areas of activity where decisions can be made to go this way or that. Street and block lengths vary, though most are shorter (less than 400 feet) and the long ones are rarely straight.

It is streets and buildings together that really count in Bath. The Georgian architecture is elegant at the same time that it is simple. First, the warm Bath stone, a light tan-pink-beige-orange, has to it a softness that is inviting and appropriate to the small-scaled buildings. Narrow streets mean that buildings are always close and can be seen, even their tops and their chimneys, in rows, because they are usually low; two and three stories for homes, up to four stories on the shopping streets. As narrow as the streets are, a sense of verticality might be expected, but the low buildings and continuous horizontal line created by the modest eaves at the roofline avoids that. Doors at street level, often less than 25 feet apart, and two or three levels of finely paned windows that march along the streets, speak of habitation, though residences are private enough behind iron fences at the street and curtains behind the panes. The eyes easily take in whole dwellings, each marked by a downspout or windows, within the longer rows of snugly designed and developed constructions of which they are part. Subtle differences in window arrangements and uneven maintenance of dwelling facades by tenants and owners over the years give a sense of individuality within an overall unified physical structure.

"Domestic scale" is an appropriate term for these buildings and streets. It is easy to think of people at home and of home activities and family intimacy in the buildings. It is hard to miss people on the streets or coming out of doorways. So much is seeable, graspable. Beauford Square, more a street than a square, is like that, with a total right-of-way width of about 20 feet and two- and three-story buildings. It would seem a physical environment easy to emulate, but its simplicity can be deceiving. Beauford Square becomes Trim Street, across Barten Street. At the corner there is a new building that tries but fails to fit in. Color and height and window sizes are similar to those in the older buildings, but there are fewer shadow lines and fewer details to the windows, no cornice line, and no fences. There are fewer doors, and the one that is visible is larger than those on Beauford Square, a major entrance. A sense of habitation is missing. On closer inspection, it is a public office building.

Brock Street, toward The Circus

Beauford Street

There are many finely scaled residential streets in Bath. They are similar but not the same, repetitive without being endless. Doorways, windows, frames, fences, and other details vary. So do street lengths, the nature of their endings, views, and the topography. Activity and liveliness are only short distances away on the commercial streets, the spas, and at the abbey church in the city center. Visual surprise and grandness are created by the "big" features: the Circus, Royal Crescent, Great Pulteney Street. Within the larger urban small street–small building framework they are not really expected. Regardless of their architectural achievement—a unified Palladian-inspired ensemble of private houses conforming to John Woods–designed facades—the larger and more famous compositions are somewhat cold and austere. The buildings are too much present. What the smaller residential streets may lack in surprise they gain in comfort.

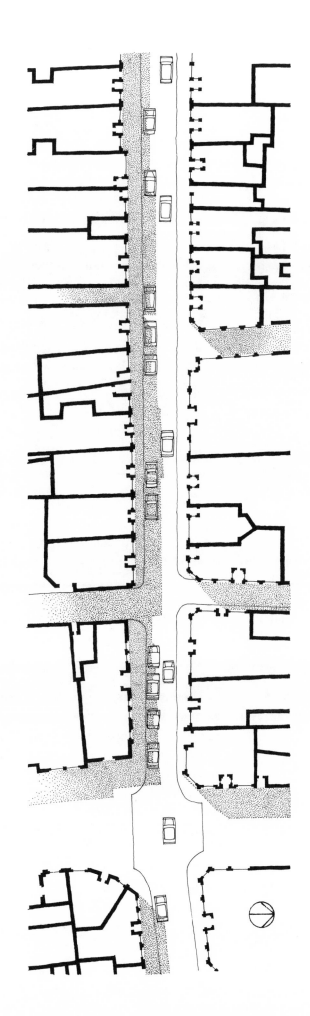

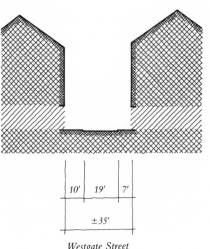

Westgate and Cheap streets: plan and sections

10' | 19' | 7'

±35'

Westgate Street

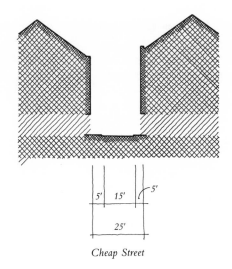

5' | 15' | 5'

25'

Cheap Street

Approximate scale: 1" = 50' or 1:600

Great Street Ensembles

Westgate Street

Commercial streets, for example York Street, Cheap Street, Westgate Street, are for the most part busier versions of the residential ones. There are no fences, and individual doorways and store windows occupy the whole of the ground floors. Signs and displays are there to catch the eye. There is a greater variety of building designs and sizes. Scale and building material and basic design style remain the same. Cars, where permitted, move slowly.

There is a density factor that at once contributes to and is a consequence of the physical arrangement of streets and buildings. Tightness of streets and continuity of buildings makes for a net density (not including streets) of 17 to 18 dwellings per acre in many places, and a gross density (including streets) of 12 to 13 dwellings per acre. That may be considered high by U.S. suburban standards, but is lower by far than what multi-family, multi-floor buildings would produce. Nonetheless, these densities permit private gardens, direct access from home to ground, supportable local stores and services within walking distances, and, consequently, active streets.

The street-building environment of Bath has remained a most livable one for over 200 years. It is an adaptable environment. There is an urban physical unity here that was achieved not by one or two designers intent on one grand design for the whole city, but by many builders using local materials and adhering to a set of building rules directed to achieving a single, identifiable community.

Bologna _____

Bologna's porticoes are renowned. Other cities have them, but none as many or as noteworthy as Bologna. The arcaded streets of Bern are more regular and may be better kept than those in Bologna, and the streets wider and lighter, but Bern is smaller, so they cannot be as extensive, nor are they as complex. In Bologna, the porticoes are the pervasive street type, not just a remnant of the past. Individual building designs are less a part of a porticoed street than of other streets, especially narrow ones. The covered walks block their view. The focus must be on the public way itself. That is most certainly the case in Bologna.

The porches of Bologna streets are not simply covered sidewalks appended to buildings that line the street. They are integral to the buildings themselves, walkways of various widths covered by one or more stories of the adjacent buildings. Typically, the central lane of a street is for vehicles and is usually not wide, varying generally from 16 to 23 feet (5 to 7 meters) in major streets. The central traffic lane is defined on either side by rows of columns that support the upper stories of buildings. Column spacing varies but rarely exceeds 25 feet. Inside the columns are the covered walkways that

Along Via Maggiore

Great Street Ensembles

vary in width from about 10 to 16 feet (3 to 5 meters). Heights of the covered walkways vary, too, depending on street type, width, and building design, but on major streets they seem to be from 15 to 20 feet. There are arches, barrel vaults, and flat ceilings of many designs. Walkways can be at the same level as the street or one or two steps higher. Variety characterizes these streets; the porches may be continuous or not; they are on one or both sides; they can have different heights. The columns are of different shapes and heights, with different spacing. The uses along them vary as well.

The experience of walking along a Bologna street is of being in an enclosed, even cloistered space at the same time that it is open. The walks are generous; no sense of crowding except rarely, perhaps approaching the Piazza di Porta Ravegnana in the late afternoon rush, or at the university along the Via Zamboni at noon, and then only momentarily. There are building facades on one side of the walk, with lighted stores and windows, or with doorways alone (to building interiors) or blank walls, and there are columns on the other side. Beyond the columns is the space for cars or buses, open to the sky. A glimpse of upper stories is possible, more if one walks close to the column line. Across the street there is another line of columns and another covered walkway. Distances are short, generally less than 30 feet from the viewer to the far wall, so it is possible to see and recognize people walking there and to see inside stores. The major focus, though, is along the path; linearity characterizes the walkway. Arches and columns recede in perspective. The many columns on both sides of the street give a sense of verticality, regardless of the proportion of the walk itself. The view, mostly, is straight ahead, more so than in a nonporticoed street. If there are stores then one is attracted to them, by their window displays and lights, which stand out. Mostly it is a walk in the shade, even at times in quasi darkness. Sunlight, when it comes into the walkways, is likely to be at sharp angles and can be dramatic; bright angular contrasts cast the shapes of columns and arches on the walks. They are comfortable.

Comfort is a significant reason for the porches, though certainly not the only one. It rains and snows in Bologna and the sun in the summer can be unrelenting, so protection from the weather is important. The same porches, however, don't do much to help air circulation in the summer, when any breeze is welcomed. On balance, local people agree that the city is far more comfortable because of them. At the end of the Middle Ages, though, needs for housing and movement within the walled, land-short central area of the city may have been more compelling reasons than protection from the weather. Up to 12,000 students and continuous immigration from the countryside crowded Bologna. There had been a long tradition of building upper floors over streets, and later of columns down to the ground to support them.[17] The porches, increasingly under community control, afforded privately maintained, sheltered public passageways in return for private building space. Today they remain part of "the social tradition that puts the interests of the community above private interests." The porches also provided safe

Approximate scale: 1" = 400' or 1:4,800

places for people from the countryside to stay during wars. It is clear that people of Bologna are proud of them, value them as something special that makes their city unique, at the same time considering them to be aesthetically pleasing. They are the symbols of the city, perhaps as much as the Piazza Maggiore at the center and the Basilica di San Petronio. There are laws and policies in Bologna to maintain the porches and to require new ones in new developments.

Of all the porticoed streets, a group of five that lead to and from the Piazza di Porta Ravegnana, at the two towers, stands out: Via Zamboni, Via San Vitale, Strada Maggiore, Via Santo Stefano, and Via Castiglione. Too even in their spacing to be anything but a rational, preconceived plan for development, their pattern is repeated on the western side of the city.[18] Each street leads to a city gate. During the Middle Ages, they provided access to the country and also served as spines for social quarters that lined them on each side. It seems they may still serve that function, each street being somewhat different from the others in the nature of people that live along it. But they are not and never were intended to be the spine or focus of the city as a whole. The Piazza Maggiore and Piazza del Nettuno, as well as the Piazza Galvani and adjacent central streets and market, are the citywide walking, strolling, shopping, and meeting grounds. The five streets are the spines of their areas, but they nonetheless come to a single focus point. Each of the five and the side streets that connect them have physical qualities that are similar, not the least of which is their common starting point at the two

Along Via San Vitale

towers. The Via Zamboni is the center of the university and student quarter, and it is a manifestation of student life that one sees: bookstores, inexpensive places to eat, announcements on walls, more blank-walled walks than elsewhere, and many students doing what students do—hanging around and talking. The center would seem to be at the Piazza Verdi, where there is also a major theater. The stores along the narrower Via Petroni, leading across the pielike sector to the second of the five streets, slowly change from an almost wholly student orientation to a larger, community-based orientation at the Via San Vitale, where there is another piazza, the Piazza Aldrovandi, and what seems to be an old city tollgate that arches over the street. Open space breaks are important on these kinds of streets and each of the five has them at points along the way. Walking back to the towers on the Via San Vitale, one side of the street is lined continuously with stores, less so the other.

Via San Vitale at toll gate

A high point along Strada Maggiore is the opening at Via Guerrazzia. It is a simple church courtyard surrounded by a covered walk, this time without buildings above. The walkway continues the covered passageway at the same time that it defines the space. On the Via Santo Stefano, as if to take advantage of the irregular open space in front of its namesake church, the buildings that face it are more grand, elegant, their arches larger. One walks under arches and alongside columns, along lengths of small local-serving shops mixed with blocks where there are no stores at all and where the eyes are attracted across the street, then back again to the walk and to other shops, some elegant, some not. The perspective is long, lineal, deep. It is shady. The pace is more intense toward the city center, where the porches give way to buildings that were there long before, and to the two towers where the five streets start.

Via Santo Stefano

Along Via Castiglione

The streets of Bologna and their very special physical design represent a triumph of community. Regardless of the various ways in which they started, the decisions to maintain, require, and continue them, decisions that have been made over and over again for hundreds of years, must have been difficult. Whether they were arrived at democratically or arbitrarily imposed, a feisty population would not have supported and maintained them for all these years if the porticoes were not useful and meaningful, at the same time that they have been adaptable to changing conditions over the years. There must have been great pressures to change those streets, almost certainly to widen them, in favor of modernization to make movement easier. The covered walks would not likely have been reproduced along new replacement streets. In the face of such pressures, there has been commitment—call it stubbornness—to a street-building design that is unique, and held to be of community value, as a symbol certainly, but as the source of great streets, too.

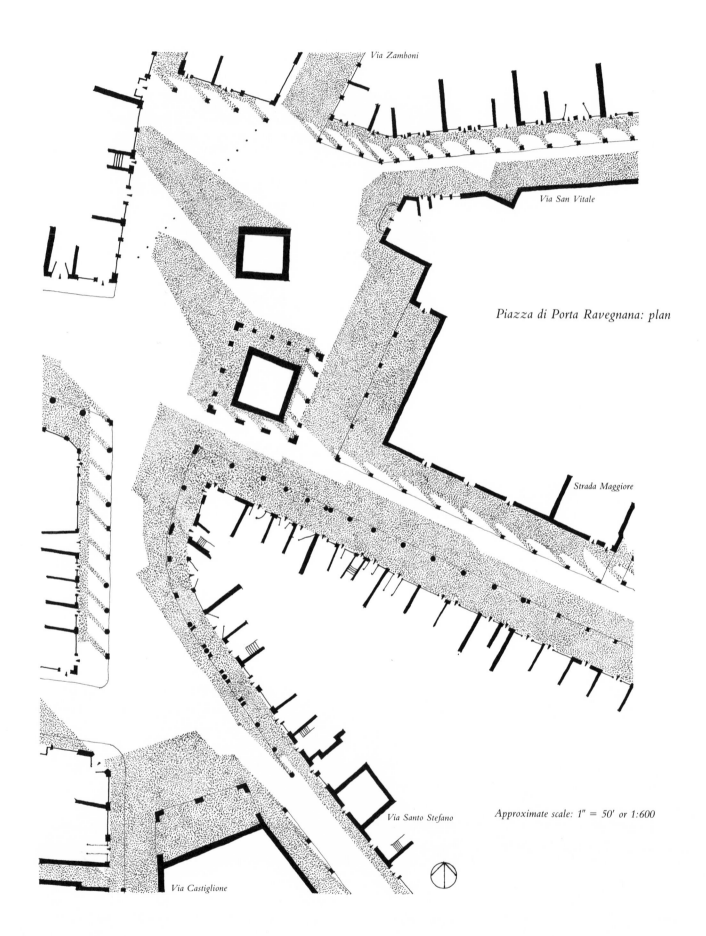

Via Zamboni

Via San Vitale

Piazza di Porta Ravegnana: plan

Strada Maggiore

Approximate scale: 1″ = 50′ or 1:600

Via Santo Stefano

Via Castiglione

*Typical cross sections of streets leading
to Piazza di Porta Ravegnana*

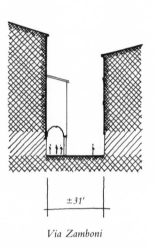

Via Zamboni

±31'

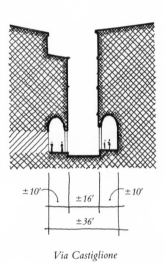

Via Castiglione

±10'   ±16'   ±10'

±36'

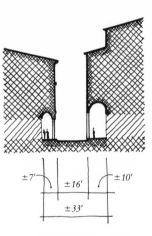

Via San Vitale, near tollgate

±7'   ±16'   ±10'

±33'

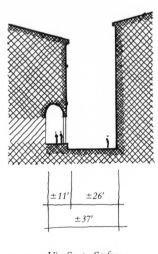

Via Santo Stefano

±11'   ±26'

±37'

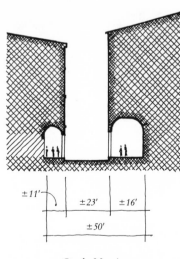

Strada Maggiore

±11'   ±23'   ±16'

±50'

Great Street Ensembles

The very best streets, the great streets and the once great streets of the previous section, are not the only ones to learn from. There are many outstanding streets—some historic, some famous, some unique, some emblematic of a type—that have much to teach. Not-so-good streets can be instructive as well. Knowing street sizes alone and what is in them is a major step in determining what is possible. Ancient streets are also informative, for knowing sizes and knowing the origins of present-day streets. If, in addition, streets can be compared one to another, including such characteristics as building height and length, store sizes, frequency of doorways, numbers of people that pass, then so much the better. The following compendium of street plans and cross sections, all drawn to the same scale, and attendant notes and data expand upon the great streets and provide a source for continuing decisions on the construction of the public realm.

Any collection of street plans and cross sections is likely to be arbitrary and incomplete. To include one is to exclude many more. The bases for what is included here are many. Research to find the very best streets, the great ones, included looking at and gathering information about many. Inquiries of professionals and surveys of street users led to other streets. Professional and academic colleagues, over the years, have suggested streets to be studied at the same time as they have inquired about the physical characteristics of one street or another. Would that all of the suggestions and requests could be answered. Space and time, the cost of getting to streets for observation and measurement or of otherwise getting information about them, have been limitations. In short, the collection will always be incomplete, but it is one that can be expanded and built upon.

Field notes are by far the major source of information about the streets. Sometimes it was possible to measure more accurately than others the sizes and cross sections of streets and what is on them. Many of the dimensions were measured by pacing. Observations in the form of notes as to the nature of the street may be less objective but are important for understanding the streets' contexts.

Some of the street plans are more detailed than others. They are drawn consistent with the level of detail available while at the same time being made comparable with each other. When individual building lengths along streets are known they are shown by a line perpendicular to the street at the break between buildings. If building lengths are not known then only the building line along the street is shown, with no further detail. Individual building subdivisions for ground-floor stores, offices, residences, or upper-floor entrances are also shown, where known, by shorter and lighter lines than those used to denote buildings. Doorways, windows, and other entry arrangements are also shown, where known.

The section at which the street plans are drawn is either at shoulder height or further above, above trees and sometimes above the buildings. The most significant factor in determining the height to use for the plan sections was, of course, the need to present the streets in a manner that permits comparisons. Beyond that, the most important consideration was to choose a height that best gives a sense of the street while giving the crucial information about the street. In all cases the plan sections work in tandem with the cross sections.

The groupings and sequences are ones that seem most appropriate to how the street information is likely to be used by designers and policy makers; the aim has been to permit ease of comparison of like streets (of those that serve the same functions or are of a distinct type). Boulevard streets are therefore grouped, as are ancient streets, streets of trees alone, and streets with central walking areas. In a functional sense, the latter may also serve as major commercial streets—another category—but that is the nature of streets; regularly they do more than one thing, serve more than one category of need or function or design.

A Compendium of Streets

Pompeii Streets

Herculaneum Streets

Ostia Antica

- In the field, a sense of scale for these streets is difficult without the buildings.

- At Herculaneum, where buildings remain, the scale is a pleasant one for a pedestrian: no sense of crowding despite small dimensions. This might have been different if there were many people on them. Nonetheless, the term "human scale" is appropriate.

- Walkways, as opposed to cartways, take a large proportion of any of these streets.

- Streets are regular in layout.

- The basic physical elements of contemporary streets are all there.

- Commercial uses, such as corner eating places, existed on these streets.

- Street dimensions were a matter of choice. They could have been larger had there been a desire or need.

- Proportions and dimensions are remarkably similar to those in the Paddington section of Sydney, Australia.

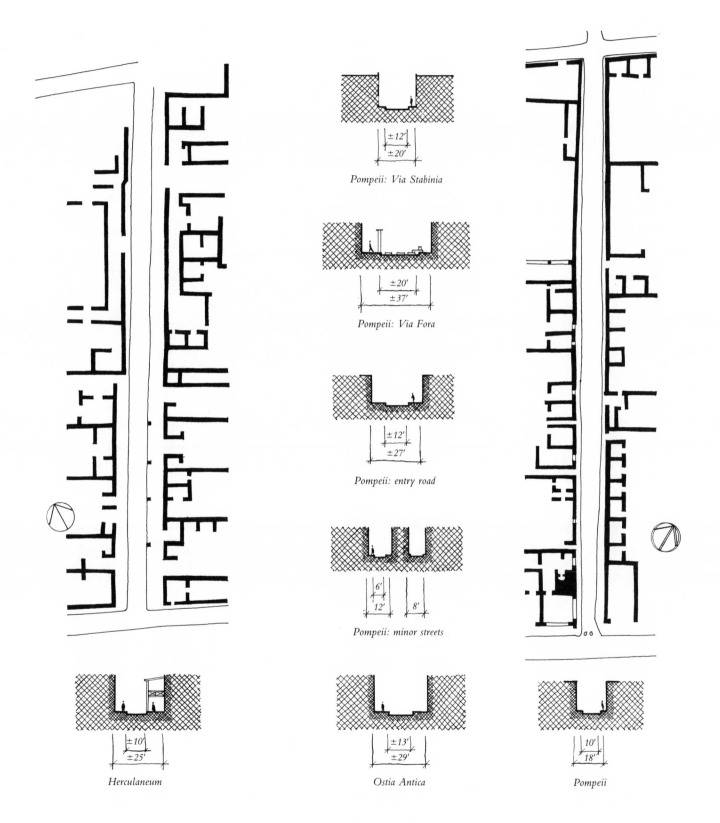

Pompeii: Via Stabinia

Pompeii: Via Fora

Pompeii: entry road

Pompeii: minor streets

Herculaneum

Ostia Antica

Pompeii

Approximate scale: 1" = 50' or 1:600

A Compendium of Streets

Via dei Coronari, Rome

- Narrow street of four- and five-story buildings.

- Many furniture, antique, and art stores.

- Residential above ground floor.

- Approximately 13 feet between entryways on either side of the street.

- A strong sense of habitation, even on a quiet, winter Sunday morning.

- Buildings are not lined up. They move in and out, slightly, more on one side than the other.

- Though it is possible to see from one end of the street to another, there is a sense of movement to it. It does not take much in the way of offset buildings to make a regular street seem irregular. Compare to Via Giulia.

- No curbs.

- Streetlights at about 20 feet above the pavement are attached to buildings on the north side, projecting about 5 feet (1.5 meters) into the street.

- Piazzetta di San Simeone is a welcome opening out. There are two other *piazze* at the approximate quarter points along the street.

A Compendium of Streets

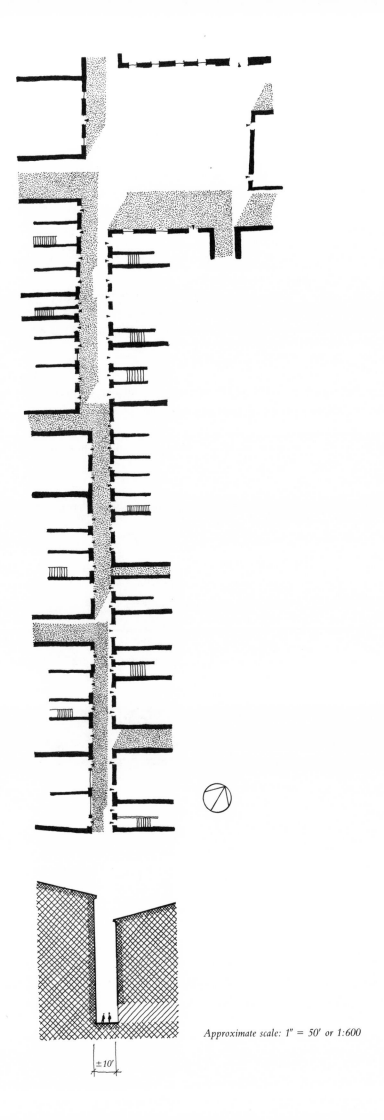

Approximate scale: 1" = 50' or 1:600

±10'

Via Giulia, Rome

- Dates from 1513 under Pope Julius II.

- Stands out in central Rome for its length and straightness.

- Buildings, particularly at the northwest end, tend to grandness. Ground floors are as high as 25 feet.

- Current ground-floor uses of many buildings—art galleries, antiques, upscale furnishings—make it a stylish destination.

- Little sense of transparency where there are high and grated ground-floor windows.

- Many basement windows, in wells, come above the pavement from 1 to 3 feet.

- Street proportions are pleasant but it is not a terribly inviting street, except where there are ground-floor shops. One has a sense of intruding on a foreign turf.

- Building facade lengths average 51 feet (15.6 meters), but include a wide range. Entryways are approximately 23 feet apart on one side and 40 feet apart on the other.

- Pavement of cobble; no separate walks.

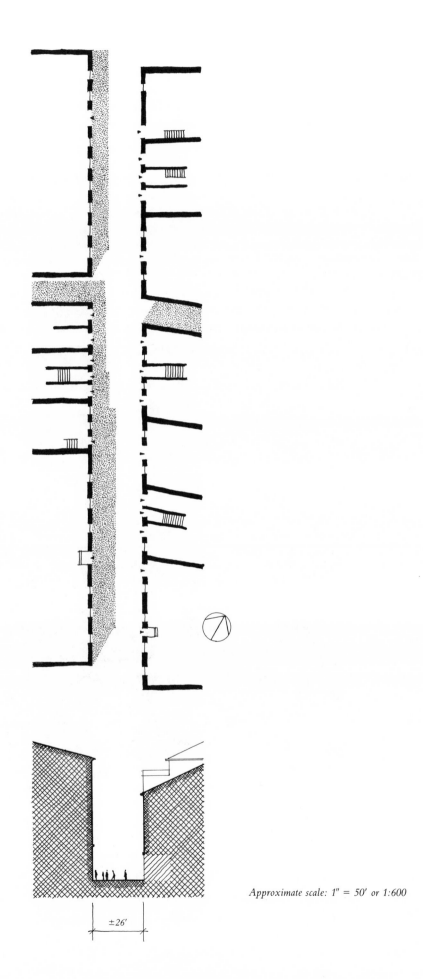

Approximate scale: 1″ = 50′ or 1:600

±26′

A Compendium of Streets

Ringstrasse, Vienna

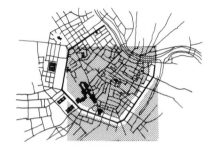

General Observations

- Well designed and magnificently maintained, with close attention to detail at every scale.

- Truly "rings" the central city, marks it unequivocally. One knows where one is on the Ringstrasse.

- Activities (stores, people, exchange) seem concentrated at turning points, e.g., where Schwarzenberg meets Kärntner Ring.

- No major concentrated activity *along* the Ringstrasse, not even at hotels, which seem to locate there increasingly.

- More people by far walk in the central planted promenade areas than on the side walks.

Ringstrasse at the Opera House:
street and building context

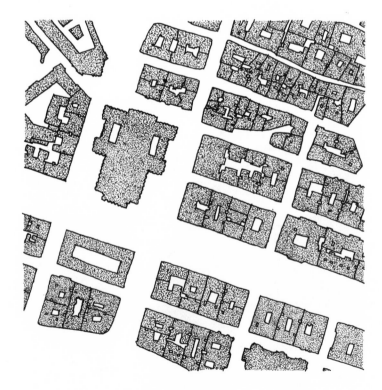

Approximate scale: 1″ = 400′ or 1:4,800

A Compendium of Streets

Along the Ringstrasse

- Generally, buildings along the street are major, singular destinations—Staatsoper, Rathaus, Borse, university, Parliament, museums—but do not do much for the street except (and then not always) to define it. Where there is a sense of transparency, enabling one to look into buildings, there is not much of interest to see, or there are barred or blank windows and too few doors.

- In front of the Staatsoper, at Kärntnerstrasse, the street is just a very large auto street intersection.

- Turning points, from a distance, give a pleasing sense of closure and/or direction.

- Some of the smaller plazas, often at minor intersections on the inside of the ring, e.g., at Wagner's post office, or at Liebenberg, work well; there is a better sense of enclosure.

- A strange street! Much of it is beautiful and the public right-of-way design is well thought out and executed. The trees and walkway paths work, especially where they border a park or where the auto access road is removed on one side. Then it becomes a linear park in itself. When bordering a park it becomes part of the park. But the buildings do not do anything for the street. The big institutional buildings stand *alone*. Where there are commercial buildings lining the street, including the apartment blocks, they don't enliven the street either. Only in short sections are there stores and restaurants; even the hotels do not help. There is hope or anticipation at the major intersections, where the Ringstrasse turns, but the activity doesn't spread along the street. At the intersection, the hope is not realized. The spaces are too large, and the view is outward. By and large the intersections are just big spaces with considerable traffic movement. Does the problem come from the reality of it being a ring? It goes around. It would be hard to enliven it all. But why is aliveness critical? Was it ever really a bustling place? The importance may lie in the making of community. Maybe the best was always elsewhere. As a ring, as a distributor, it seems to have a centrifugal force, tending to move away from the center, even away from itself. It may not be a street to walk on normally, to get from here to there. It is not direct; other paths are surely faster. It is much more direct to walk across the city than around the ring. But if many people lived nearby, this would be a wonderful strolling street. Or does its distribution role hinder that function? Probably a wonderful street to stroll upon on Sundays and holidays, when other activities are closed. Certainly a great street for visitors walking from one historic building to the next.

Details

- The central roadway, about 50 feet (15 meters), is a reasonable width: three lanes in one direction plus two streetcar lanes, one running opposite the auto flow.

- Streetcars at the curb work well. Autos do not enter these lanes. Streetcar stops can be major transfer points, associated with underpasses, toilets, waiting kiosks, above-grade shelters, snack stands, and newspaper-magazine kiosks.

- Trees are in raised grass planting strips. At the central roadway the strips are continuous, presumably to discourage midblock crossings. Elsewhere they rarely run longer than three trees and permit walkers ease in crossing the street.

- Bicycle paths are marked and used.

- Trees, about 20 feet (6 meters) apart, create a canopy, meeting overhead in both directions.

- At intersections, the first trees are larger than others, perhaps to mark the intersections.

- Lights, in a diagonal pattern, are about 130 feet (40 meters) apart.

- Kiosks are also located in planting strips.

- Along parks and at some other locations, the marginal access road drops off, creating a park ring approximately 69 feet (21 meters) wide.

A Compendium of Streets

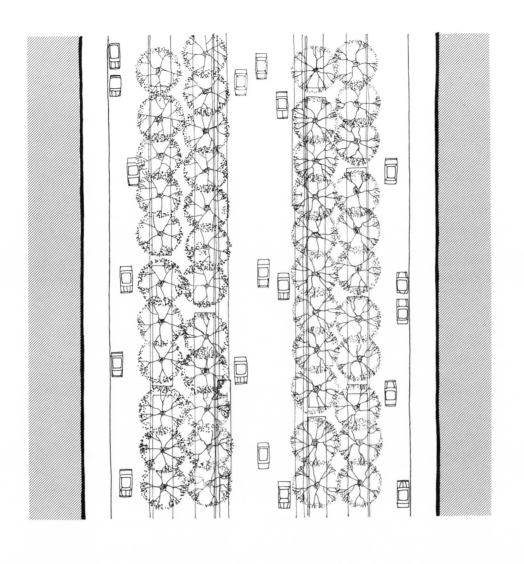

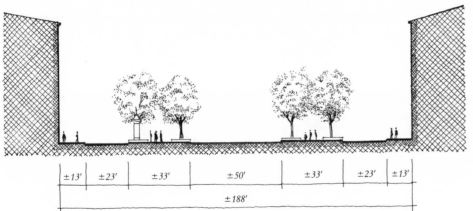

Approximate scale: 1″ = 50′ or 1:600

±13′ ±23′ ±33′ ±50′ ±33′ ±23′ ±13′

±188′

- The small glass and wood waiting shelters are as elegant as any to be seen anywhere.

- Iron fences, such as at the Burggarten or the Volksgarten, provide excellent, pleasant-to-walk-along street definition that is more interesting than that provided by some of the buildings.

A Compendium of Streets

Rambla de Catalunya, Barcelona

- A sense of intimacy, despite the wide, almost 100-foot right-of-way, due, at least in part, to narrow sidewalks, narrow auto cartways, bay windows, signs, awnings. There is a great deal in the right-of-way.

- Many attractive stores.

- Each roadway, about 21 feet wide, can handle one parking lane and two moving lanes, though generally there is only one moving lane.

- Buildings are five to seven stories tall.

- Streetlight spacing varies: 45 to 70 feet apart.

- Trees are 21 feet apart.

- The central walkway, with benches, has a planting strip along the curb integrated with trees. This one-meter-wide planting strip stops before intersections and for about 75 feet in the center of the block.

- Cafes under temporary canvas structures are set up along parts of the central walkway during spring and summer.

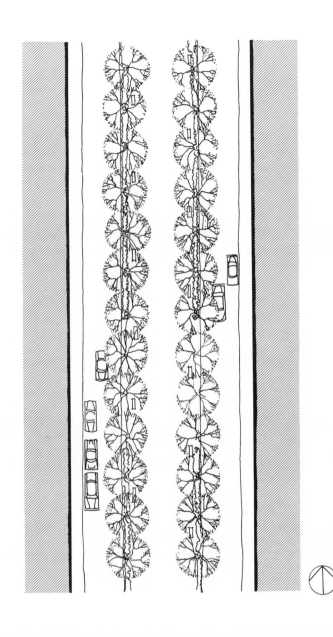

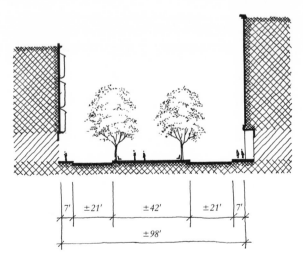

Approximate scale: 1″ = 50′ or 1:600

A Compendium of Streets

Unter den Linden, Berlin

- The street section is reminiscent of the Ramblas, Barcelona, but with wide sidewalks.

- Buildings along the street, mostly post–World War II, are generally dull, lifeless at street level. Long stretches of blank walls or screened windows. When there is a storefront, even if poorly executed, it attracts people and interest.

- Older buildings, of five or six stories, are about 10 feet taller than equivalent post–World War II buildings.

- The street deteriorates totally at the monument in front of the university, becoming a roadway–parking lot.

- An 1820 drawing shows 42 buildings on the university side, to the canal. Buildings then had about the same height, 55 to 65 feet, as now.

- There are two lines of trees in the 1820 drawing.

- An 1825 colored etching shows tall, mature trees.

- The lindens are uniformly 8 meters apart; the smell is beautiful, a reason to go there.

- The streetlights line up, between every two sets of trees.

- There seems almost no relationship between the street of the early 1990s and the street Paul Lindau wrote of so warmly in "Unter den Linden," in *Great Streets of the World,* in 1892.

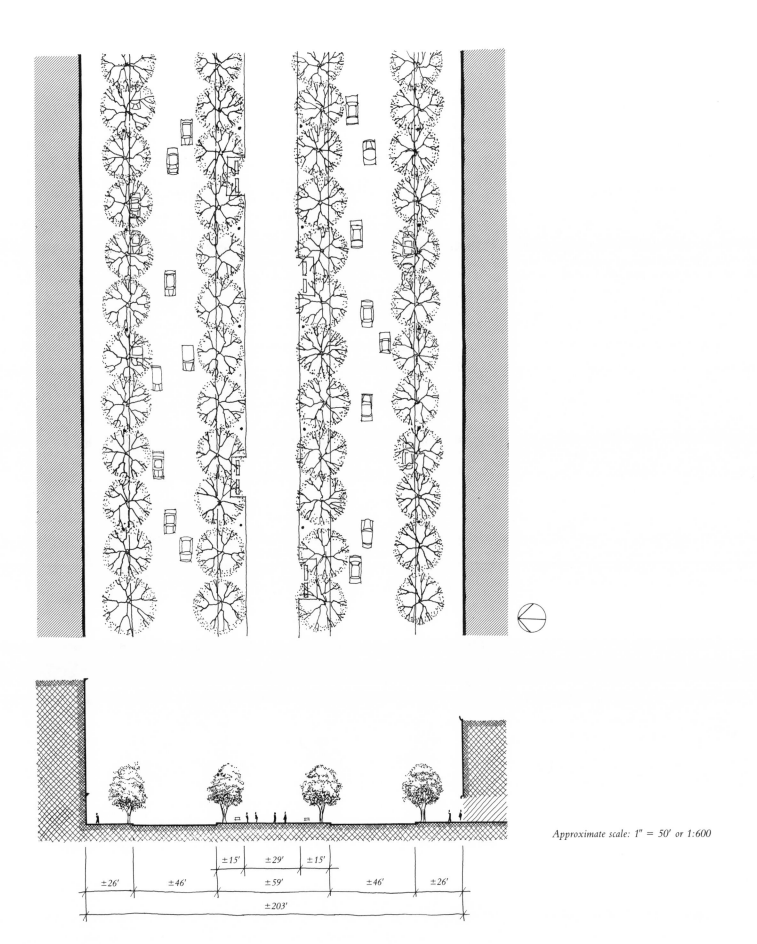

Approximate scale: 1″ = 50′ or 1:600

±15′ ±29′ ±15′

±26′ ±46′ ±59′ ±46′ ±26′

±203′

A Compendium of Streets

Motomachi, Yokohama

- This street shows how much can be designed, successfully, into an amazingly small cross section.

- The basic street cross section is approximately 28 feet, between facing buildings that range in height from two to five stories.

- The upper floors of newer buildings are set back to permit sunlight to penetrate to the street.

- Ground floors of buildings have been altered to set back from the building line, approximately 5 to 6 feet, to achieve wider sidewalks. This has been achieved, apparently, by regulation.

- Building widths along the street are from 12 to 20 feet; most are about 15 feet.

- There are small stores and many, many doorways.

- Materials, details, and workmanship are of a very high quality.

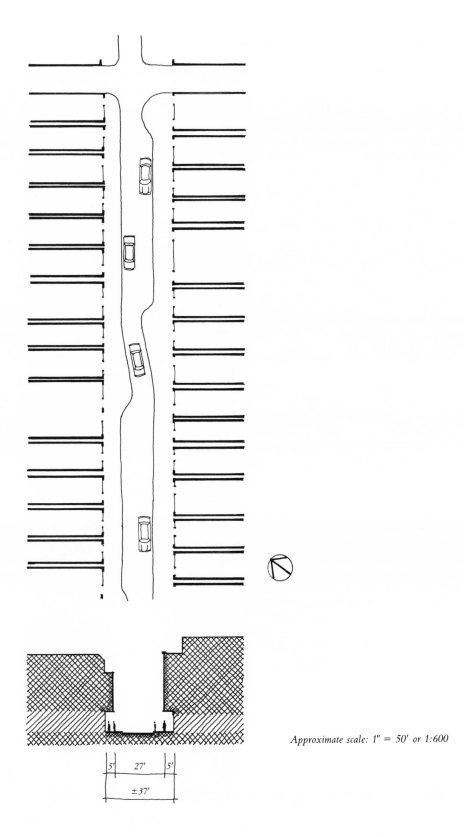

Approximate scale: 1″ = 50′ or 1:600

| 5′ | 27′ | 5′ |

± 37′

Bahnhofstrasse, Zurich

- An elegant main street with significant changes in character and uses from its start at the railroad station to its end at the Zürich-See: it changes from a shopping and eating street near the railroad to banking (in self-conscious buildings) toward the lake.

- A relatively new street, over the course of what was the Froshengraben Canal for much of its length. The canal existed as late as 1860.

- Truly the central, organizing street of the central area.

- At least two significant changes in direction over its length.

- No special ending at Zürich-See, but the railroad station is a very strong focal presence at the other end.

- Streetcars enter and leave it at many locations.

- Two or three open areas for sitting and gathering along its length.

- Seems an ever-changing street that has been adapted to new demands and possibilities.

- Parades take place on the Bahnhofstrasse.

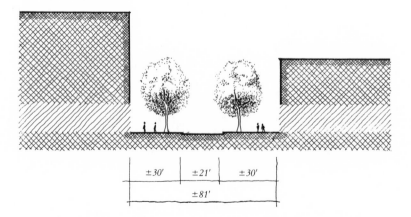

A Compendium of Streets

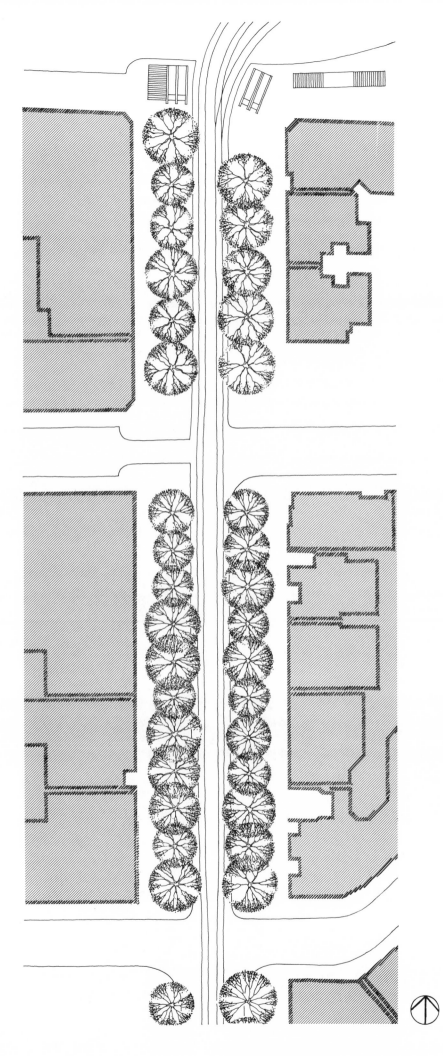

Approximate scale: 1″ = 50′ or 1:600

A Compendium of Streets

Via Cola di Rienzo, Rome

- The major street between Piazza del Popolo and Piazza del Risorgimento, near the Vatican.

- A middle class, bustling shopping street with offices, housing, institutions above stores, in five- to eight-story buildings.

- Generally similar building heights at from 70 to 80 feet.

- Very crowded during late afternoon and early evening shopping hours. Hard to walk rapidly on the sidewalks, especially on Saturdays, due to the crowds.

- The street is well defined, and the cross section is a pleasing one.

- A widening about two-thirds of the way to the river is a welcome pause on the street; effectively ends the main shopping area.

- Buildings are generally large, but there are many small stores at ground level with many windows and doors: typical buildings are 116 feet (35.5 meters) long, the average store length is 23 feet (7 meters), and the average distance between doorways is 20 feet (6.3 meters).

Via Cola di Rienzo:
street and building context

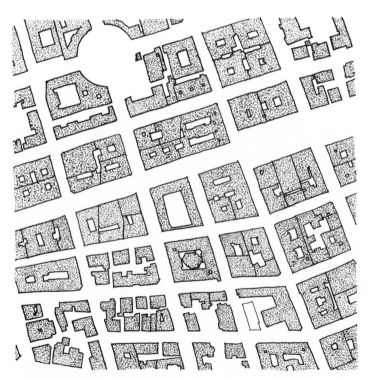

Approximate scale: 1" = 400' or 1:4,800

A Compendium of Streets

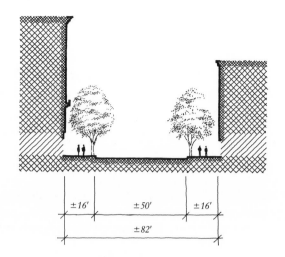

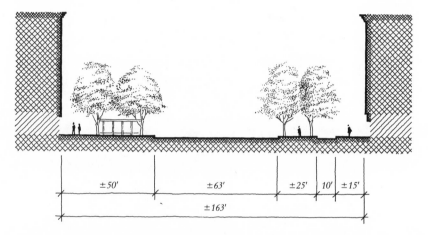

Approximate scale: 1" = 50' or 1:600

- Open stands at some corners sell mostly leather goods, shoes, clothes.

- Typical neoclassical buildings have many facade breaks and there is a constant play of light and shadow over them.

- Trees are important on this street; *Cercis occidentalis*.

- The trees are not tall, but are planted 15 to 18 feet apart and come to the corners.

- Trees are absent in front of the public market; this is unfortunate.

- Streetlights hang over the center of the street on wires attached to buildings. Very effective; they take the eyes down the street.

- Auto traffic moves slowly. Parking is permitted at curbs. No double parking here; police enforce the rules.

- Side streets are full of parked cars oriented to this street.

- Lack of parking doesn't seem to keep people from coming.

A Compendium of Streets

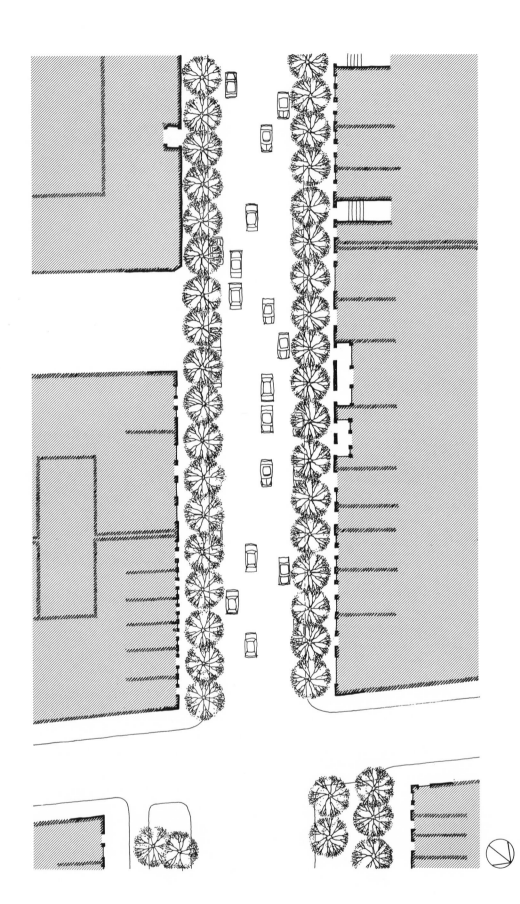

Approximate scale: 1″ = 50′ or 1:600

A Compendium of Streets

A Compendium of Streets

Kurfürstendamm, Berlin

General

- A central, significant street with a long history, dating as a boulevard from around the late 1800s. It continually changes and evolves.

- A fine street. A better street in 1991 than in 1973, when there were no trees in the center planting strip.

- Many people of all ages and perhaps of many incomes. A true, central community street? Many are strolling, talking. A place to walk. There is a pleasant sense of informality.

- The street has a distinct starting point, at Kaiser-Wilhelm-Gedachtniskirche, but no sense of an end, despite appearances of a bending or turning point, at Leibnizstrasse and at Brandenburgische Strasse.

- Many stores sell a wide variety of goods, all with windows that invite looking inside. There are also many eating places and movie houses, especially at corners. Department stores are closer to the center.

- Upper floors appear to be used mostly for offices and businesses, though some are residences, especially in older buildings.

- Side streets are developed with apartment blocks: high density in buildings of less than 10 floors. The ground floors have commercial uses.

- Moving westward from the central area, the buildings and stores get larger, with more housing. Some higher-style, more expensive stores but also larger stores, less oriented to comparative, fast-turnover shopping—oriental rugs, office furniture—and fewer eating places.

- Generally, in summer, the view is kept low, of branches, leaves, storefronts, not of buildings.

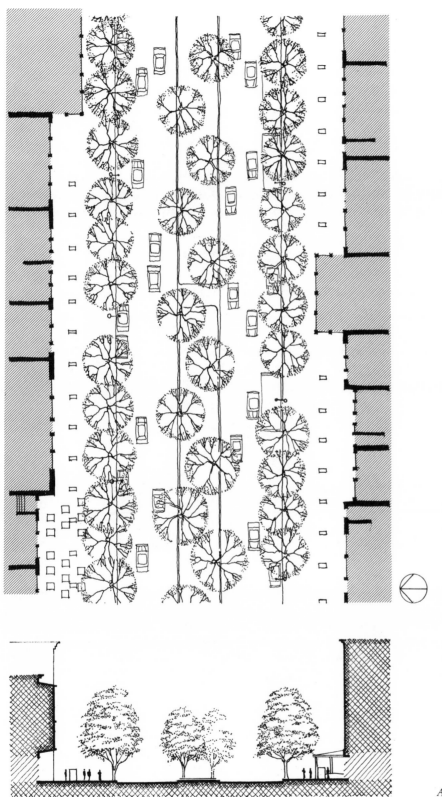

Approximate scale: 1″ = 50′ or 1:600

±33′ ±33′ ±23′ ±33′ ±33′

±155′

Buildings _____

- Older buildings are somewhat heavy but richly detailed. Newer buildings, in the International Style, generally have nondescript, extruded aluminum details and panels. A few larger ones, out from the central area, have setbacks and the street suffers. The newest buildings, toward the center, visible from Joachimstaler Strasse, are better suited to street life.

- Buildings seem limited to about 72 feet high, five to seven stories. At times, a top setback permits one or two more floors.

- Some older buildings set back approximately 2 meters, and some of these have 2-meter projections above the ground floor.

- Many awnings, signs, large marquees from buildings over walks.

Trees _____

- The presence of trees is very strong; London planes.

- Along walks, the tree spacing varies but is generally 20 to 24 feet. Occasional "missing" trees are replaced with large, ornate streetlights that vary in spacing from 80 to 105 feet. Sidewalk trees are taller and older than those in the median.

- Branches of the sidewalk trees can come within 8 feet of buildings and do a good job of hiding the least lovely.

- The trees in the median are about 26 feet apart; branches overlap.

- In summer the trees direct and limit the view. It is a low, horizontal view, under the branches, to lighted stores. Overwhelmingly the color is green.

Corners

- There are major openings at corners, partly due to wide intersections, partly to diagonal orientations of many buildings, but also because the trees stop.

- Intersections are not always pleasant despite sidewalk cafe locations here. Partly they are too open, partly it is the traffic and noise, partly that the defining buildings are architecturally poor.

Traffic, Parking

- Constant traffic but not high-speed.

- Two moving lanes and one parking lane on each side.

- No turning lanes intrude on the central planted strip.

- Subway entrances are sometimes at street corners, sometimes in the central strip.

- Past Uhlandstrasse the trees remain, but the center is used for diagonal parking and the curb lane in the outward direction for parallel parking.

Sidewalks

- The most notable aspects of sidewalks are the cafe "intrusions." "Temporary" cafe structures can come within 20 feet of curbs, and are anything but temporary. They do not seem to have proliferated since 1973.

- Display boxes, about 20 feet from the curb, are about 50 feet apart and measure about 2 by 3 feet.

- Clocks, advertising signs, and kiosks have no location or spacing patterns.

- Handsome, ornate streetlights are hidden by the tree leaves in summer.

Kurfürstendamm light

A Compendium of Streets

Regent Street, London

- Most notable for its wide, clear, purposeful shape in an otherwise fine-scaled, irregular street pattern, and its large, formal, meant-to-be-impressive buildings in a surrounding environment of much more modest, intimate structures.

- It is most impressive at the starting point, Piccadilly Circus, and the crescent section leading in an arc northward toward Oxford Street.

- Leaving or approaching Piccadilly Circus one has a sense of anticipation, a desire to see where it ends or what it leads to. The curve gives a sense of closure, a sense of place. It is one of the few places where one can examine both a concave and a convex street.

- Basically a very simple street section: walks 15 to 18 feet wide on either side of a 50-foot auto cartway.

- Building heights are similar if not uniform, six to seven floors, about 70 feet.

- Building material is noteworthy; light gray or gray-brown limestone.

- Buildings have been designed to address the street: columns, major entrances, domed corners, many windows, strong cornice lines.

- Diagonal corner entryways to most buildings.

- An architecturally unified block front may really be five or more separate buildings.

- In one block, from Conduit Street to New Burlington Street, there are 18 entrances, or approximately one entrance per 20 feet in what appears to be one building.

- Small irregular streets off of Regent Street are inviting, more so than Regent Street itself. They complement each other.

- A major traffic street: cars, noise, fumes.

- Many people, most walking fast; very little or no strolling, though any pace is possible.

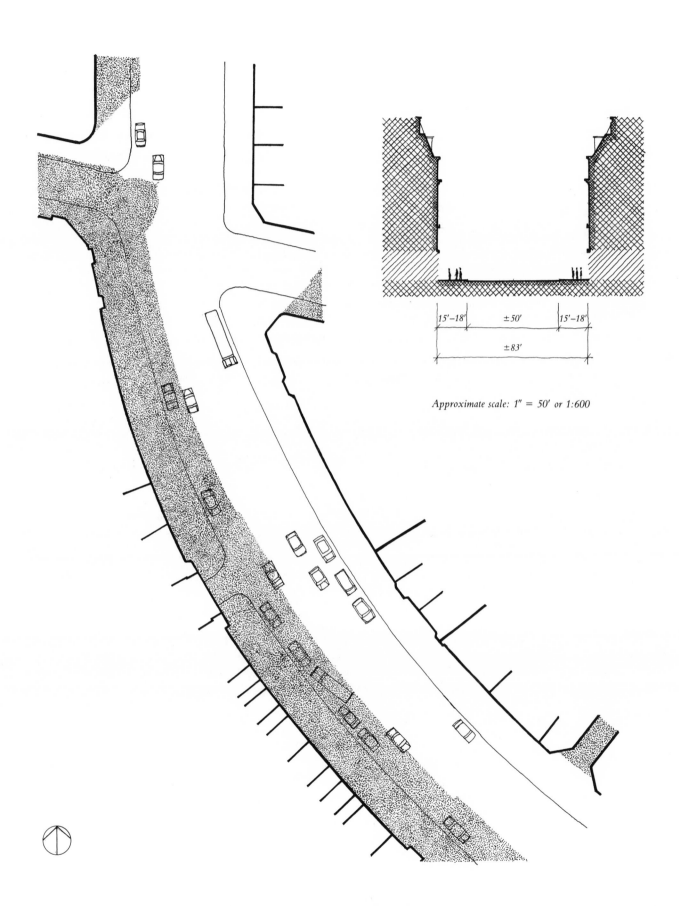

±15'–18'   ±50'   ±15'–18'

±83'

Approximate scale: 1" = 50' or 1:600

- A special crossing arrangement at street corners resembles a maze, presumably to discourage jaywalking; most notable at Oxford Street.

- The street calms down, people-wise, north of Oxford Street.

- All Souls Church tower that ends the street is not very effective, in part because of the hodgepodge of buildings behind it.

- If this is a special street, it is the uses—Waterford, Wedgewood, Jaeger, Burberry, Liberty, etc.—and maybe the similar complementary architecture that make it so. The Piccadilly approach is not enough to hold the street.

- The earlier Regent Street in the early 1800s, designed by John Nash, must have been much better: porticoes and colonnaded walks gave it a smaller, lower section, with more architectural interest.

Note: See Steen Eiler Rasmussen, *London: The Unique City* (London: Jonathan Cape, 1937).

Regent Street

A Compendium of Streets

Borgo Pio, Rome

- The Borgo area is like a small town, nestled between the wall–escape route leading from the Vatican to the Castel Sant'Angelo on the south, Via del Mascherino on the west, Borgo Angelico and Via Vitelleschi on the north, and the Castel itself on the east. Borgo Pio is its main street. Or it can be considered the main street of a distinct, small district of the city.

- Another block on the west, just before the Vatican, is of large institutional buildings, unrelenting in scale, that border the area and damage the integrity of Borgo Pio.

- A mix of local shops, religious and tourist-oriented stores, small hotels.

- A sense of neighborliness. A few benches are very inviting.

- One or two small knots of men talking and small kids playing soccer in the street at 7:30 P.M., end of February.

- The street is about 1,000 feet (300 meters) long and has a distinct beginning and end.

- Buildings are three to six stories, mostly four.

- Five to six buildings per block face, averaging 37.5 feet (11.4 meters) in length.

- The average store length at the street face is 18.2 feet (5.5 meters).

- The average distance between doorways on the street is 12.5 feet (3.8 meters).

- Streetlights hang in the center, over the street, from wires at the third floor. They give upper definition to the street, and create a line that the eye follows along the street.

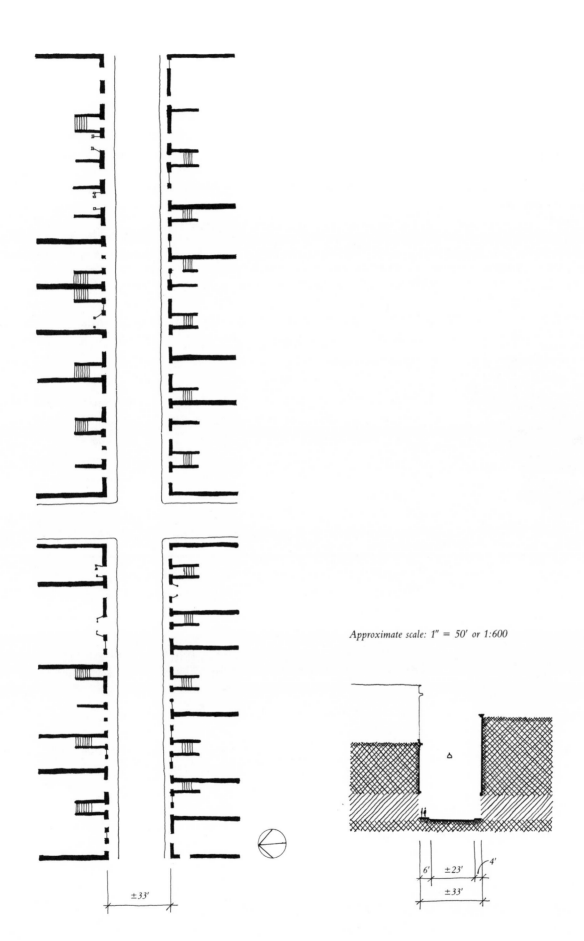

Approximate scale: 1″ = 50′ or 1:600

±33′

6′ ±23′ 4′

±33′

A Compendium of Streets

**Castro Street,
Mountain View, California**

- A delightfully executed new street, circa 1990.

- A street of subtle changes in level and of flexibility within a strong, clear design concept.

- A street on three levels: sidewalk, parking, auto cartway.

- The sidewalks, at the highest level, separate pedestrians from cars more effectively than on other streets and give a better than normal view over cars to the opposite side.

- The parking apron, with trees planted along its outer edge toward the street, provides a flexible transition zone that is clearly in the domain and at the pace of the pedestrian.

- The trees could be spaced closer together, but will be better when more fully grown.

- The slight elevation change and the line formed by the parking apron clearly separate it from the street.

- The apron is available for use for outdoor restaurants or cafes as well as for exhibition space on special occasions.

- Well designed and located passageways from Castro Street to rear lot parking space help focus activity onto the street, not to the rears of buildings.

- Plenty of seating.

- Economic vitality of the street leaves much to be desired, but that is not due to the street design. Rather, the design is a draw to the area.

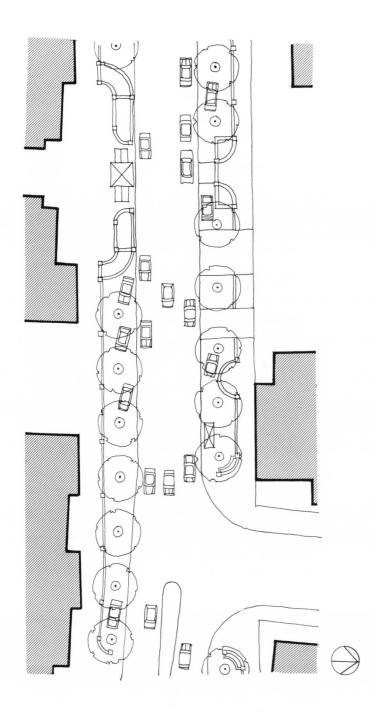

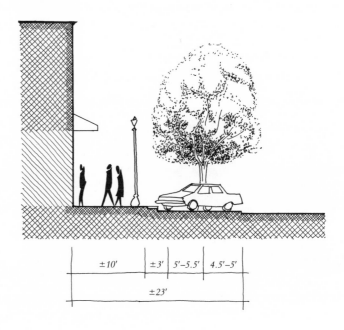

An adaptable section: for cars or for cafes or exhibits

±10′	±3′	5′–5.5′	4.5′–5′
±23′			

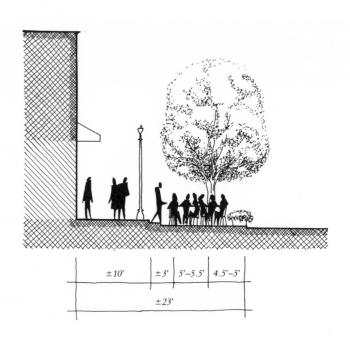

±10′	±3′	5′–5.5′	4.5′–5′
±23′			

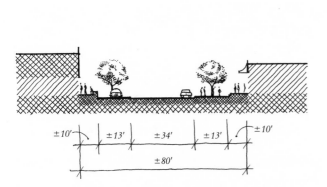

±10′	±13′	±34′	±13′	±10′
±80′				

Approximate scale: 1″ = 50′ or 1:600

**Main Street,
Disneyland, California**

- All fake, all stage set, yet it represents an idealized dream-memory of what made a great street, with stage set physical qualities that exist on the best streets: buildings lining the street, architectural details over which light constantly moves, transparency at ground level, pedestrian comfort, a hint of housing and habitation, a beginning and an ending.

- Many doorways, one every 18 feet, but some aren't real and what appear as different stores outside are the same store inside.

- An appearance of many buildings, one every 22 feet on average.

- Many windows and signs.

- Upper floors are proportioned correctly but are smaller in actual dimensions than real buildings: a less than full-scale model.

- Cleanliness.

- Despite the artfulness of concept and high quality of execution, there is a sense of physical thinness, as if the walls aren't really walls, as if it's all being held up with props.

- An example of how little area it takes to create a sense of urbanity.

- Central trolley tracks reveal ambivalence as to what this is—main street in a small town or main street in a city.

- All in all an exercise in giantism made to look like populism.

Main Street, Disneyland

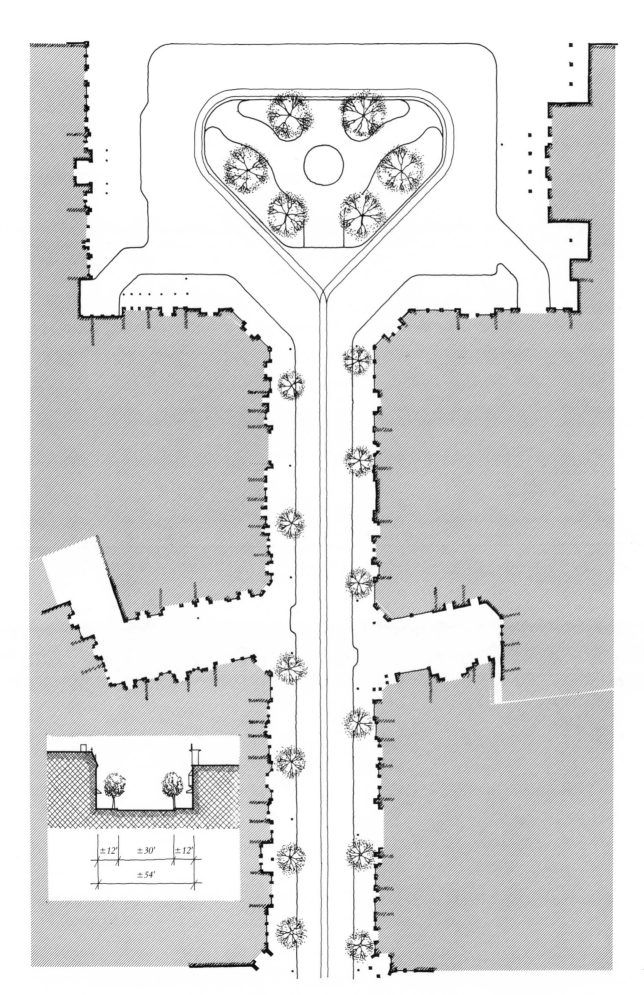

±12' ±30' ±12'

±54'

Approximate scale: 1" = 50' or 1:600

Strada Nuova, Venice

- Parallel to the Grand Canal, part of a long, continuous walk of many street segments from the Rialto Bridge to the railroad station.

- Seems more a local street, for local people, than others.

- Ponte San Giovanni Crisostomo seems a break point from tourist to more local orientation.

- Many school children, older people, mothers with infants at about 3:30 to 4:30 P.M., early March.

- Many people strolling, most walking leisurely, few fast.

- In a one-hour period some people were seen a second or third time.

Strada Nova.

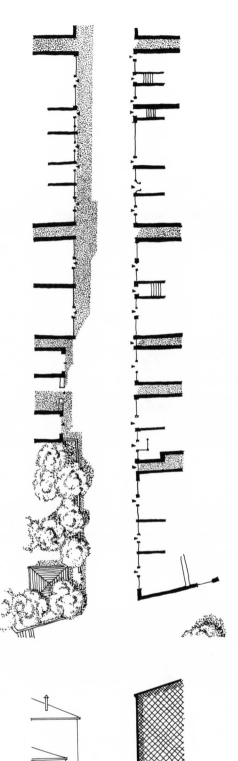

- The street stays mostly local until at least Ponte Sant'Antonio.

- Buildings vary from one to five stories, mostly four, but they are not tall stories.

- Most buildings are modest in scale and design; vernacular architecture.

- Many small stores: average store width 20–25 feet (6–7.5 meters); average building width 42 feet (12.7 meters).

- Though not wide in actual dimensions, it is very wide for Venice.

- Many small breaks, with very narrow public ways running perpendicular to the street; passages to housing.

- A delightful street!

30'

Approximate scale: 1″ = 50′ or 1:600

**Fairmount Boulevard,
Cleveland Heights, Ohio**

- A not-wide, sensuous, lightly curving residential boulevard lined with large houses, well set back from the street, on well-planted lawns.

- There is a pleasant, memorable start at Cedar Road, where Fairmount peels off, winding upward. A sense of place moving in either direction.

- The curving street allows continuous views of green and glimpses of houses. Because of the turns it does not get boring.

- Street dimensions, adequate but not large, nevertheless give a sense of space, probably because of deep landscaped setbacks to houses and their spacing.

- Two to three houses per block front.

- The trees along the street have no pattern, may once have been regularly spaced at 27 to 36 feet but not now.

- Where trees exist it is especially nice to walk.

- Larger pin oak trees are 60 to 70 feet tall.

- Large slate sidewalk slabs, 6 feet wide, are a notable surface.

- A general quietness to the street, a lazy graciousness.

- A setting for smaller, excellent residential side streets that intersect.

- Auto cartway widths of 18 feet allow two lanes but are not wider than necessary: a distinct plus.

- The central planting median is wide enough to be a presence, but is not one.

- The median, once a streetcar line, is now haphazardly planted, with groups of small trees and self-conscious spacing. It would be much better with regular, larger trees.

- Overall it is the houses and apparent wealth more than the street itself that are most compelling, especially the landscape in the private realm.

- Although the street right-of-way is kept very clean, it is not maintained otherwise, with an understanding of its history and the linear tree planting that the median and tree lawns require.

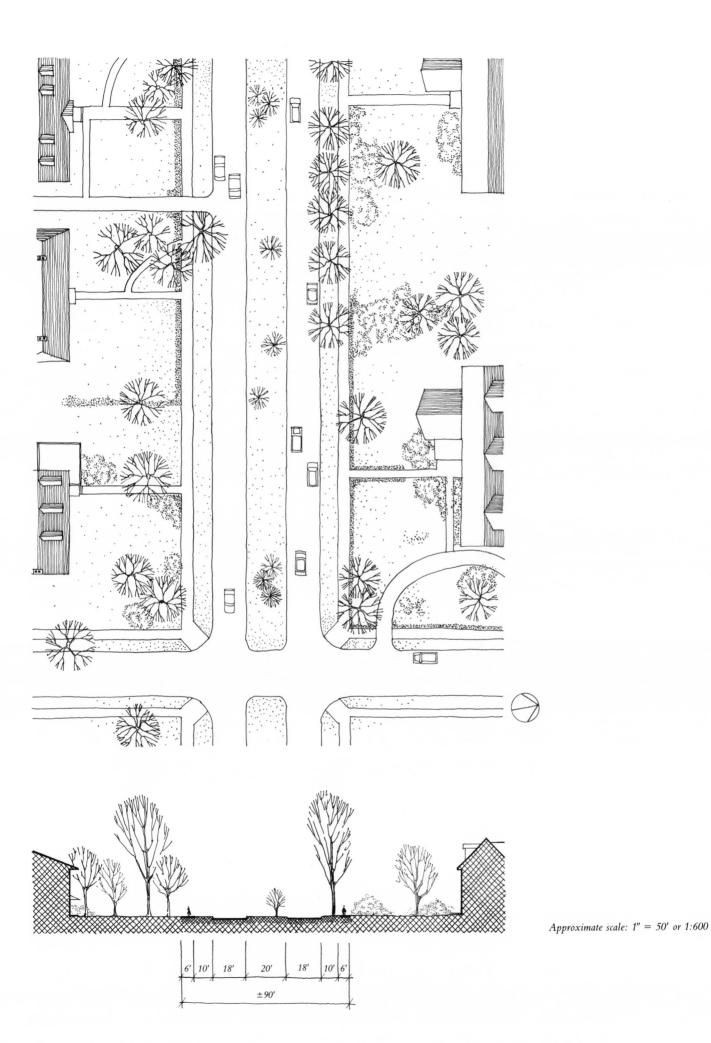

Approximate scale: 1" = 50' or 1:600

6' | 10' | 18' | 20' | 18' | 10' | 6'

±90'

**Orange Grove Boulevard,
Pasadena, California**

- Extraordinarily compelling from a distance or moving at moderate speed in a car. Trees are alternating tall California fan palms *(Washingtonia filifera)* and lower, deep green, spreading magnolias, in front of which is a line of opaque white streetlight globes. The overall background is heavy dark green foliage.

- The streetlights, white in strong contrast to the green, are crucial in catching the eye and directing vision along the street.

- Glimpses of houses with large lawns suggest wealth.

- Closer up, walking the street, it is pleasant but not as compelling as from a distance. The two tree types do not in fact alternate and the spacing is erratic.

- Streetlight spacing varies as well.

- For one long stretch all palms are missing and the street suffers.

- The palms are about 40 feet high to where fronds start; the fronds spread about 6 to 10 feet on either side of the trunk.

- The magnolias are from 25 to 30 feet high with a branch spread of 30 to 40 feet. Low branches are 10 to 12 feet above ground, sometimes less.

- Buildings, a variety of large one-family residences and multiple-family apartments, vary from two to three floors. Buildings are set back 40 feet from the right-of-way.

- The maintenance of street trees is not uniformly adequate.

- The gentle curve at Colorado Boulevard offers the best view of the street.

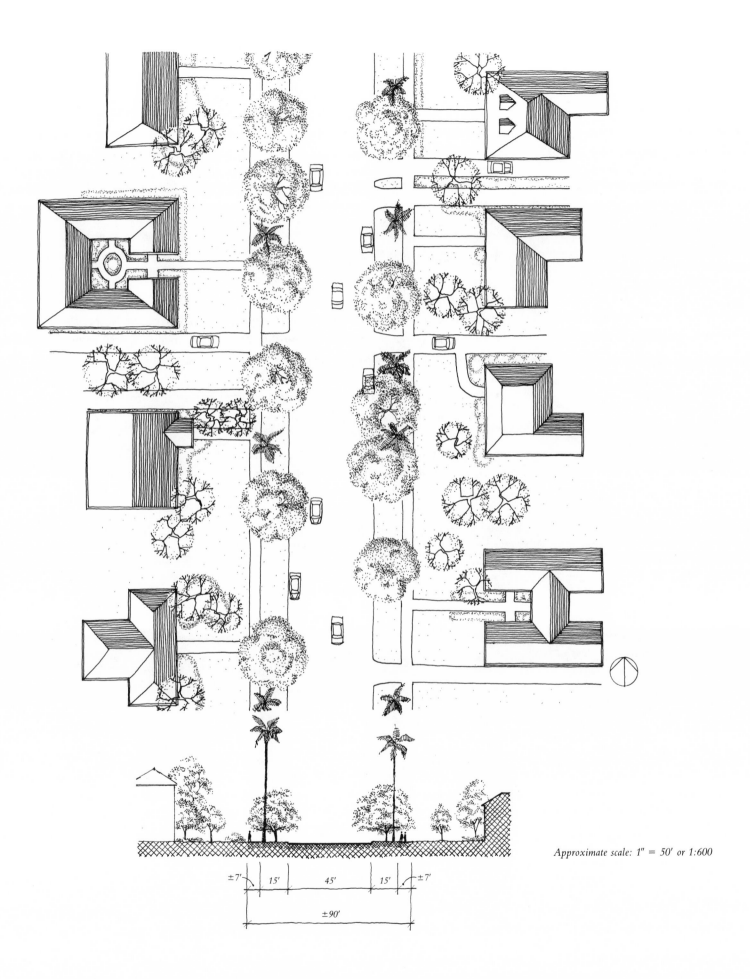

Approximate scale: 1″ = 50′ or 1:600

±7′   15′   45′   15′   ±7′

±90′

A Compendium of Streets

**Yohga Promenade,
Setagaya, Japan**

- A connected series of magnificently detailed streets in an area of mixed uses—residential, some industrial—to create a quiet, traffic-protected area next to a very busy thoroughfare.

- An epitome of what a protected residential area can be.

- Fine examples of how much can be designed into a small cross section: trees, sculpture, a soft edge rather than a curb where paving meets landscape, inventive play areas for children, mini-theater, water elements, special paving tiles of local materials in an ever-changing yet unified design.

- Automobiles are permitted even on the smallest street—a 12-foot cartway—but the feeling throughout is pedestrian.

- A continuous water element on the surface recalls that a stream once flowed along one of the streets. The original stream has long since been channeled into a culvert, but the design recalls it.

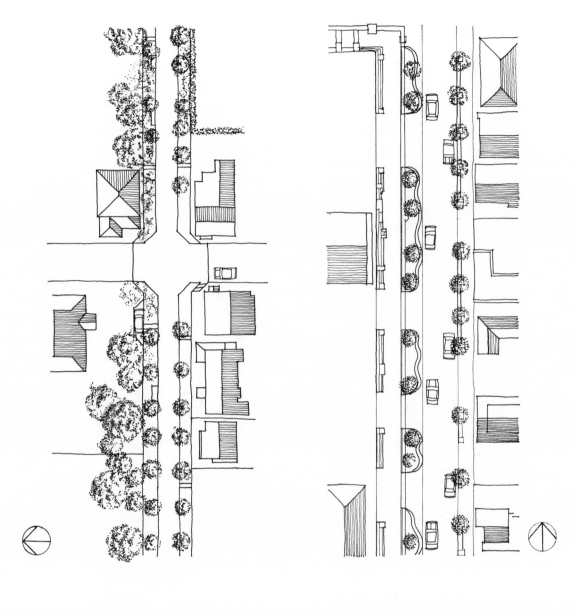

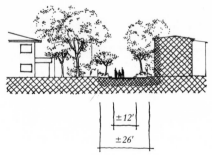

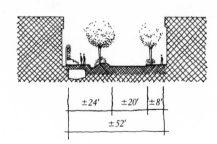

±12'

±26'

±24' ±20' ±8'

±52'

Approximate scale: 1″ = 50′ or 1:600

**Roxboro Road and Tutor Road,
Cleveland Heights, Ohio**

- Exemplary American suburban streets of the early 1900s. Individually designed and built homes on large parcels: 65-foot frontages, 10,000-square-foot lots, about four dwellings per net acre. Conceived and executed with well-to-do residents in mind.

- The streets themselves are compelling, particularly their dimensions, which are in strong contrast to much larger streets built for much less opulent homes in the 1980s and 1990s. Roxboro and Tutor are tight (for U.S. streets) but with houses set well back on heavily planted front yards (not just lawns), as opposed to much wider streets with equally large setbacks on sparsely planted lawns.

- Tree lanes along the street, 6 to 8 feet wide, make the streets appear narrower than they are.

- The curb-to-curb width of 22 to 24 feet is wide enough to permit parking on both sides.

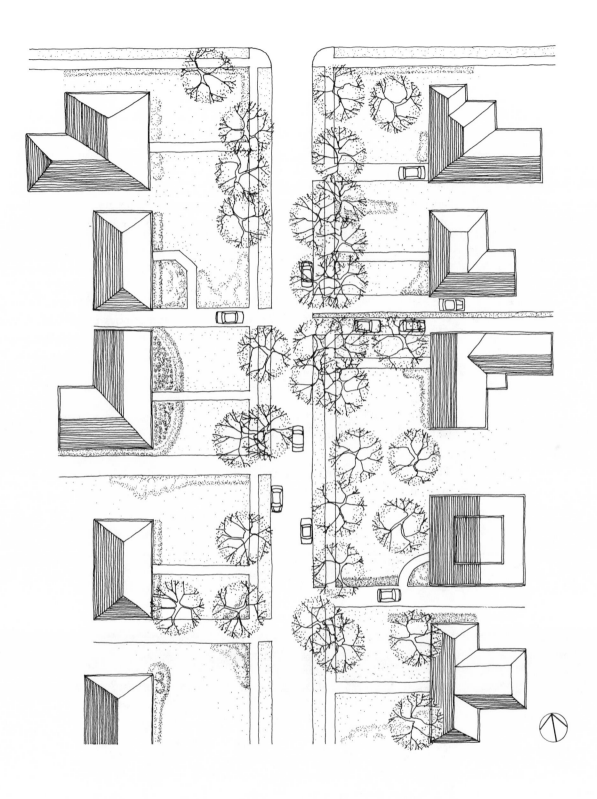

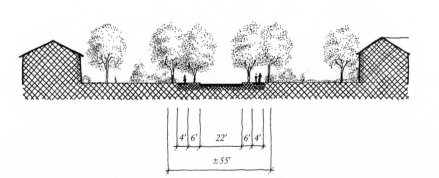

Approximate scale: 1″ = 50′ or 1:600

4′ 6′ 22′ 6′ 4′

±55′

Paddington Streets, Sydney

- Amazingly dense, small-scaled, single-family, terrace housing streets. Many houses are as little as 12 feet wide. Net residential densities are 50 dwelling units per acre along some streets; truly high for single-family homes.

- Public rights-of-way of 40 feet are common.

- No off-street parking, so cars park on narrow (20-foot) streets that are crowded and slow-moving. The entire right-of-way becomes pedestrian-oriented.

- Some 4-foot-wide sidewalks have trees planted along them.

- Building setbacks of 5 feet are often planted with shrubs. Setbacks and narrow porches are major socializing, community-building areas.

- The street right-of-way is not unlike Roslyn Place, in Pittsburgh. Essential differences are the closeness of Paddington homes to the street and their continuous facade.

Paddington area, Sydney: street and building context

Approximate scale: 1" = 400' or 1:4,800

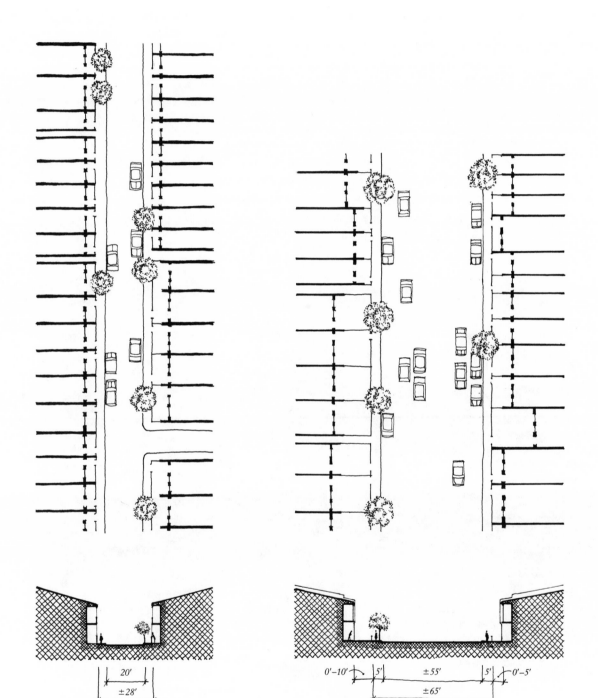

Approximate scale: 1″ = 50′ or 1:600

20′
±28′

0′–10′   5′   ±55′   5′   0′–5′
±65′

Amsterdam "Streets"

- Even the narrower canal streets are wide compared to many residential streets in the United States—Achterburgwal in the center is about 75 feet and Looiersgracht is about 86 feet—but are experienced as narrow and tightly defined. In part this is because of the height of the buildings that line them, and in part because there is so much in them: distinct level changes from street walks to water, lines of trees that divide the space, entry stoops, a sense of enclosure created by the bridges that cross the canals at a level higher than the walkways, and the boats.

- Buildings are generally three to five tall stories plus high, sloping roof areas. There is more brick than other materials.

A Compendium of Streets

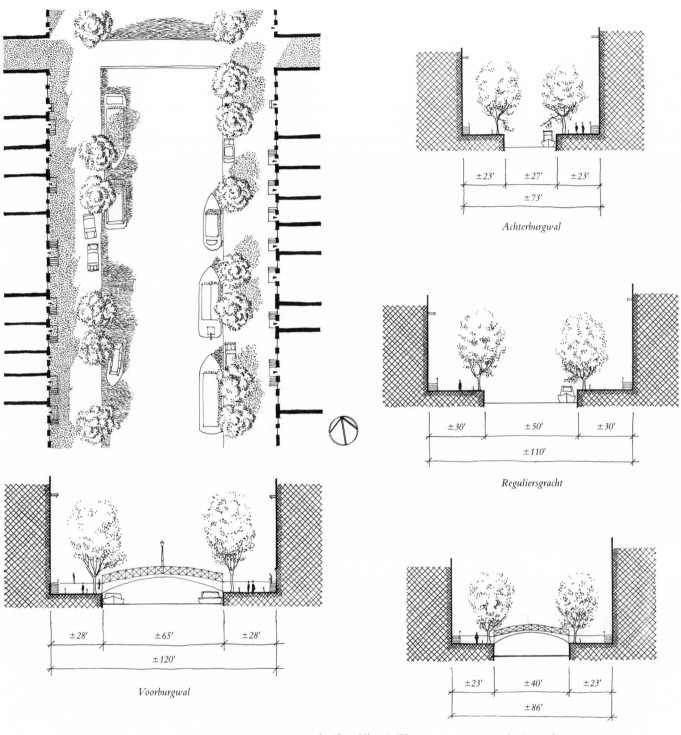

±23' ±27' ±23'

±73'

Achterburgwal

±30' ±50' ±30'

±110'

Reguliersgracht

±28' ±65' ±28'

±120'

Voorburgwal

±23' ±40' ±23'

±86'

Approximate scale: 1" = 50' or 1:600 *Looiersgracht*

A Compendium of Streets

- Buildings are generally narrow, emphasizing verticality and height: an average of 20 feet wide on Achterburgwal, for example, and 21 feet on the wider Prinsengracht. Newer buildings tend to be wider.

- At canal crossovers the streets rise to meet the bridges, which must start high enough to permit barges to pass beneath them. These elevation changes permit a pleasant viewing of the canals and parallel walks from a slightly elevated position.

- Trees along the narrower canals are generally closer (20 feet) than on the wider, circular canals (often over 43 feet). Tree canopies sometimes meet over the narrower canals.

- Paving is often a pinkish brick or light pink-purple aggregate brick.

- Small bollards, where used to clearly mark parallel parking limits, make a positive difference, resulting in uninterrupted walking areas.

- Many physical details contribute to a sense of inhabitation along the canals, especially the smaller ones: many doors (often more than one per building), stoops, many windows, window boxes with flowers, benches at corners, inhabited and individualized barges and houseboats.

- The smaller canals are more compelling as potential places to live than the larger ones.

A Compendium of Streets

**Botanical Gardens,
Rio de Janeiro**

- A wonderful example of a public way created by trees alone.

- A compelling space created by tall, stately palms, only 12 feet apart, defining a walkway 33 feet wide.

- A high, vertical, long space, about one-third of a mile; the space itself rather than anything at the ends is the most attractive part of the composition.

- A space with a light, open, Gothic-cathedral feeling.

- The trees, approximately 50 to 60 feet high, seem taller.

- Heavy planting along either side helps define a larger space, but is not an essential part of the whole: the trees alone would do it.

- The central walkway is of crushed granite.

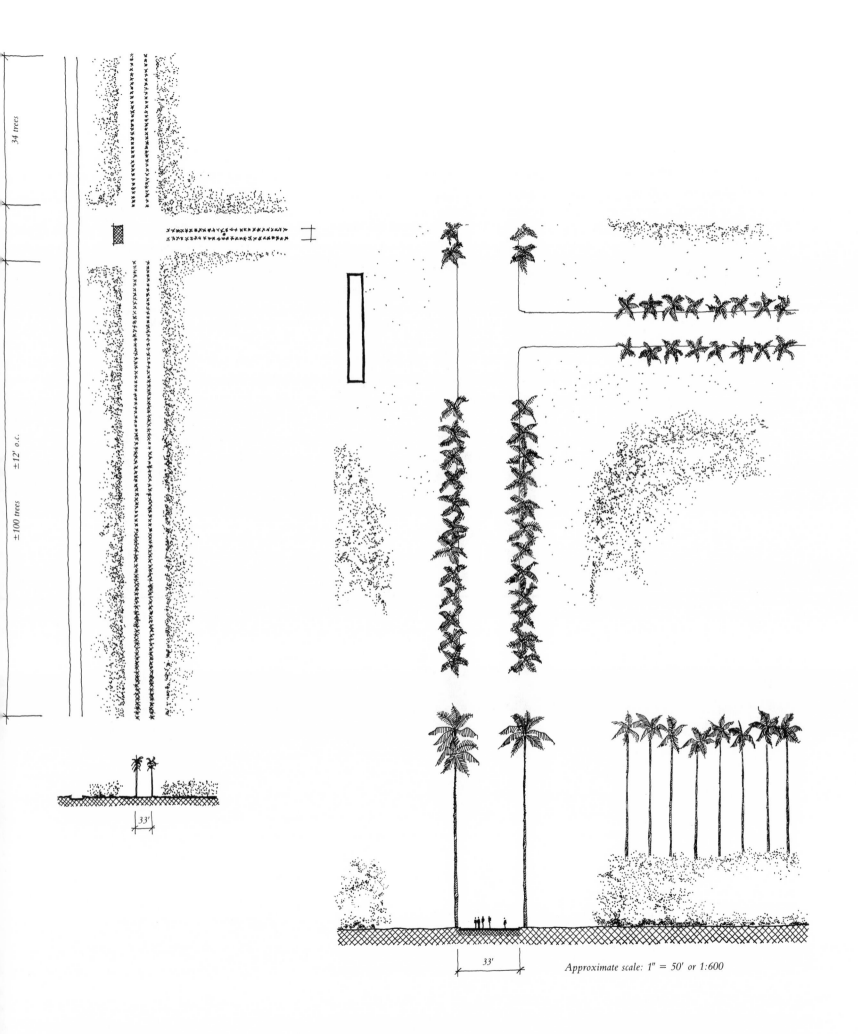

34 trees

±12' o.c.

±100 trees

33'

33'

Approximate scale: 1" = 50' or 1:600

A Compendium of Streets

**Champs-Elysées
(Place de la Concorde to
Rond-Point), Paris**

- Save for the wide central auto roadway, this could be a wonderful street, made only by trees. The ten traffic lanes divide the street into three separate environments and it is hard to experience one side from the other: wholeness is lost.

- Each side is very well done, each a wonderful environment in which to stroll, sit, stroll again.

- The buildings, often behind additional landscaped space, are not a significant part of the street.

- The south side is a linear bosc of four rows of a variety of elm trees, planted 16 feet (5 meters) apart in both directions. The north side has three rows, generally, but the fourth row is added at the intersections.

- There are quiet, shady places to walk, on a crushed granite surface; also a sunny open walkway, of smooth aggregate gray pavers in a bond pattern (about 0.5 meters square), a good place to walk when sunlight is desired.

- Streetlights mixed with large London planes along the center roadway vary in spacing from 33 to 50 feet (10 to 15 meters). The London planes are 26 to 33 feet (8 to 10 meters) apart.

- Outstanding details: rain shelters, benches, lights, toilets, refreshment stands.

- All trees come close to corners and cross streets.

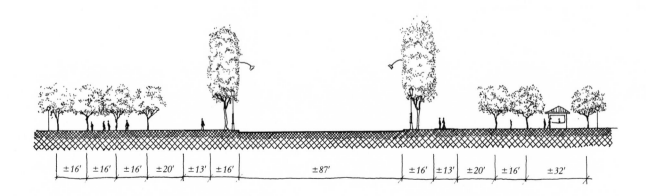

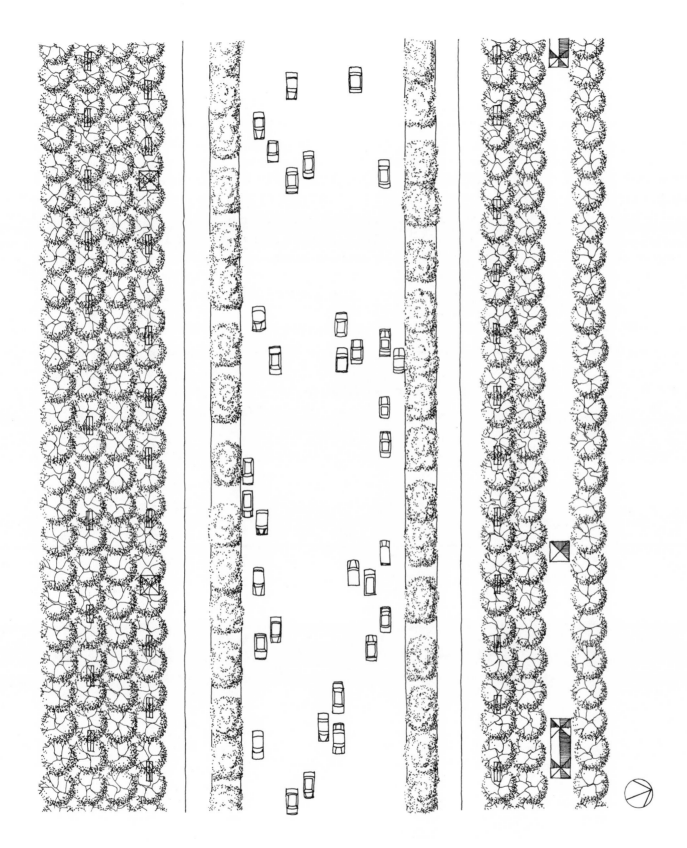

Approximate scale: 1" = 50' or 1:600

A Compendium of Streets

**Royal Palm Way,
Palm Beach, Florida**

- Four lines of palms, like columns, are the essence of the street.

- The palms in the central median are uniformly 30 feet apart. The palms along the walks are spaced unevenly, with no apparent attempt to match those in the center or on the other side.

- A grand entry street, at its beginning at the inland waterway, but without a focused ending.

- The buildings on the south side, though at the building line, are not a major presence because of their simplicity, colors that blend with surroundings, and the strength of the lines of palms that draw attention.

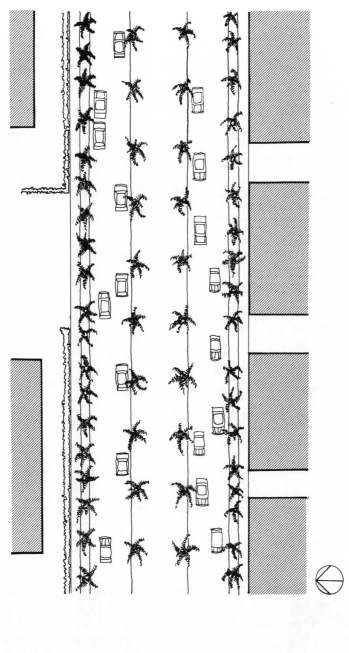

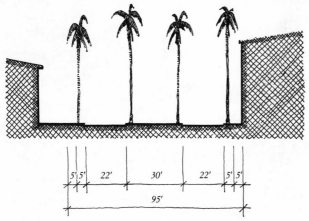

Approximate scale: 1" = 50' or 1:600

5' 5'   22'   30'   22'   5' 5'

95'

A Compendium of Streets

Princes Street, Edinburgh

- Designed and intended to be a great street, it is the focal street of the city, a city with many examples of first-rate urban design.

- It is a "one-sided" street in that one side is defined and lined with buildings while the other is mostly a promenade flanked by park and open space.

- The irregularly sized and designed buildings and the building gaps detract from the street.

- A long street, approximately 4,250 feet (1,300 meters), it has distinct but distant beginnings and endings, not on the street itself but in the form of church towers beyond the western ending point and centered monuments on the hillside above the eastern end. The actual endings-beginnings on the ground are somewhat unresolved, seem to peter out.

- The western end of the street is an intersection of five streets that might be more comfortable as a circle.

East on Princes Street

- There are distinct focal points along the street, at each intersecting street in the form of a building or statue, and these are reflected by statues at intersections on George Street, one block away and approximately 12 to 15 feet higher in elevation. Princes Street is not the "high" street in this area, but it is clearly integrated into its district by the statues.

- A very busy street, the one side lined with major downtown stores and hotels. Also a major bus and auto street.

- Lots of people at lunchtime on the store side, people walking briskly, no dawdling, a sense of crowding. About 10 to 15 percent as many people on the park side.

- The street width narrows along the park side at a number of locations to accommodate major buildings: hotel, monument, art museum.

- The combination of shopping on one side of the street with the promenade that borders the park on the other and the wonderful views of the old city, including Edinburgh Castle, make this a special street.

- On the park side, large trees are 30 feet apart; branches come together overhead.

- Flowering trees west of Frederick Street overhang most of the walk, not high overhead.

- The benches are simple, wooden, sturdy, all of a similar design and very frequent. Benches have been donated by groups or individuals, each one with a simple commemorative message.

- A pleasant place to stroll, pass time, enter the park with its many levels.

- Aluminum and glass bus shelters and strange structures built to hold flags (about 240 feet apart) detract from the park side of the street.

A Compendium of Streets

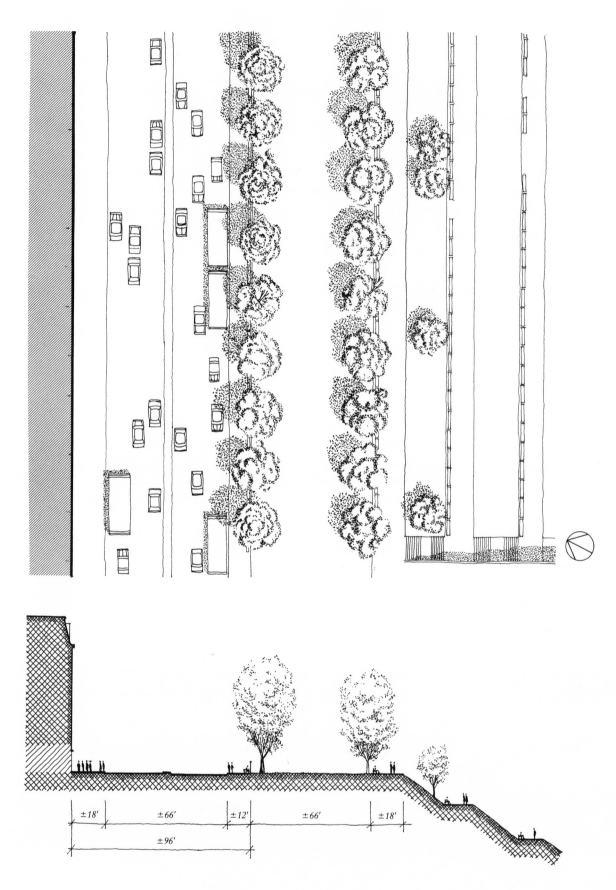

Approximate scale: 1″ = 50′ or 1:600

View from Princes Street

- The sidewalk is an attractive, smooth, dense paver, typically 36 by 20 inches by 2 inches deep, in a bond pattern.

- An early map suggests that the built side of the street was originally composed of three- to four-story townhouses. Taller buildings, of 60 to 70 feet, if similar in height, might suit it better.

Fifth Avenue (along Central Park), New York

- An elegant, compelling street, much more so along Central Park than it is below 59th Street.

- A one-way, high–traffic volume, fast-moving street.

- As many as five buildings per block front, usually less.

- Some buildings have small planted areas in front.

- Walkways along the buildings are graciously scaled. The trees here follow no special pattern.

- Though building heights vary, the overall impression is of a line of tall, expensive apartments interrupted by older, lower buildings (once mansions, now museums or private clubs).

- The older, smaller buildings give a sense of history and continuity.

- A passerby, on the east, may understand that he is not welcome inside these buildings without an invitation, but the windows give a sense of habitation and of other people nearby.

- The western, park side of the street is clearly for everyone.

- Double rows of trees on the west have no distinct spacing pattern but clearly define the street on this side.

- Paving materials on the park side are most handsome: hexagonal asphalt pavers in walks, cobble paving in tree areas.

- Low walls and benches invite pause and give visual access to Central Park. Both park and street seem accessible.

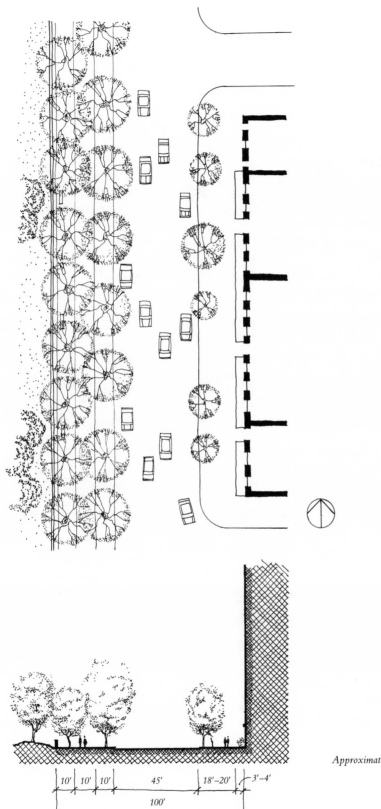

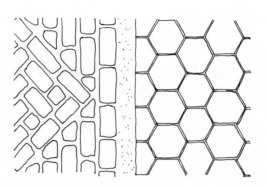

Paving detail

Approximate scale: 1" = 50' or 1:600

10' 10' 10'   45'   18'–20' 3'–4'

100'

Street and City Patterns:
Settings for Streets and People

17 March 91

If you were to walk all of the pathways and travel all the canals of one square mile in Venice you would pass more than 1,500 separate intersections and circle at least 900 blocks. By contrast, in Brasília you would find fewer than 100 intersections in a square mile and less than 50 blocks. The numbers alone bespeak vast differences in the physical nature of cities: in city scale, in visual and spatial complexity, in the sheer numbers of things in one area versus another, in the amount and sizes of spaces, and in the numbers of individual choice points that are available to people. At every intersection in each city—where two different public paths meet—there is at least one choice that can be made, to go this way or that, to follow one street or another. In that sense, there are over 1,500 points of choice available in a square mile of Venice, and fewer than 100 in Brasília.

Street and block patterns reflect differences among cities beyond those of scale, complexity, available choices, and the nature of spaces. They relate to the time period when the city was built, to geography, to differing cultures, to city functions or purposes, to design or political philosophies, and to technological demands, to name some of the more obvious. They are, as well, the settings within which great and not so great streets are to be found.

Our concern with street plans and city block patterns derives from an interest in the physical, designable characteristics of the best streets. In the process of determining what the best streets are and what makes them so, we want to know something of their settings, if for no other reason than to be able to locate them in their cities; to know where they are. But the more we find out about the street and block patterns, the more compelling they become in their own right. It is not only individual streets that are designed and redesigned, but whole sections of urban areas, to say nothing of new cities. Totally new cities, so much of the essence of which is the layout of streets, may not be frequent at the turn of the twenty-first century, but new urban areas are plentiful. Subdivision designs may be as plentiful in the 1990s as were surveyors' and engineers' layouts for whole cities in the United States during the eighteenth and nineteenth centuries.[1] City redevelopment schemes, with new street layouts for large urban areas, at times with the objective of achieving great streets, regularly capture our attention.[2] Models that permit comparison of what has worked with what we may be contemplating building, for street plans and block patterns just as for individual streets, are therefore of interest. Then, too, we would like to know if we might reasonably say that the particular layout of streets and blocks within which an exceptionally fine street exists contributes to or helps determine that street's special quality. A knowledge of physical context, we presume, will help us better understand differences in streets, while at the same time helping us to understand the difficulty in pinpointing what it is that makes a particular street stand out in our memories; is it the street itself that is so special, or is it one or more of the contextual physical variables that makes the street stand out?

The Via dei Giubbonari, we have seen, is narrow and bends, but may be considered regular and even ordered within its immediate context. Next to the Via del Corso, which is certainly straight, long, and wide in its context, the Via dei Giubbonari would be anything but regular. In Venice, however, the Via dei Giubbonari would be both wide and direct. In turn, the Via del Corso would be perceived as narrow compared to the Grand Canal, to say nothing of the Champs-Elysées which it influenced. The Grand Canal, so very wide in Venice, in such contrast to its setting, is significantly narrower than the Champs-Elysées, whose largeness stands out not only in relation to the size of streets around it, but also because of the relative infrequency of intersections with it. We want to know about settings, then, so that comparisons of streets and explanations about what makes them stand out can be more easily made.

Some streets may be called "ordering" streets. They bring comprehension or order to a city or district. They may form a boundary, such as the Ringstrasse in Vienna, or an attracting spine, such as the Bahnhofstrasse in Zurich or the Kurfürstendamm in Berlin. They let you know where you are. To a considerable extent, it is street patterns, by themselves or in relation to each other, that may give an initial order or disorder in relation to which individual streets can play their roles. The street and block patterns are the starting points.

There are many reasons, then, to know about the physical patterns and scales of urban streets and blocks, not the least of which is that they are compelling in their own right, just as patterns. But which city patterns shall we show and how shall we show them? To try to understand both the nature of a particular city or area and the differences between cities, it is important to compare areas of the same size at the same scale. It is difficult if not impossible to understand the differences between two or more cities by looking at different-sized areas—say one square mile of one versus 200 acres of another—to say nothing of what happens if the areas are presented at different scales. At issue is the difference between experience and knowledge. We may experience a part of Los Angeles over time, probably quite often in an auto, and get to "know" that area. We may do the same in the center of Rome, almost certainly on foot. We may see two different maps of the same areas and, without thinking about scale, acknowledge that we are familiar with those cities. But if the two areas are drawn at the same scale and cover the same amount of space on a drawing, we are likely to be surprised at their relative sizes, the sizes of the streets, the blocks, etc., because we did not experience them comparatively. To look at different cities drawn at the same scale and for the same area is to gain a knowledge of relative sizes that is almost certainly different from our experiences. Here we want to increase the objectivity of the comparison. We have chosen one square mile (2.59 square kilometers or 259 hectares) and a scale of one inch to one thousand feet (1″ =

1,000' or 1:12,000). It is an area within which patterns of various sizes can be seen (often more than one pattern appears) and it covers a surprisingly large part of many older cities. The size of drawing produced permits easy visual comparison.

The choice of which cities and which parts of cities to include was another matter. The choice has been determined by a number of factors, not the least of which is the need to show areas within which lie particularly noteworthy streets: the urban contexts of the Ramblas, or of Market Street, or of Strøget, for example. Also, there is an attempt to include cities that may be considered as typical: ancient, medieval, old, new, Middle Eastern, Asian, European, Western, industrial, capital, hilly, central, peripheral, and so on. Choices are sometimes eccentric or personal, responses perhaps to an offhand comment like "I wonder how Tokyo looks at this scale," or "You should see Cairo." The presence of great streets, geographic coverage, and the availability of information have been the main determinants of the choices of cities shown.

AHMEDABAD

INDIA

0					1 Mile
0	1000	2000	3000	4000	5280 Feet
0		500		1000	1609 Meters

AIX-EN-PROVENCE

FRANCE

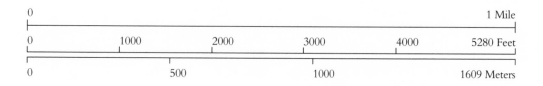

Street and City Patterns

AMSTERDAM

THE NETHERLANDS

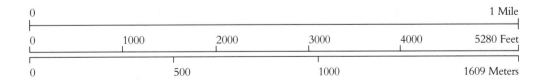

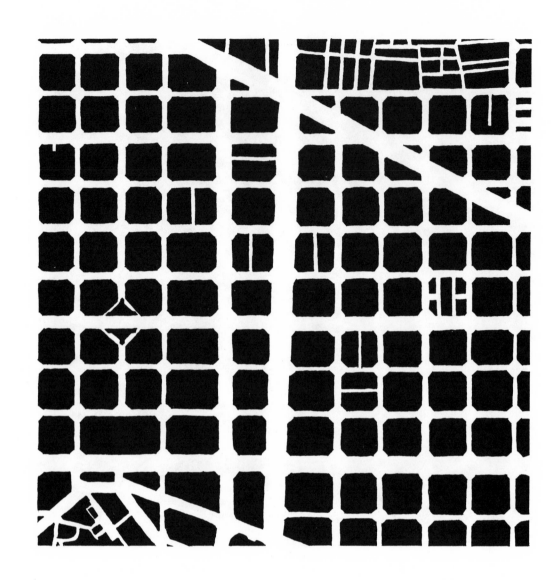

BARCELONA

(Paseo de Gracia)

SPAIN

0					1 Mile

0	1000	2000	3000	4000	5280 Feet

0	500	1000	1609 Meters

BARCELONA

(Ramblas)

SPAIN

0					1 Mile
0	1000	2000	3000	4000	5280 Feet
0		500		1000	1609 Meters

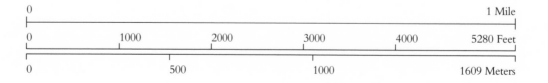

BARI

ITALY

0					1 Mile

0	1000	2000	3000	4000	5280 Feet

0	500	1000	1609 Meters

B A T H

E N G L A N D

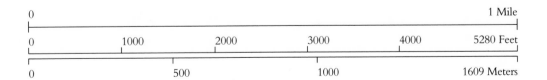

Street and City Patterns

BERLIN

(historic center, 1750)

GERMANY

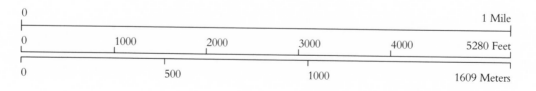

Street and City Patterns

BERLIN

(historic center, 1986)

GERMANY

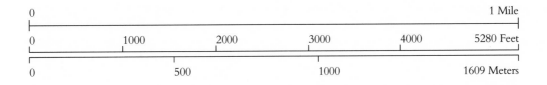

BOLOGNA

(city center)

ITALY

0					1 Mile
0	1000	2000	3000	4000	5280 Feet
0		500		1000	1609 Meters

Street and City Patterns

BOLOGNA
(Via di Corticello)

ITALY

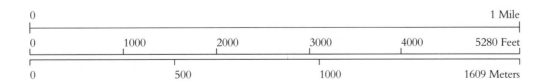

0   1 Mile

0   1000   2000   3000   4000   5280 Feet

0   500   1000   1609 Meters

BOSTON

(1980)

USA

BRASILIA
(city center)

BRAZIL

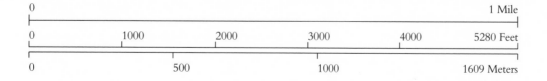

Street and City Patterns

CAIRO

EGYPT

Street and City Patterns

COPENHAGEN

DENMARK

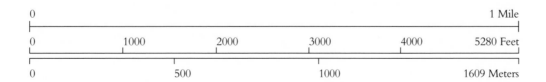

Street and City Patterns

FLORENCE

ITALY

0					1 Mile

0	1000	2000	3000	4000	5280 Feet

0	500	1000	1609 Meters

Street and City Patterns

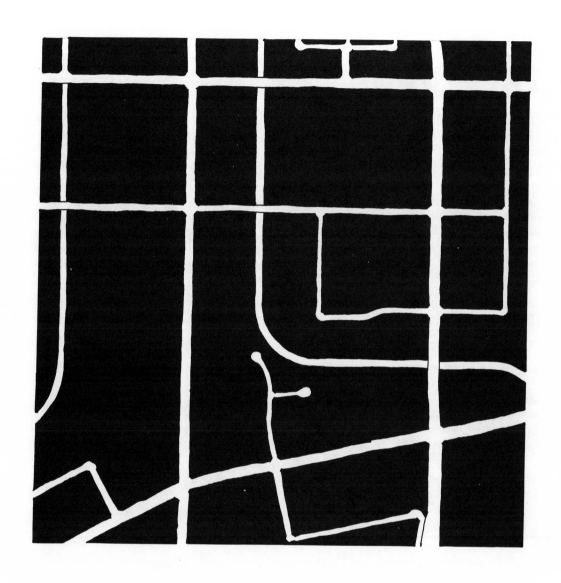

I R V I N E

(business complex)

U S A

0					1 Mile
0	1000	2000	3000	4000	5280 Feet
0		500		1000	1609 Meters

Street and City Patterns

IRVINE

(residential area)

USA

0					1 Mile

0	1000	2000	3000	4000	5280 Feet

0	500	1000	1609 Meters

LONDON

(Mayfair)

ENGLAND

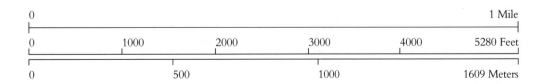

LONDON

(the City)

ENGLAND

0					1 Mile

0	1000	2000	3000	4000	5280 Feet

0	500	1000	1609 Meters

LOS ANGELES

(downtown)

USA

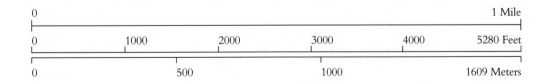

Street and City Patterns

LOS ANGELES
(San Fernando Valley)

USA

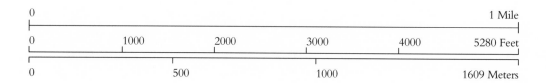

LUCCA

ITALY

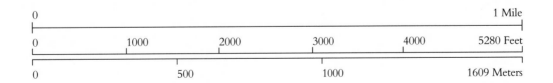

Street and City Patterns

MADRID

SPAIN

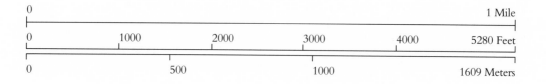

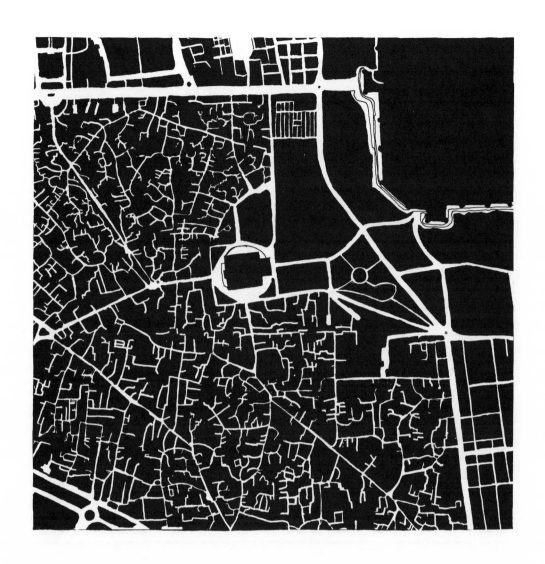

NEW DELHI

(old city—Red Fort)

INDIA

0					1 Mile

0	1000	2000	3000	4000	5280 Feet

0	500	1000	1609 Meters

NEW DELHI

(India Gate)

INDIA

Street and City Patterns

NEW YORK

(Lower Manhattan)

USA

0					1 Mile

0	1000	2000	3000	4000	5280 Feet

0		500		1000	1609 Meters

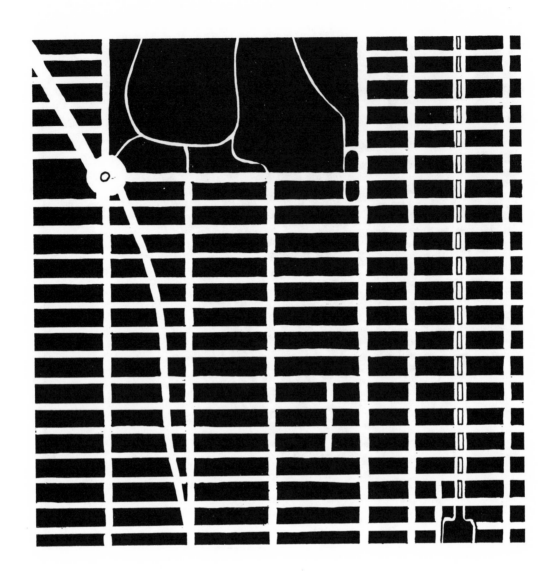

NEW YORK

(Midtown Manhattan)

USA

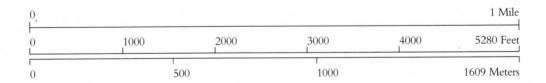

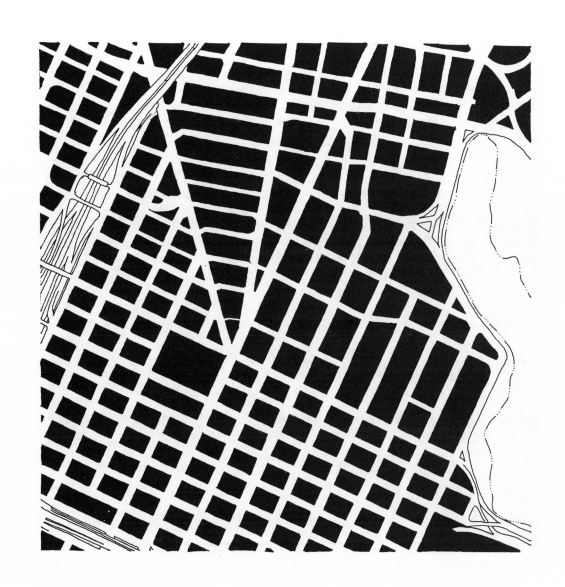

OAKLAND

USA

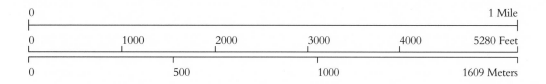

PARIS

(Etoile—Rond-Point)

FRANCE

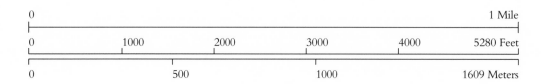

0					1 Mile
0	1000	2000	3000	4000	5280 Feet
0		500		1000	1609 Meters

PARIS

(Louvre—Palais-Royal)

FRANCE

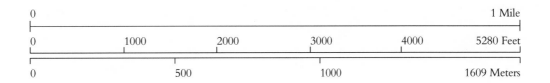

PHILADELPHIA

(downtown)

USA

0					1 Mile
0	1000	2000	3000	4000	5280 Feet
0		500		1000	1609 Meters

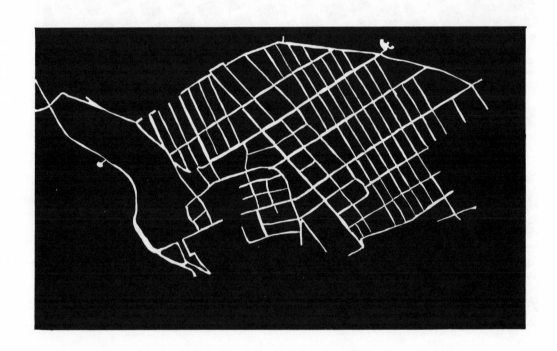

POMPEII

———————————————

ITALY

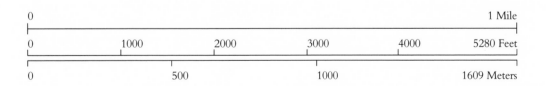

0					1 Mile
0	1000	2000	3000	4000	5280 Feet
0	500		1000		1609 Meters

Street and City Patterns

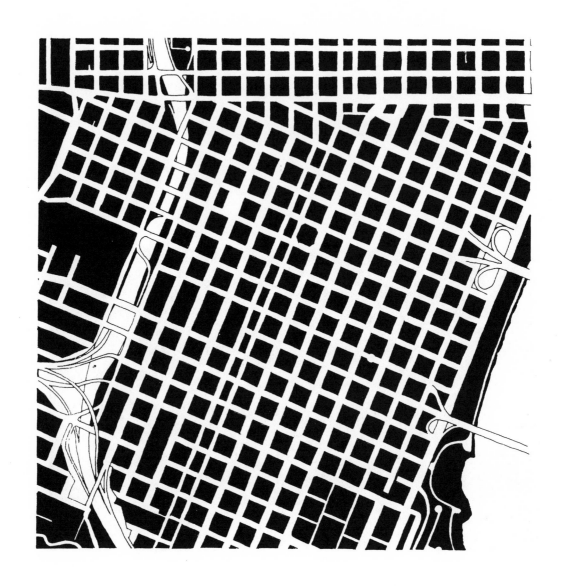

PORTLAND

USA

0					1 Mile

0	1000	2000	3000	4000	5280 Feet

0	500	1000	1609 Meters

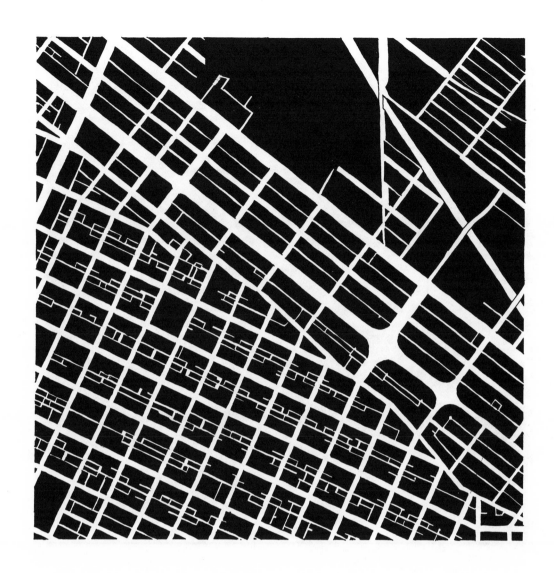

RICHMOND

USA

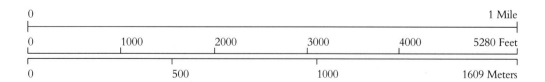

ROME

ITALY

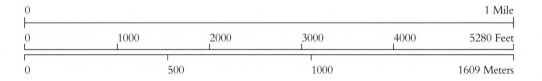

SAN FRANCISCO

(downtown)

USA

0					1 Mile
0	1000	2000	3000	4000	5280 Feet
0		500		1000	1609 Meters

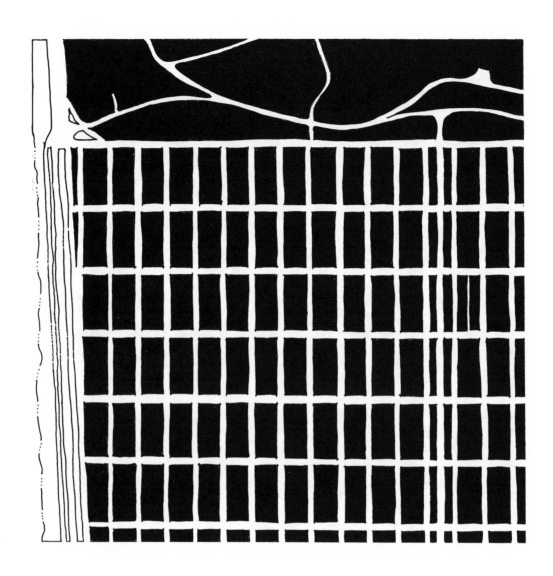

SAN FRANCISCO

(outer Sunset)

USA

0					1 Mile
0	1000	2000	3000	4000	5280 Feet
0		500		1000	1609 Meters

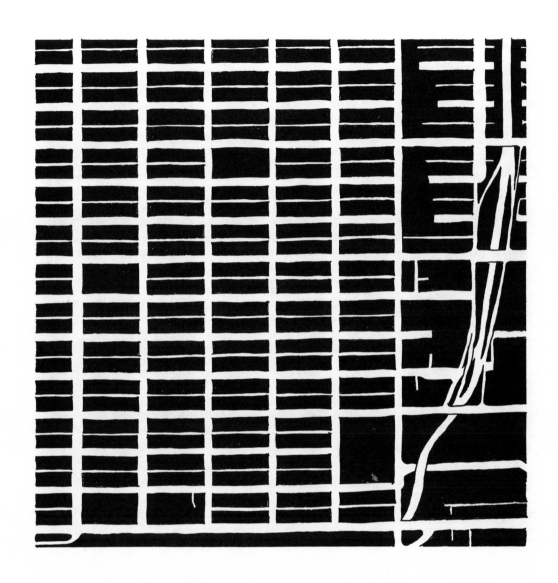

SANTA MONICA

USA

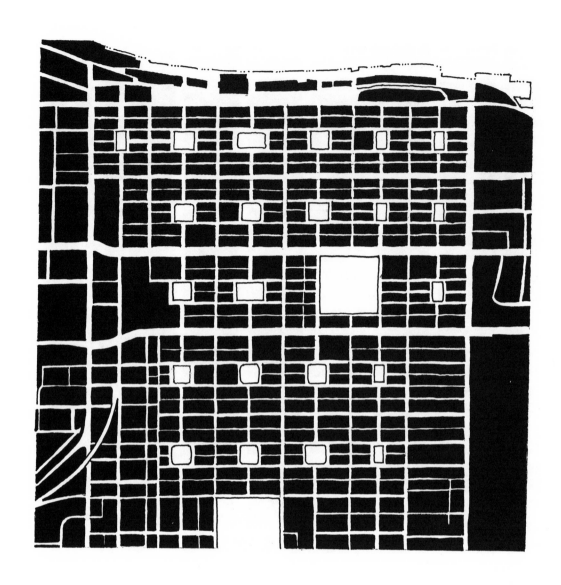

SAVANNAH

USA

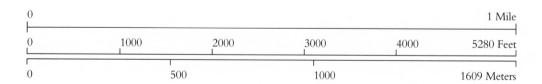

Street and City Patterns

SEOUL

KOREA

TOULOUSE

FRANCE

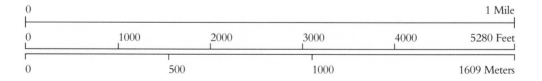

　　　　　Street and City Patterns

TOULOUSE-LE-MIRAIL

FRANCE

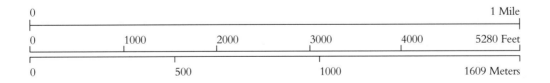

Street and City Patterns

TOKYO

(Nihonbashi)

JAPAN

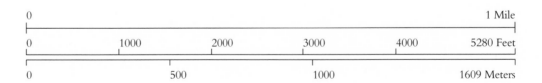

0   1 Mile

0   1000   2000   3000   4000   5280 Feet

0   500   1000   1609 Meters

VENICE

ITALY

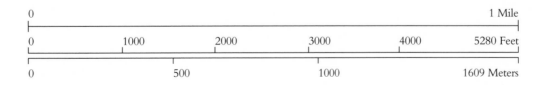

Street and City Patterns

VIENNA

(Ringstrasse)

AUSTRIA

Street and City Patterns

WALNUT CREEK

(residential area)

USA

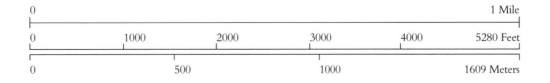

Street and City Patterns

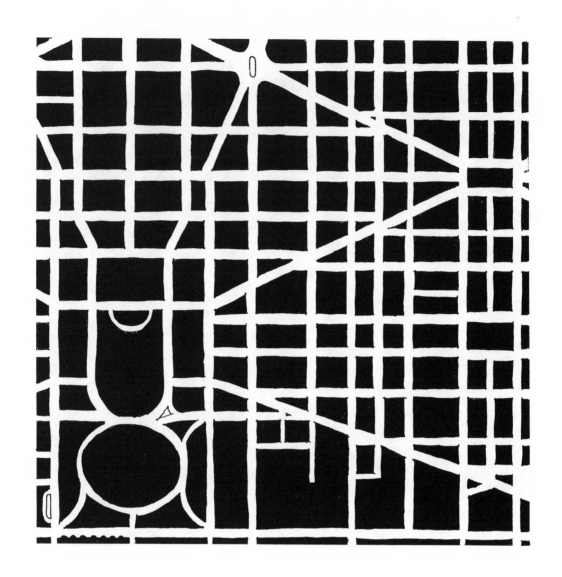

WASHINGTON

(city center)

USA

```
0                                                    1 Mile
├────────────────────────────────────────────────────┤

0         1000        2000        3000        4000    5280 Feet
├──────────┼──────────┼──────────┼──────────┼─────────┤

0                   500                   1000    1609 Meters
├─────────────────────┼─────────────────────────────┤
```

ZURICH

(1860)

SWITZERLAND

0					1 Mile
0	1000	2000	3000	4000	5280 Feet
0		500		1000	1609 Meters

ZURICH

(1985)

SWITZERLAND

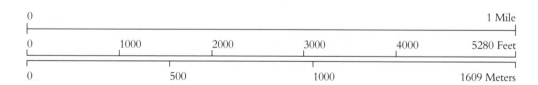

The square mile drawings make it abundantly clear that city street patterns are wonderfully varied, and that many are individually memorable. Even the ubiquitous American grid, so often considered a city pattern characteristic of North America, is anything but uniform upon even the most superficial examination. There are also similarities between city patterns, but what stands out first is the variety. Once seen, there is no mistaking Rome or Venice or the tip of Manhattan, or Paris, Amsterdam, Cairo, Brasília, or Irvine, California. Beyond the different types of patterns—grids, curvilinear, diagonal overlays, eccentric—there are vastly different block sizes and shapes, street widths and lengths, and different mixes of these elements. For some there is considerable white space indicating large areas in streets, as compared to the black area of blocks, and for some we find the opposite. For some there seem to be focal points or ordering streets, while for others there is pattern made up of uniform elements—nothing stands out.

Major cities of the same general development period may share many overall structural similarities, but their street and block patterns are often easily distinguishable. The patterns of Lucca, Bologna, Copenhagen, and early Barcelona, for example, are not alike. Three straight, direct streets that fan out from the Piazza del Popolo through the warren of central Roman streets identify Rome. Of much later vintage, the grid pattern of Savannah, Georgia, is like no other we know in its fineness and its distinguishable squares. The grid of turn-of-the-century Barcelona stands out because of its diagonal corners, even from a similar grid by the same designer in Madrid. Paris and Seoul may have large-scaled street patterns laid over more finely scaled earlier ones, but the resemblance ends there. Venice is unique. A square mile of Brasília bears little resemblance to other cities, except perhaps another new one, maybe Irvine. The underlying grid of Washington, D.C., even including one of its diagonals, is strangely similar to that of Bari, in Italy; distances between parallel streets in both cities are unaccountably varied. But to see them together, drawn at the same scale, is to focus immediately on their differences.

For similarity, one anticipates United States grid plan cities—the grids, for example, of outer San Francisco, mid-Manhattan, Santa Monica, and downtown Los Angeles. The sizes of blocks and the widths of streets appear similar in such cities, at least in proportion. It is difficult, too, to distinguish in memory one U.S. suburban residential area from another (one in Walnut Creek, California, from another in Irvine, California, from still a third one on the outskirts of Phoenix, Arizona, for example), though they may indeed be different. They have overall patterns with similarly placed streets, generally without focus.

For a very few cities, the patterns of streets and blocks have a certain abstract elegance of design that alone makes them memorable. The Savannah grid once seen is unforgettable, and it carries over into real life experience. See it once, in person, on the ground, and it is not difficult to draw. See it in plan, on a map, and you will recognize it on the ground. The Amsterdam public way pattern, driven by its canals, is both memorable and elegant. The tartan-plaid-like patterns of the Nihonbashi area of Tokyo is another example.

Similarities exist. How could they not? But at the start, it is the differences that are most striking.

Topography and Natural Features Show _____

At some point, topography and natural features such as rivers show in street patterns, including those patterns that were arbitrarily laid over hilly terrain.

The fine-grained medieval street pattern of Zurich stayed huddled along the lake and river's edge until development pressures together with advances in technology permitted larger but nongrid patterns of development into more hilly terrain. The street and block patterns of early European hill cities reflect topography. Similarly, the impacts of rivers show, not only as undulating linear bands of public space between areas of streets and development blocks, but as determinants of the development patterns themselves. Difficult to cross, major waterways often confined development to one side. Where development forces and technology persisted, however, river crossings and development took place, often in significantly different patterns from previously, on the other side of the river. Freeways and expressways are often like rivers or waterfronts in this regard. They either break patterns or come where there were already pattern changes, in the no-man's lands that sometimes exist where two patterns join. San Francisco's Central Freeway and Embarcadero Freeway were examples. Freeways also come at points of major topographic change. None of which explains the freeway in central Boston, an exercise in human perversity. Perhaps most dramatic, however, are areas built relatively recently where a grid pattern runs into difficult topography. The determination of early San Francisco surveyors and engineers to disregard topography in the layout of their city is well known. But at some points it became impossible to continue the grid, the topography was too steep, and either development ceased, to be continued only years later when preplatted public streets could be replatted to follow land contours, or the designers were not so hard-headed in the first instance and let land forms determine street and block layout. In either case, the changes in land form are reflected in the street patterns.

Street and City Patterns

Either by design or evolution, city street and block patterns can give order and structure to a city, district, or neighborhood. In considerable measure that is their purpose. The object is not only to facilitate communication but also to help people know where they are, in their neighborhoods, in relation to the larger community and to a larger region. Individual streets can be wider or straighter or longer or more focused than others, and as such can help give a sense of orientation to users. Patterns themselves, by their nature or design or juxtapositions one to another, can do the same thing. Often, it seems, the great street in an area or city is one that gives focus or structure. All of this can happen at a two-dimensional level, without regard to a third dimension of topography or building height or to a fourth dimension that includes land uses and density of habitation—factors that can in themselves give order and structure, either reinforcing the two-dimensional patterns or running counter to them.

The Roman *cardo* and *decumanus* were meant to give order and focus to a city, and so they still do in central Bologna after some 2,000 years. Interestingly, though, the more compelling street pattern in Bologna, the one that draws one's attention forcefully both from the maps and on the ground, is that of the five streets that focus on an old eastern gate of the city. Similarly, the three straight and relatively wide streets that focus on the Piazza del Popolo order central Rome, just as the wide boulevards structure Paris. The Ramblas running through the Gothic Quarter of Barcelona and the Paseo de Gracia in the later extension of the city are the most powerful ordering, structuring streets of their areas and, taken together, of the city itself. The Grand Canal, Venice's great street, so much wider, longer, and more gentle than any other canal, is that city's orienting structural spine, and this might well be so regardless of what buildings lined its path. The streets that radiate from Broadway, Telegraph Avenue, and San Pablo Avenue in Oakland, California, are long streets that give focus to the downtown. City Hall is where they come together. Market Street, in San Francisco, once a great street, is wider and longer than other streets and is the joining street of two different grids.

One can only wonder how orienting the street and square pattern of Savannah would be if the pattern continued for another mile or so in each direction. Would it become monotonous, even disorienting? To which someone might respond, "Better elegant, urbane monotony than mundane, curvilinear, faceless suburbia." The answer may lie not in the continuation of the pattern but in subtleties within the pattern—for instance, the two wide east-west boulevards in the center of the pattern. The horseshoe-shaped canal system of Amsterdam focuses on a central core and on the railroad station now at the water's edge. It is easy to know where one is.

For a series of cities with grid street patterns like Portland, Oregon, Los Angeles (in the center), Santa Monica, outer San Francisco, and to some extent even Manhattan, the street and block patterns alone are not particularly ordering. They provide a regular arrangement of parts, they organize the city, give a sense of succession, and they regulate their areas, but taken alone they are not much more than patterns without focus or contrast. To be sure, the north-south streets in New York are generally wider than the east-west streets, and Broadway and Park Avenue differ from other streets. In Portland, there are 60-foot versus 80-foot rights-of-way, but there is a general blanket pattern that persists over an entire square mile of these cities. Building height, landmarks, land uses, and topography—the view of the Pacific Ocean in outer San Francisco—become more important. Broadway breaks the New York grid and some would reasonably argue it is the best Manhattan street.

Some cities were designed at such a large scale that very little can be discerned in a given square mile. Brasília's overall airplane shape is unmistakable from the air, but much less so on the ground, or for any given square mile. The same is true of Canberra.

Regent Street, Oxford Street, Park Lane, and Piccadilly give order and orientation to the Mayfair area of London. Some other major streets—Fleet Street in the City, for example—do the same for other areas. There are old high streets that are the centers of their districts. But orientation in London is often difficult. The street and block pattern alone doesn't help, and even confuses. On the ground this can be pleasant, especially in small neighborhoods where small foci in nonregular street patterns "just appear." At a city scale, even a square mile scale, it can be disorienting. One imagines that the cul-de-sac byway system of interior streets in Ahmedabad can be even more disorienting, except for the person who really knows them or lives there, but then the objective was not necessarily to order things for outsiders or newcomers. Interestingly enough, the same can be said, both as to pattern and purpose, of residential subdivision patterns in Walnut Creek, Irvine, Phoenix, and many more such places.

Ordering and city structure, then, seem partly a matter of regular patterns of arrangement, methodological organization and successions of parts, and of contrast. Even at a small, two-dimensional scale, many of the most notable streets give order and focus to their surroundings, often but not always by virtue of contrast. Streets that are longer, wider, and more regular than surrounding streets, such as the Ramblas or the Grand Canal or the Champs-Elysées, seem to stand out from their surroundings more than shorter, narrower, and less regular ones. Broadway, in New York, however, is irregular in a very regular pattern. Strøget, in Copenhagen, on the other hand, is actually hard to pick out in its two-dimensional context.

Differences in the scale of street and block patterns, particularly between older and newer cities, stand out. The scale of older cities is generally much smaller and finer than that of newer cities. Shown a square mile of Venice after looking at a square mile of each of ten or fifteen major U.S. and European cities, an observer is likely to ask if the map of Venice is truly drawn at the same scale as the others; isn't there some error? And then look at Ahmedabad, India, so finely scaled and yet so different from Venice.[3]

For the cities studied, it seems clear that the scale of blocks and of street patterns has become larger with time, especially over the last 150 years, and with distance from the center of the community in question (which, of course, may well be just another way of expressing time). This seems as much so in a city like Bologna as in the San Fernando Valley area of Los Angeles. Over time, also, the patterns become less complicated. It is not very difficult to look at the maps of Barcelona or Bari or Rome or Paris or Boston or other older cities, and to identify the later additions to them. The newer is almost always simpler, more regular, larger-scaled. Even in a relatively new city, like Oakland, California, the original grid was smaller and more complex than the newer grid to the north. For startling contrast, one need only look at cities like Brasília or Irvine to see how far the scale of blocks and public ways has moved toward giantism in the late twentieth century. Compare any block pattern of a twentieth-century city with one of a city of more than two centuries and the contrast in scale will be striking. To a considerable extent the most recent jumps in scale may be explained by technology, most notably the advent of automobiles. Faster speeds make greater distances both possible and desirable. Things are bigger. But largeness started well before the auto, as the patterns of New York and San Francisco will attest. The auto has adapted well to those street sizes and patterns just as fine-scaled cities, such as Zurich, have made those adaptations that were necessary to their survival, adaptations that include limitations on the auto.

Complexity and fine-grainedness are not characteristics of all early cities. The patterns of Pompeii or Herculaneum were remarkably straightforward though the blocks were generally small. And certainly the earlier, usually Roman grids of cities like Bologna, Florence, and Lucca do not bespeak particular complexity, though their simplicity may have been lost later during the medieval period.

We experience different cities differently and have varied lasting impressions. Sizes of the things experienced, their numbers and their closeness, can become confused with the overall space or settings within which our experiences have taken place. Horizontal distances in any case are difficult to judge and remember. If I spend an afternoon walking in Brasília, another in Zurich, and yet another in Venice, do I know, when I think about all three, how much space I have covered, do I have a sense of what content of each of the three cities would be contained in a given surface area? Not likely. If I know one or two of those cities really well, will I fare much better in terms of understanding the relative scales of the second or third? Not likely. Maps, each the same scale, each covering a same-sized area, help. How much and what we might find in a square mile of land area (2.59 square kilometers), an area containing distances of which we might have some idea, can tell us something about how easy or difficult it is to get from one place to another and about an area's walkability. Better yet, the maps permit us to compare an area that we know well with another, less familiar area of the same size.

An amazing amount of Venice, compared to almost any other major city, can be found in one square mile. Most of the Grand Canal is in that area, as is everything from near the railway station at the northwest to the Arsenal on the east. To compare that mile with what can be found in a mile of Brasília or Irvine is almost cruel if one values compactness, intensity, and density, but a relatively compact community like San Francisco does not fare that much better. To know a square mile of Venice is to know most of that city. Only a part of San Francisco's downtown takes place in a square mile. On the other hand, one square mile of Rome could easily include the Piazza Venezia to the southeast, Piazza del Popolo to the north, Castel Sant'Angelo, Via dei Giubbonari, Via del Corso, Piazza Navona, the Pantheon, the Trevi Fountain, and even a corner of the Villa Borghese. Paris is much more grand in scale. Almost all of central Amsterdam, including its major canal system, fits into such an area. Most of Soho and Mayfair in London and much more than the central area of Zurich fit into one mile. Most of downtown Boston, once called the Hub, easily falls within one mile.

A consequence of the various scales of cities and of how much is in a limited area is the amount that can be experienced intimately, on foot, in one compared to another. The square miles with more in them seem also to have more streets in them, more different places for people to be, though not necessarily a greater surface area taken up by streets. Most of the great streets that we have encountered are also in areas where there are more things.

Dimensioning and Measuring Two-Dimensional Scale _____

The square mile maps of different cities permit quantifiable comparisons of some two-dimensional aspects of urban scale, such as the numbers of public intersections and blocks in those areas. It is also possible to know the distances between intersections and thereby to know how far one may travel before having the opportunity (or challenge) of making choices. Straightforward observation of a square mile of Venice as compared to lower Manhattan or Irvine, California, speaks volumes in terms of scale, block sizes, complexity, and the physical manifestations of differing cultures at different times. Knowing, in addition, that Venice has over 1,500 intersections, that lower Manhattan has about 220, and that the Irvine business area has 15 gives some dimensions to those differences. In 1989 the mayor of Irvine, interested in having a "downtown" in his city, one that had some street life as well as a mixture of uses that included housing, and supportive of a plan that might achieve such a center, looked at the one-square-mile map of his city next to others of Los Angeles and Santa Monica and San Francisco and said, "Ah, that explains it."[4] There are few streets in Irvine upon which a street life might take place.

Most apparent, and not unexpected, is that older cities have a finer two-dimensional scale than do newer cities when measured in terms of intersections or blocks per square mile. The Asian and Middle Eastern cities observed—Ahmedabad, Tokyo (Nihonbashi area), Cairo, and Seoul—are among the finest scaled, after Venice. This is so regardless of the basic patterns, whether grid or nongeometric. The data shows that Venice is a unique city in terms of this measure of scale. For the cities for which data is available—Bologna, Barcelona, Los Angeles area, and San Francisco Bay area—scale does indeed get larger with distance from the center. Of the European cities observed, the late nineteenth-century and early twentieth-century area of Barcelona has the largest scale, with some 164 intersections and 138 blocks in a square mile, compared with 486 intersections and 330 blocks in the older Gothic Quarter. Gridiron street patterns can be very fine-grained: observe Tokyo (988 intersections), Savannah, Georgia (530 intersections, which is more than central Rome), and Richmond, Virginia, whose alleys account for its small scale. Central Boston was once the finest-scaled U.S. city, more so than most European cities, but that is no longer true. Portland, Oregon, with its uniform 200-foot-square blocks, is as finely scaled as contemporary Boston. Generally, there is an inverse correlation between numbers of intersections and blocks per square mile and the distance between intersections; as the former decrease the latter increases. Intersections in Irvine are about one-quarter of a mile apart. For an older U.S. city, Savannah, they are regularly 125 to 300 feet apart.

Changing Scales _____

We know that street and block patterns change over time. Depending on what we are trying to show, the evidence available to us, and the time periods we compare, we might conclude that there is hardly any change, or that change takes place slowly and incrementally, or that change is dramatic in remarkably short periods. Or we may observe that, despite change, something significant of the past almost always remains. Our concern is not with change from largely undeveloped rural land to an urban environment (such as depicted in the two drawings of Zurich over time), but with change from one urban development pattern to another. Tragedies (wars or fires), changing community values and perceived economic imperatives, fads, and design philosophies are among the reasons for change.

City (and area or date)	Intersections	Blocks	Distances between Intersections (feet)	
			Mean	*Median*
Venice	1,725★ (1,507)	987★ (862)		
Ahmedabad	1,447	539		
Tokyo (Nihonbashi)	988	675		
Cairo	894	301		
Old Delhi	833	244		
Seoul	718	496		
Boston (1895)	618★ (433)	394★ (276)	190	150
Amsterdam	578	305		
Savannah	530	399		
Boston (1955)	508★ (356)	342★ (240)		
Rome	504	419	198	150–175
Barcelona (Ramblas)	486	330		
London (City)	482★ (423)	295★ (259)		
Zurich (1985)	425	275		
London (Mayfair)	423	273		
Bologna (center)	423	272	224	300
Paris (Louvre)	418	315	245	200
Boston (1980)	373★ (261)	245★ (172)	235	300
Portland	370★ (351)	318★ (302)		
Zurich (1890)	369	243		
Aix-en-Provence	362	233		
Pompeii	347★ (151)	246★ (167)	224	300
New York (Lower Manhattan)	339★ (218)	275★ (177)	274	260
Toulouse	331	242		
San Francisco (center)	293★ (274)	216★ (202)	353	350
Paris (Etoile–Rond-Point)	281	214		
Pittsburgh (center)	277★ (143)	197★ (124)		
Copenhagen	244	170		
Pittsburgh (Shadyside)	242	188		
Oakland (center)	208	153		
Santa Monica, CA	185	147		
San Francisco (mid-city)	182	137	409	325
New York (Midtown)	181★ (159)	166★ (146)	423	260
Santa Cruz, CA (center)	179	108		
Los Angeles (center)	171	132	390	360
Barcelona (Paseo de Gracia)	164	138		
San Francisco (Sunset)	161★ (131)	130★ (106)	461	300
Bologna (Mazzini)	160	88		
Bologna (Corticello)	158	104		
Washington, DC	155	122		
Toulouse-Le-Mirail	146	112		
Irvine, CA (residential area)	119	43		
Walnut Creek, CA (center)	116	64		
Walnut Creek, CA (2.5 m from center)	113	50		
Brasília	92	47		
Los Angeles (San Fernando area)	81	47		
Irvine, CA (business complex)	15	17	1,290	1,300

★For cities where the square mile includes a large body of water—bay, ocean, river, lake—that area has been deducted and the numbers shown are the adjusted proportions of intersections and blocks per square mile. The number in parenthesis is the actual count. For San Francisco's Sunset area and New York's Midtown area, Golden Gate Park and Central Park have been deducted.

An intersection is counted as a point where two or more different public rights-of-way meet and where it is possible to go from one to another. An overpass of one road over another is not an intersection, nor is a pathway over a canal, unless it is possible to move from one to another. Both walkway and canal intersections are counted in Venice and Amsterdam.

A block is an area of land surrounded by a public right-of-way. Parks are shown as blocks.

1895

1955

Central Boston: 1895, 1955, 1980

1980

Approximate scale: 1″ = 400′ or 1:4,800

Consider downtown Boston over time. It has changed. The changes were
intended, even desired. But do we understand how much? Three maps of the
same area spanning about 100 years show dramatic changes. One hundred
years ago, one mile of Boston's downtown area had over 400 intersections
and approximately 276 blocks. In two-dimensional layout, scale, and complexity, it compared with cities like Rome, Bologna, and Paris. When people
said, as they did, that among U.S. cities Boston was the most European in
layout, they were correct, at least in these respects and about the irregularity
of its street pattern. By the 1980s, Boston's downtown had more than 170
fewer intersections and about 100 fewer blocks, and change had accelerated
over the last 30 years. The scale and complexity of Boston, at least in the
physical terms we are speaking of, had become more like those of San Francisco, to which it is presently often compared, or like lower Manhattan. The
changes are consistent with earlier observations on larger city scale over time
and might well reflect a compulsion to be up to date, to achieve a kind of
modernity.

What happened to all those blocks and intersections? Highway and public
redevelopment projects took their toll, and the downtown lost some complexity and became more like others. But that explanation only begs the
question: Where and to whom did the blocks go? By and large, small city
blocks became consolidated into fewer but larger blocks, and the streets and
intersections that had separated blocks became part of the larger pattern and
scale. What happened at the area scale also took place within development

Approximate scale: 1″ = 400′ or 1:4,800

projects and within individual blocks, and continues to do so. Land parcels became larger and presumably more efficient to develop, in consonance with reigning social-economic-physical beliefs that extolled the efficiency of fewer, wider streets with fewer inhibiting, congesting intersections. The story is clearly told by "footprint" maps, such as those of Boston, that permit seeing and counting the sizes and numbers of buildings in a given area before and after change. Change in San Francisco's Western Addition area, as documented by Anne Vernez Moudon, is as dramatic.[5] If one can generalize from experience and from growing evidence, the land went not only to fewer and larger private landholders-developers, but also to large public institutional developers. With the land went the streets.

Fewer but larger blocks and fewer streets and intersections may or may not be more efficient than more blocks and intersections. If, as seems to be the case in Boston and other cities, the larger blocks are accompanied by fewer and larger landholders-developers, then it might also be argued that the newer pattern provides fewer opportunities for fewer actors to take part in city development. Presumably, the larger the developer, public or private, the wealthier. The new pattern, the pattern brought about by *public* policy and *public* actions, favors bigness and wealth at the expense of participation by large numbers of smaller actors. For many cities this was and is an invitation to large-scale national and multinational developers and financiers at the expense of locals who may not have the organizational and fiscal resources to get into the game. Cooperatively held developments are not much different.

There may be many owners of a project but they act as one, and the number of actors participating individually in the nature of city development is fewer than before. At the same time, these large projects can be vulnerable to economic depressions that see the one large developer run out of funds and development over a large area stalled and left incomplete. Be that as it may, the very large-scaled pattern of Irvine is an example of a developed area with relatively few landowners and a preponderance of big players. And the streets, what of them? They become part of the larger blocks and parcels. In total they come to a considerable amount of land, easily 25 percent of all land before redevelopment. It could be argued then that large areas of the public domain—streets—have been ceded to large, generally wealthy private interests and to large, perhaps not-so-public, public institutions.

Lost intersections, in turn, can be viewed in terms of diminishing choices and perhaps in terms of diminishing freedom. As we noted, each intersection represents an available choice or challenge to a user, to go this way or that. To be sure, they are not the only places where pedestrians have choices, nor are the streets the only places where they can walk. The Boston City Hall block may have removed many streets and intersections, but the building itself takes up only the center of the site and there are innumerable paths that people can take across the block. But are there more new choices, if any? From the point of encountering the more open plans, one has the opportunity of making directional choices. Certainly it is possible to walk in some instances over land or through buildings that are on the new larger blocks and parcels. Not all of the choices are evident. But that is not the general case and, over time, easements have a way of not always being open to the public or of being highly regulated, and public institutional stewardship in no way means public access or choice.

We look at the Boston maps again, marvel at the changed and perhaps less interesting emerging pattern, and wonder about choice and freedom. There are about 170 fewer locations—intersections—where people can exercise choice. Of course, the same observations could be made about Paris before and after Haussmann's insistent boulevards opened up the city and about so many other American cities that have been caught up by a national enthrallment with highway building and redevelopment.

At some point, if the street and block patterns are small and complicated enough, it may well be that freedom is replaced by confusion, except for the most knowing inhabitants of an area. Those 1,500 intersections in Venice or the 1,400 in Ahmedabad or those in almost any other older Middle Eastern city come to mind. It is not for nothing that there are myriad signs in Venice to lead the pedestrian to where he or she may want to go. Street layouts and patterns have objectives beyond those having to do with pedestrian choices. In any case, the maps permit comparison and provide a common scale base for inquiry and design.

Just as it is possible to see the ideas and rules that guided Roman and Spanish urban thinking in the street and block patterns of cities that they built, and just as the patterns of Bari and Lucca (and many other cities) reflect the purposes of fortification and defense, so do more contemporary city patterns reflect the design ideas of their creators. Garden city, superblock, and neighborhood theory are clearly visible in residential developed areas like Irvine or the San Fernando Valley area of Los Angeles. It is easy to know where the elementary school or the shopping center or the park or park system would fit in their patterns of streets and blocks. The notions dear to followers of the International Congress of Modern Architecture (CIAM), with their clear distaste for street orientation, are visible in either Brasília or Irvine. One does not think of looking for great streets in either of these types of modern city. Nor does one look for great streets in new cities like Toulouse-le-Mirail, where it is in fact difficult to know what is or is not a street, in such sharp contrast to the older, fine-grained Toulouse. And one does not look for them in large-scale developments like the Barbican in London, where streets have been avoided.[6]

Ad Hoc Observations ————————————————————————————

Beyond certain general characteristics, street and block patterns of individual cities have peculiarities that stand out and are noteworthy. For example:

- Having many streets and intersections does not necessarily mean having a large percentage of land in the public domain and less in development. Central Bologna has well over 400 intersections and almost 275 blocks in a square mile. But the streets are narrow, leaving rather large blocks compared to other cities. The "white" area or street area of many contemporary cities—central Los Angeles, for example—with many fewer intersections and blocks appears to be much greater, leaving less land for development.

- Barcelona's memorable pattern of streets and blocks is achieved by the diagonal corners of every block over a large area. The city's abundance of fine streets, where buildings are built to these street lines, may be accounted for in part by this pattern. The scale of blocks, however, is not particularly small. It may simply seem small, because one may experience the block as ending at the start and finish of the diagonals, which become part of the intersections. Portland's square grid is in fact much smaller.

- The Parisian overlay of boulevards (for the areas mapped) is not outstandingly discordant with the earlier, medieval pattern. Many of the earlier, smaller streets run parallel or normal to the boulevards, or have a similar kind of angularity. Just as the boulevards are straight, neither, by and large, did the earlier streets meander.

- The overlay pattern in Seoul, Korea, stands in sharp contrast to the narrow pedestrian path system that it covers. As in Paris, however, the overlay pattern has similarities to the original; much of the earlier pattern is also a grid. The imposition of one pattern over another usually shows.

- Ahmedabad and non-Western parts of Cairo have distinctly different block and street patterns from those of Western cities: small, winding streets, few continuous, none very wide; cul-de-sacs; a much finer scale. But this cul-de-sac characteristic can be found in contemporary U.S. suburban development; witness the San Fernando Valley area of Los Angeles or a residential pattern in Irvine. The difference is in scale more than in layout.

This examination of streets and block patterns starts from a concern with the physical, designable qualities of the best streets. Having identified outstanding streets, we want to know of and to communicate their contexts. The patterns help us to understand the importance of contrast, scale, ordering and structure, focus, starting and ending points; and they permit us, simply, to locate the street of interest.

Street and block patterns do more than help us understand individual streets. They are informative and useful in and of themselves, not least in showing how different so many of them are in scale, geometry, and design. Knowing of the relative compactness of different urban places should at least suggest caution when we compare cities, particularly by means of social, economic, and political data. Politically and administratively, a San Francisco, where scale and pattern permit easy access to City Hall from the furthest reaches of the city, may be expected to be different from a Los Angeles, where access is difficult and time-consuming. The political and administrative organization of one might well be required to be different from the other's. Social organization and ways of communication will surely be different in an Irvine than a Rome, based solely on the physical scale differences between them. Yet physical scale and urban patterns are rarely taken into account as integral, important information for comparative, nonphysical studies.

The street and block patterns permit some dimensioning and measuring of differences and similarities and of how those seem to change over time and distance. Most interesting, perhaps, is how areas themselves change over time, notably in recent years, to a more coarse grain of streets and blocks. On the other hand, the mayor of Irvine found a one-square-mile map of his city helpful in explaining why his community lacked the kind of street life he thought would be an improvement. That, really, can be their greatest purpose—to help people have better understandings of their communities as a basis for doing things or for not doing others.

PART FOUR

Making Great Streets

Certain physical qualities are required for a great street. All are required, not one or two. They are few in number and appear to be simple, but that may be deceptive. Most are directly related to social and economic criteria having to do with building good cities: accessibility, bringing people together, publicness, livability, safety, comfort, participation, and responsibility. These designable qualities are the subject of this chapter.

Not unexpectedly, the course is full of caution signs. The connections between what can be built on a street and the socioeconomic criteria for a fine street are not always easy to make. If you cannot walk along a street or go from one side to the other, then you aren't likely to meet anyone on it. At the same time, it remains difficult to isolate physical features from social and economic activities that bring value to our experiences: to what extent is it the experiences that we have on a street rather than the physical setting that make it memorable in a positive way? These problems, hopefully a bit less formidable than when we started, will remain.

Walking in comfort

An inherent difficulty with asserting universal requirements is that one need recall only one fine street without one of the qualities and the game seems lost. To assert that all the best urban streets have trees, and to be reminded that neither Strøget nor many others are so endowed, is to invite more than a little skepticism. In anticipation of trouble seekers, we also want to recall that we are concerned with *city* streets. Can a country road be a great street? Yes, of course, but our subject is urban streets.

Anticipating such counterexamples, there is a tendency to arrive at requirements for great streets that are so general that they can include or exclude almost any street, depending on the whim of the observer. It is one thing to say, for example, that a great street needs definition, but quite another to be explicit about what constitutes that quality. Explicitness is striven for, alas not always achieved. Ambiguity will remain but can be significantly reduced. At the same time, few of the measurable requirements are so precise as to demand specific numbers, such as for tree spacing or building heights. There are ranges within which fine street designs have been and will be achieved.

A major objective of this work is to provide knowledge of the best streets for designers and urban decision makers, a reference for current work that might answer such inquiries as "I remember that the median of the Kurfürstendamm had certain size characteristics and I wonder what they are," or "What, generally, is the height of those buildings along the streets in Barcelona that I remember best?" or "What is the Savannah grid size?" or "How large is the space that I am designing for Mission Bay compared with Piazza San Marco?" People can use the information however they wish; as models, as guides, as points of departure for new designs, or to find out just how much or how little can take place in a given cross section of street. It is just as well, then, that the conclusions on urban streets are inexact or come in ranges. The intent is not to provide formulae or recipes, but to provide knowledge as a basis for designs of future great streets.

By themselves, as a group, the required qualities will not assure a great street, but they are necessary. Overall, though, a final ingredient—perhaps the most important—is necessary, and I call it "magic"—the magic of design. All of the parts, all of the requirements have to be put together into a whole street, and the ways of doing that, at least in detail, are infinite. It is hard to believe that all of them have been tried. There are new great street designs to come. Whatever is designed, though, will share with other great streets a few critical physical qualities.

Places for People to Walk with Some Leisure

The point of view and interest of this inquiry has mainly to do with the best streets for people, mostly on foot. We take for granted that the functions of streets include gaining access to abutting uses and getting from one place to another within and through cities, often by mass transit or car. Good streets have to do that, and the best, for drivers or passengers in mass transit vehicles or private cars, make the journey comfortable, safe, pleasing, and even enlightening in terms of the experience they offer of the city. Vehicles often share public rights-of-way with people on foot: no problem, that has been and can be accounted for in design. But you do not meet other people while driving in a private car, nor often in a bus or trolley. It's on foot that you see people's faces and statures and that you meet and experience them. That is

Requirements for Great Streets

how public socializing and community enjoyment in daily life can most easily occur. And it's on foot that one can be most intimately involved with the urban environment; with stores, houses, the natural environment, and with people. Marshall Berman, though he is speaking of one street, Nevsky Prospekt, in his book on modernism, might be talking of so many of the best streets when he observes, "The essential purpose of this street, which gives it its special character, is sociability: people come here to see and be seen, and to communicate their vision to one another, not for any ulterior purpose, without greed or competition, but as an end in itself."[1] His references to Gogol are apt, including "This is the one place where people don't show themselves because they have to, where they aren't driven by the necessary and commercial interest that embraces the whole of St. Petersburg," and "The Nevsky is the common meeting ground and communication line of St. Petersburg." Great urban streets are often great streets to drive along as well as great public places to walk, but walking is the focus here.

Shanghai : Pedestrian overflows into streets

Every fine street that has been identified in this book is one that invites leisurely, safe walking. It sounds simple and basically it is. There have to be walkways that permit people to walk at varying paces, including most importantly a leisurely pace, with neither a sense of crowding nor of being alone, and that are safe, primarily from vehicles.

Variables abound in deciding the right amount of walking space, including what people are accustomed to, the reasons for walking, and the nature of the street.[2] The arithmetic for walking in comfort is not as precise as traffic engineers would have us believe it is for vehicles, that is, the kind of number combinations that determine how many traffic lanes and their widths. Such calculations have often been used to widen and add auto lanes at the expense

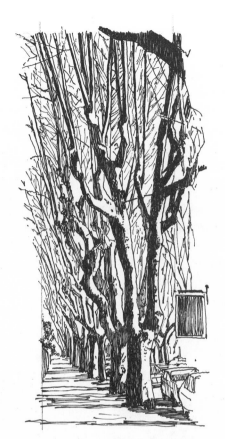

Closely spaced trees, Rome

of sidewalks in the absence of any data on what would happen to the comfort of people on the sidewalk. In any case the matter is too important to be left only to numbers. Nonetheless, some numbers may be helpful in gaining a sense of how people walk on various streets.[3] The Via dei Giubbonari at its narrowest and Strøget have among the highest numbers of pedestrians, measured in terms of people per minute per meter of width, almost 17 and 14.3 respectively. With these numbers there is a sense of crowding; people can get in each other's way, not all walking speeds are possible. Yet amid the crowds there is leisurely walking, even strolling, people going back and forth talking to each other, and even mothers out for a walk with babies in prams in Copenhagen. The Via del Corso has similar numbers: over 13 people per minute per meter in one location where there are 4-foot sidewalks and during a Saturday afternoon rush hour, over 15 people per minute per meter at a location where it is not required to stay on the walks. There are places on the Corso where people cannot stay on the walks even where there are moving cars. The pedestrians spill over into the roadway up to 6 feet normally and sometimes up to 12 or 13 feet. Leisurely walking is difficult. So is fast walking. In Shanghai the crowds are so great that pedestrian barriers are placed one traffic lane out into the street to accommodate them. On the Paseo de Gracia and the Ramblas, where the counts are from about 7 to 9 people per minute per meter of walkway, all paces are possible, while there is a sense of crowding in front of the stores at the Plaça de Catalunya that joins the two streets—here the count reads 13 people. Walkways never seem crowded at 3 or 4 people per minute per meter; at under 2 the walks may seem empty. Any kind of walking is possible with up to 8 people per minute per meter. Then, it seems, speed picks up even though leisurely walking still takes place, and crowding starts at perhaps 13 people per minute per meter, when overall speed slows. People, it seems, make do in walking just as in so many other things; some can shut out distractions and walk at a leisurely pace even among large crowds. But at the high counts they must at times move to avoid people, and that cannot be too pleasant. And when people are forced off of walkways into streets because of too little space, then certainly safety is an issue.

Curbs and sidewalks are the most common ways of separating and thereby protecting pedestrians from vehicles. They may physically separate but do not necessarily offer a sense of safety or tranquillity. Trees added at the curb line, if close enough to each other, create a pedestrian zone that feels safe. An auto parking lane at the curb also creates separations, but while some great streets have parked cars, that is not one of the things you think of to create a great street. No physical separation at all between vehicle and pedestrian paths, that is, no curbs, can be a better solution, particularly on crowded, small streets; let cars and people mix. The Via dei Giubbonari is such a street and there are many others. The auto is forced to move at the pedestrian's pace. In part, the woonerfs of the Netherlands and other countries, notably Denmark, use this principle successfully to achieve safe residential streets.[4]

Requirements for Great Streets

The requirement for a great street that people be able to walk easily and safely on it is, on its face, obvious and easy to achieve. These qualities are not much to ask for on any urban street, great or not, where there are people. Still, they are often absent from many streets.

Physical Comfort _____

There are streets and places that we avoid because we know them to be physically uncomfortable. I will always avoid Golden Gate Avenue at Polk Street in San Francisco because of the cold, hard wind that rushes down from the Federal Building there. The sidewalk in front of the Fox Plaza Building, on Market Street, can be worse. The plaza in front of the Bank of America Building seems always to be in shade, and sunshine is important in cool San Francisco. It is not for nothing that the large, black marble sculpture near the corner is referred to as the "banker's heart." There were two choices for

Choreographed by the wind at Fox Plaza, Market Street, San Francisco.

Bank of America, San Francisco: "Banker's Heart"

where to locate the plaza and where to put the building, a 50-50 chance for sun and someone made the wrong choice. In Rome, during the summer when it is hot and humid, the Via dei Giubbonari is shady, and a much better street to walk on than others.

The best streets are comfortable, at least as comfortable as they can be in their settings.[5] They offer warmth or sunlight when it is cool and shade and coolness when it is hot. They offer reasonable protection from the elements without trying to avoid or negate the natural environment. It is a contextual requirement for good streets: it is too much to expect a street in an Alaskan city to be warm in the winter, but it can be as warm as possible under its circumstances and not colder than it need be. A good urban street gives shelter from the wind. On urban streets winds will measure 25 to 40 percent of the winds outside the city in the open field, unless placement and height of buildings are such that winds are accelerated.

Boulevard Saint-Michel

Requirements for Great Streets

People understand and respond to comfort. They seek out sunny or shady places, depending on the climate.[6] The best street designers have understood that. The trees on the Boulevard Saint-Michel bring shady relief on hot sunny days, making it a delightful place to be, and they provide some protection from rain, as do the shop awnings. Sun reaches the street during the winter, not always but during the midday hours, because the leaves are gone. Bologna is cold and can be rainy or snowy in the winter and so its arcaded streets offer winter protection as well as shade in the summer, as do the arcaded streets of Vicenza and Bern. The people of San Francisco voted for sunlight as a requirement on at least one sidewalk of their downtown streets during critical hours and require that buildings be tested for their wind-producing qualities before they are built.[7]

Climate-related characteristics of comfort are reasonably quantifiable and there is every reason that they should be a part of great streets. Sensitive designers of the past understood the requirements in planning their streets, often intuitively. It is possible to do better than that now, through measurement and pretesting of future street environments.

Bologna Porticos

Great streets have definition. They have boundaries, usually walls of some sort or another, that communicate clearly where the edges of the street are, that set the street apart, that keep the eyes on and in the street, that make it a place. But what does that mean in operational terms? What does it take to define a street? If building facades or walls are the answer, how big do they have to be or how small can they be? What can be their spacing? These questions are more difficult to answer, but it is necessary to try.

Streets are defined in two ways: vertically, which has to do with height of buildings or walls or trees along a street; and horizontally, which has most to do with the length of and spacing between whatever is doing the defining. There is, as well, definition that may occur at the ends of a street, which is both vertical and horizontal. Usually it is buildings that are the defining elements, sometimes walls, sometimes trees, sometimes trees and walls together, always the floor.

Regarding vertical definition, it would seem to be a matter both of proportion and of absolute numbers. The wider a street gets, the more mass or height it takes to define it, until at some point the width can be so great that real street definition, not necessarily space definition, stops, regardless of height. For example, it has been observed that, when the small dimensions of places exceed 450 feet (137 meters), spatial definition is weak and becomes "more that of a field than of a plaza, despite the great height of the structures."[8] At another extreme, most buildings along the southern edge of the Giudecca Canal in Venice are only two or three stories high, yet they certainly define the Giudecca, at a distance of about 1,100 feet (335 meters) from the Zattere, across the canal. But that is not street definition or plaza definition. Rather, it is a clear definition of an urbanized shoreline.

Although the subject of street width and shape has long been a concern of architects and city designers, the focus has not generally been on definition. Understandably, Alberti and Palladio seemed mostly to be concerned with matters such as ease of movement, safety, sun, wind, visibility, and military access.[9] They were also attentive to ways of achieving mobility and views of buildings, and the roles of these in making noncity streets more pleasant and healthy, but they did not directly address ways to achieve definition. They may well have taken it for granted. Harmonious proportion has, at least since 1784, been a major objective of regulations of building height along Paris streets. The two (street width) to three (height to the cornice line) proportion of streets had existed traditionally and was then formalized.[10] Later, Haussmann would change to a square section for streets but without changing cornice height, although height above the cornice lines became greater for the city as a whole. Sunlight may well have been a factor in these height limits, but not, it seems, the idea of height to achieve street definition.

Giudecca Canal, Venice: Defined Urban Skyline

Again, given the width of most streets and the height of buildings permitted and generally built, always to the property line and without side yards, it may have been natural to take definition for granted.

Hans Blumenfeld, relying heavily upon work by H. Maertens, is concerned with urban scale and principally with defining what can be meant by human scale, but he does, indirectly, get to street definition.[11] Basing their work on physiological optics and experience, Maertens and then Blumenfeld use distances at which they report it is possible to recognize people (human scale) and distances at which facial expressions can be perceived (intimate human scale), together with angles at which objects can be perceived clearly, to judge the scale of buildings. They conclude that a building height of three stories (approximately 30 feet) and width of 36 feet, with a street width of 72 feet, are the maximum dimensions for a building of *human scale*. The smaller *intimate scale* requires a building height of 21 feet, a building width of 24 feet, and a street width of 48 feet. For our purposes two points need to be made: human scale and street definition are not necessarily the same thing; and, applied to a street, these conclusions would apply mostly to looking directly across a street, not along one. Also, while it may well be correct that a 27-degree angle is the maximum at which an object may be perceived clearly, people are ornery and keep moving their heads and their eyes, so the dimensions that are the result of the analysis may be fine for defining human scale but perhaps not for streets. More to the point of street definition, Maertens and Blumenfeld attest that

at an angle of 27 degrees (height-distance ratio 1:2) the object appears . . . as a little world in itself, with the surroundings only dimly perceived as a background; at an angle of 18 degrees (1:3) it still dominates the picture, but now its relation to its surroundings becomes equally important. At angles of 12 degrees (1:4) or less, the object becomes part of its surroundings and speaks mainly through its silhouette.[12]

Making Great Streets

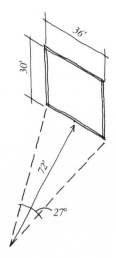

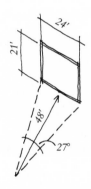

Human scale (top) and intimate human scale (bottom) according to Blumenfeld and Maertens

Generally, buildings are likely to provide a sense of definition when height-to-horizontal-distance ratios are 1:4 when the viewer is looking at a 30-degree angle to the street direction

These dimensions and ratios seem more appropriate to the dynamic nature of street experience, which takes place while one is moving and generally in perspective views. Sizes between those where the objects still dominate—the buildings or walk, whose job it is to define the street—and those that permit silhouette may be those that are most important in street design.[13]

There have been other, more recent assertions on the subject of appropriate street sections and of definition.[14] All of the great streets discussed here have definition. In sections, their vertical to horizontal ratios range from 1:4 in the case of Monument Avenue, a residential street, to 1:0.4 in the case of the Via dei Giubbonari. Most of the streets we have studied seem to fall within a range (vertical to horizontal) of from 1:1.1 to 1:2.5. For the widest streets, where width is significantly greater than height, such as along the Champs-Elysées or the Paseo de Gracia, it is the intervening trees as much as or more than buildings that strengthen or provide definition. That is one of their purposes and speaks to the necessity of their closeness and fullness.

Field observations and measurements can help determine the dimensions or proportions at which street definition is most likely to be experienced. Taking into account width of street, building height, topography, and intervening visual intrusions (e.g., signs or trees), preliminary field research suggests that buildings along streets are likely to provide a sense of definition when height to horizontal distance ratios are at least 1:4 with the viewer looking at

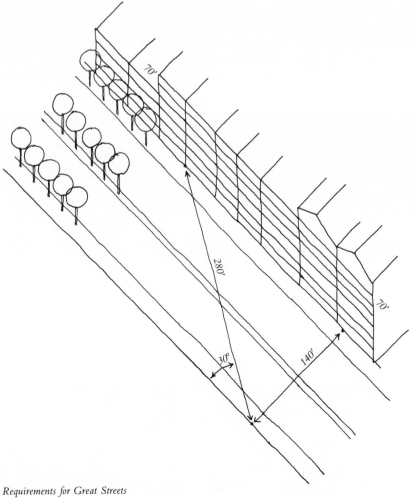

Requirements for Great Streets

Outer Market Street, San Francisco

a 30-degree angle to the right or left of the direction of the street.[15] Put another way, if, walking along a street on its left side, you turn your head about 30 degrees to the right, a rather normal, unforced thing to do, and if the building height across the street where your vision intersects with it is one-fourth of the horizontal distance to that point, then it is likely that you will sense that the street is defined, albeit sometimes weakly. At height to distance ratios of 1:3.3 there always seems to be definition, and at 1:2 definition is strong. Interestingly, these ratios correspond with the Maertens and Blumenfeld conclusions. As the ratios get smaller, to 1:5 and beyond, there is not a sense of the street being defined. Looking straight ahead or slightly skewed to the right or left, the eyes tend to focus on discrete points and a sense of street definition is harder to come by, unless the street actually does end in some way, such as at a crossing street.[16] This may account for why focal points—e.g., obelisks, fountains, statues—or crossing streets that provide street endings are important to creating a sense of place. The 1:4 ratio at the 30-degree angle translates into a street cross section design ratio of one (height) to two (width).

Noticeably, many fine streets are lined with trees, and these may be as important as the buildings in creating street definition. Of the very best streets, Monument Avenue, in Richmond, Virginia, has a height to distance ratio of 1:7.2 and the Paseo de Gracia one of 1:5.0 when looking at a 30-degree angle, but both of them have four rows of closely planted trees that create definition and enable them to give a sense of place. Nonetheless, at this angle most of the best streets have height to horizontal distance ratios of 1:4 or less, often significantly less. It is also noticeable that streets such as Roslyn

Via dei Greci, Rome

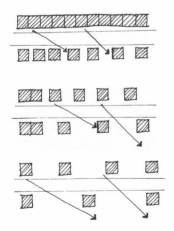

Greater horizontal spacing and less definition

Place in Pittsburgh and the unpretentious streets of Bath, with low height-to-distance ratios, are made up of both narrow streets and low buildings and generally fall within or near dimension characteristics that Maertens and Blumenfeld say create human scale.

Is there some point, some proportion or absolute height, at which the buildings are so high in relation to street width that the building wall becomes oppressive? Is there an upper limit to street definition as well as a lower? Maybe not. Building heights along the Via del Corso in Rome reach approximately 70 feet (21.3 meters) against a width of 36 feet (11 meters), giving a height-distance ratio of 1:0.5, and there are stretches where the height and the proportions seem oppressive. But the Via dei Greci has buildings of about 45 feet in height against a 15-foot width, a ratio of 1:0.3, and it is pleasant. Is that because this street is so much shorter? The proportions of the Via dei Giubbonari are similar, with taller buildings over a longer length, and is even more distinctive. It may be that the upper limits are more appropriately determined by the impact of height on comfort and livability of the street, as measured by sunlight, temperature, and wind, than by absolute or proportional height. At the same time, it may be observed, none of the very best streets can be characterized as having tall buildings. The height of buildings along the best streets is less than 100 feet.

There is another factor important to street definition: the spacing of buildings along a street. Buildings can be far enough apart so that, looking directly across a street or walking along one, it is normal to see beyond buildings to rear yards or to buildings on the next street. Again, the numbers and proportions are not clear and it is difficult to know for certain whether it is building spacing or one of the many other variables along a street—building height, setbacks, architectural quality, trees and shrubs and fences, for example—that are what define or fail to define a street. Along East and West streets in Litchfield, Connecticut, which comprise a truly grand and historic residential main street, the homes are as far as 200 feet apart and, as pleasant as the street may be as a planted way, there is little street definition at a pedestrian pace. Typical homes along Fairmount Boulevard in Cleveland Heights, Ohio, are approximately 30 to 40 feet apart (as well as 60 feet back from the sidewalk) and there is little or no street definition. On the other hand, some of the smaller residential streets off Fairmount Boulevard—Roxboro or Delaware or Tutor, for example—have a sense of definition as regards spacing, and the buildings are typically 10 to 20 feet apart. In the end, tighter spacing is more effective than looser in achieving street definition.

Qualities That Engage the Eyes _____

The eyes move. There is no stopping them, no keeping them still, unless there is nothing to see. As Gibson explains it, "In the ordinary vision of everyday life any long fixation of the eyes is a rarity. . . . It is equally rare to

Hong Kong street signs.

perceive the environment with the head motionless. . . . The visual field is ordinarily alive with motion." Or, "In the activities of everyday life the center of clear vision will shift as often as a hundred times a minute, and during reading or while driving a car the rate of fixations will exceed this figure."[17] Great streets require physical characteristics that help the eyes do what they want to do, must do: move. Every great street has this quality.

Achieving streets that prompt eye movement does not seem to be difficult. Generally, it is many different surfaces over which light constantly moves that keeps the eyes engaged; separate buildings, many separate windows or doors, or surface changes. Or it can be the surfaces themselves that move and therefore attract the eye, if only for a split second, before something else gains momentary ascendency: people, leaves, signs. Visual complexity is what is required, but it must not be so complex as to become chaotic or disorienting. Hong Kong street signs, for example, can be so demanding and insistent as to negate the street entirely and make the environment disorienting, even where the street plan is straightforward. Complexity within some holistic context, on the other hand, permits orientation.

Beyond helping to define a street, separating the pedestrian realm from vehicles, and providing shade, what makes trees so special is their movement; the constant movement of their branches and leaves, and the ever-changing light that plays on, through, and around them. The leaves move and the light on them constantly changes: thousands and thousands of moving, changing surfaces. If light filters through them, casting moving shadows on walks and walls, so much the better. Branches of deciduous trees may not move much in winter, but the light plays over their uneven surfaces, changing them always, challenging the eyes if ever so subtly. The special character of so many great streets—Roslyn Place, the Ramblas, the Mills College entry street, and perhaps most dramatically Boulevard Saint-Michel—has to do with the constant challenge to the eyes of light and leaves.

People on streets do what leaves do; they move. To be sure, streets are for people, but it is also true that many moving people help to make good streets. We see people moving at our own level and our eyes move to them, to pick them out, to take messages as to where they are and so how to get nearer to them or avoid them, to recognize them or not, to assess their dress. More than anything else we can relate to people, and so they capture our eyes' attention as we and they move. Many though not all of the best streets have lots of people on them, and, if for no other reason than their movement, they help to make the streets what they are. Cars can do the same: attract the eyes by virtue of movement. We hypothesize that cars have to move at a pace conducive to what eye-brain messages perceive as normal or not surprising or shocking-alerting in order to contribute to a great street. Or their fast movement must be sufficiently separated from the pedestrian (by the line of trees, for example) and therefore perceived as nonthreatening or as background movement. The reasonably paced movement of cars on Monument Avenue, in Richmond, seems not to be threatening, nor is that along Amsterdam canals, nor along Avenue Montaigne, while those fast-moving ten lanes on the Champs-Elysées, left unscreened by high-leafed trees planted too far apart to constitute a movement barrier, are not exactly something to follow with interest.

Buildings do not move. Light, though, moves over them, and the surfaces change, in lightness, darkness and shadow, and therefore in color, as it does. The changes may be slow but are changes nonetheless, and it would seem that the eyes, ever sensitive, are happy to respond. Complex building facades over which light can pass or change make for better streets than do more simple ones.

A look at cross sections of two different buildings along the Via Cola di Rienzo in Rome is instructive. The neoclassical building, with a total of six floors, has six major breaks in its facade from ground to roofline—cornice line, balcony, detail at top of windows, etc.—and four other less major breaks—sills, for example; while the post–World War II building has two major breaks, at the top and just above the commercial ground floor, and no minor breaks. (A major break in this case is considered a significant protrusion from the facade, more than six inches, that creates a shadow line or band on the facade, and a less major break is something smaller in size, like a sill, that protrudes and can cast a shadow.) Horizontally, in a distance of 150 feet, the neoclassical facade has 14 distinctly separate windows on each of the

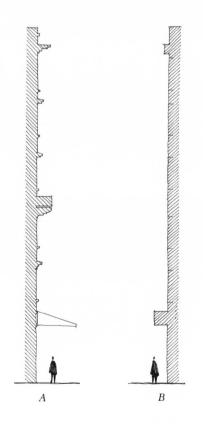

A   *B*

Building wall sections of two buildings on Via Cola di Rienzo, Rome; the more complex facade, A, *offers more surfaces, more opportunities for shadow and light changes than does facade* B

Requirements for Great Streets

Complex windows that catch light and give a sense of habitation

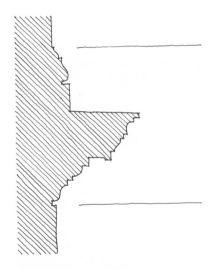

Multiple surfaces and edges on a single detail

top five floors, each with a cap and sill and with shutters that move (each one of which has as many as 30 separate slats) and create breaks when they are perpendicular to or otherwise out from the facade. The newer building has one major horizontal break and the nine windows are set into the walls, with no frames or other break around them on the wall. Looking more carefully at a major facade break in another complex building—in this case a belt course above a window, but not including the window—one can see 18 to 20 separate surfaces. Each one modulates light. Even then, none of the surfaces are absolutely smooth, so on each surface light changes. The exercise is not for the purpose of extolling older design styles at the expense of more recent, usually less complex ones, but simply to observe that with more surfaces there are more chances for light to change and to attract and interest the eyes.[18] Market Street, in San Francisco, has proven a good case in point. Older, detailed, many-surfaced buildings, perhaps not architecturally outstanding in themselves, have been replaced by fewer and larger structures, patterned, smooth-surfaced buildings over which light passes more evenly and which hold less interest for the eyes.

This does not explain the countless streets with detailed facades of many surfaces that are every bit as uninteresting and non-eye-catching as Market Street or New York's Avenue of the Americas have largely become. Not far from Strøget, in Copenhagen, near the university, there are any number of streets whose building facades may not be as plentifully surfaced as those on Via Cola di Rienzo but are certainly not flat. Superficially, particularly above the ground floor, they are similar. They have many of the characteristics of buildings that help make a good street. Still, there is a monotonous drabness about them and the streets that is not all that different from buildings and streets of flat, paneled, even-banded window surfaces. There are many possible explanations. Many of the buildings are unrelieved in that there are few breaks on a facade, no balconies at either end, nothing special to mark an entrance, no rain downspouts to arrest the eye momentarily or to mark the end of one building and the start of another. The details may not project far from the main facade so there may be a flatness about them. There may be an evenness of surface color and texture, without stains or uneven weathering. On some of these Copenhagen streets there is very little at ground level to catch the eye. On one of them there is a hotel with a few flags and a small sign in front over the doorway. That small contrast makes a difference. Mostly on these streets, however, there may be windows not far above ground level, but there is not much of a sense of anything in them. Families may have inhabited them at one time and the facades might have been enlivened by some of the visible messiness of normal family living—flowerpots, clothes, flags, wires—things that people do to places where they live. Now these buildings seem to be occupied by institutions. Perhaps most importantly, on these streets the materials themselves seem to absorb rather than reflect light, particularly if they are dirty or grimy. The light seems to die on them. There are buildings on Strøget, brick buildings not far from the City Hall end, that have this quality, and they do nothing for the street. There are

Signs of habitation

relatively new buildings in San Francisco, most notably the complex that has replaced the Hills Brothers Coffee factory, with new colors and aggregate panel materials, that belie that city's wonderful light quality and bright reflective colors, instead seeming to suck in light like a sponge. All of which is to say that this business of light and surfaces and physical qualities that engage the eyes is a complicated one.

What of streets at night? Much that was visible during the day disappears. The eyes may have less to look at. They become more focused, usually at a lower level than during the day, where the lights are: streetlights, signs, and store windows. Streets are different at night. They may almost cease to exist, like the Grand Canal, or they may exist only at night, because of the light and what it does to the eyes. The Paseo de Gracia, Boulevard Saint-Michel, and Strøget in winter stand out at night.

We remember Venice during the day and the ever-moving, ever-changing canal street floor and the reflections it offers: it is indeed a feast for the eyes!

Transparency

The best streets have about them a quality of transparency at their edges, where the public realm of the street and the less public, often private realm of property and buildings meet. One can see or have a sense of what is behind whatever it is that defines the street; one senses an invitation to view or know, if only in the mind, what is behind the street wall.

Usually it is windows and doors that give a sense of transparency

Via Cola di Rienzo, Rome

Requirements for Great Streets

Glass, but no transparency

Bank Building,
Colorado Boulevard, Pasadena

Usually it is windows and doors that give transparency. On commercial streets, they invite you in, they show you what is there and, if there is something to sell or buy, they entice you. On the best shopping streets there may be a transition zone between the street and the actual shop doorways, a zone of receding show windows and space for outside displays that are welcoming attention getters. The Boulevard Saint-Michel is as good an example as any, but there are streets the world over that do the same. Doorways do the same, with or without glass. They take you in, if only psychologically. They let you know, even if you cannot see, that something is inside. The more doorways the better. The best streets are replete with entryways, as little as 12 feet apart.

It is not just a matter of windows or glass or doorways. There are windowed buildings at street level in most cities that offer nothing but blinds or drapes or screens that one senses have never been opened and never will be, and they are just as opaque as any thick masonry wall. Colorado Boulevard, the main street of Pasadena, California, sports a black glass bank building that is more ominous than a fortress, the Darth Vader of repelling office buildings.

Clear visibility into windows is not always necessary or desirable, particularly on residential streets. But the windows are nonetheless important for the person on the street to have a sense of habitation and possible comfort or refuge inside and for the inhabitant to have visual access to the public realm. I live on the downhill side of a relatively recent San Francisco street where the homes take full advantage of spectacular views away from the street. On my side of the street there are no windows but mostly garage doors and a few entryways, often hidden from the street itself. In terms of community,

Venice Passageway

of knowing neighbors in any but the most superficial way, it is not a good street. If one knows a neighbor well, it is likely to be someone across the street, where there are windows onto the public way. Nor is my street a particularly pleasant street on which to walk. Blank walls and garage doors suggest that people are far removed, and they are.

There are subtle ways to achieve transparency; it needn't be all windows and doors. There are blank-walled passageways in Venice, less than three feet wide, with no windows and very few doorways but with the branches and leaves of a tree overhanging the wall, that offer a kind of transparency. The branches, the leaves, the vine take you over the wall, into the garden beyond.

Complementarity _____

Overwhelmingly, the buildings on the best streets get along with each other. They are not the same but they express respect for one another, most particularly in height and in the way they look.

Requirements for Great Streets

Buildings on the best streets are
generally of similar heights and they fit
with each other

Amsterdam canal

Except for buildings along the Grand Canal, those along the best streets are generally of a similar height. There are rarely big jumps or drops. On the streets with lower buildings of two to five stories—Roslyn Place, Monument Avenue, or the streets of Bath—the variations are rarely more than one or two domestically scaled floors. Above that, to seven or eight stories, the differences are usually one or two stories as well, rarely three. Even then, building heights may not be so different; a tall three-story building can be very much like a four-story one in height. Every now and then there is a church or a corner tower that is significantly different from the norm, but these are exceptions: buildings of special symbolic importance, or whose height is purposeful on the street, marking a turn or a corner. Along one of the very few fine streets characterized by tall buildings, the one-sided Central Park section of Fifth Avenue, in New York, the tall buildings have a general height complementarity. Here, though, it is the occasional lower buildings— museums, clubs, churches—that are the landmarks. Whether by norms or by regulation (which has often been a major determining factor in height of structures along these streets), they have a sense of regularity and of order, observable in their other physical characteristics as well.

Development along some of the best streets occurred all at once (Roslyn Place) or over a relatively short period (individual Paris boulevards or streets in Bath, for example). For others, development and change has been long continuing (the Via dei Giubbonari, Strøget, the Grand Canal). It is not necessarily time of building or similarity of style that accounts for the design complementarity of buildings along the best streets. Rather, it is a series of characteristics, all of which are rarely present on any one street, but enough of which are always there to express regard and respect, one for another and for the street as a whole. The variables are materials, color, cornice lines and belt courses, building sizes, window openings and their details, entrances, bay windows, porches, overhangs and shadow lines and details like downspouts. A common architectural style is not to be discarded just because it may result in sameness of buildings. Formulae and prescriptions, however, are hard to come by. Caution and individual assessment are better ways of determining what it is that holds the buildings together. On Roslyn Place, it is materials (brick and wood trim), windows (double-hung, many-paneled), size (two and one-half stories), and design style. For the Via dei Giubbonari, it is store sizes, shutters, colors (earth tones), materials (largely stucco, but stone and brick too), and all of the store windows, but not style, as it is along the Boulevard Saint-Michel. Buildings along the Paseo de Gracia may be more disparate than on most of the great streets—made up of many different sizes and styles, and different materials and colors, though not clashingly so. A generally similar building height, an overall building geometry dictated by the diagonal corners, and the bay windows are the critical pieces.

The great streets are not generally characterized by standout, individual architectural wonders. That may be a part of fitting in. The architects of palaces along the Grand Canal built to the canal line, and there seems to have been no need to set them apart from adjoining buildings. Gaudí and his colleagues also found it possible to build within height standards and norms, and to respect street lines and the scale of other buildings along the Paseo de Gracia. It was possible and desirable to build complementarily.

Maintenance _____

Ask a pedestrian on a San Francisco street what physical, buildable characteristics are most important to achieving a great street and the answers are very likely to include words like "cleanliness," "smooth," and "no potholes."[19] It is a point well taken. Care of trees, materials, buildings, and all the parts that make up a street is essential. Given a choice, and there usually are choices, people would prefer to be on well-maintained rather than poorly maintained streets.

Shopkeepers know about maintenance. People would rather not shop in poorly maintained stores if they can help it. They know, too, that boarded up windows and closed buildings (not necessarily a matter of maintenance but of occupancy) are detracting. When they can, merchants' associations keep the windows of closed shops clean, even fill them with merchandise sold elsewhere. Individually, they shine the windows of their own stores. It

Poster-filled windows of a vacant store

Strøget, Copenhagen

makes a difference, not unrelated to eye-engaging light and reflection. Even on a well-maintained street like Strøget, there are places, every now and then, that are drab. On inspection, one finds dirty windows at upper floors, which may be understandable in a cold environment that requires two sets of windows, often with many individual panes. Cleaning them represents a difficult, maybe expensive chore. But if they are not clean, the grit absorbs light and drabness results. A small insignificant problem? Maybe not. Think of an extreme case, like the Défense section of Paris, effectively a streetless area (which is bad enough) but appropriate for the point being made. So many of the buildings there are of glass panels, ground to roof, or of glass and other high-gloss materials. A critical part of those materials, and of the building designs that depend on them, is their shininess: they must be kept clean. What, though, if maintenance, the constant cleaning not just of windows that people can see through but of the rest of the building as well, a fairly costly matter, is not a normal part of building management? And what if occupancy rates, and therefore rents, in those (largely office) buildings decline for one reason or another? Is it possible that regular maintenance, in this case window and wall panel cleaning, goes down in a noticeable way relative to other more conventional buildings, thereby increasing the likelihood of their being less desirable and less occupied? The issue, then, becomes not only one of maintenance, but of the use of materials of good quality that are relatively easy to maintain, a matter that is of major concern in the public realm of streets. Untold numbers of people use streets and buildings, and natural elements like wind, rain, and snow wear and grind at them. They have to hold up and be capable of regular maintenance.

The Gaudí-designed paving tiles on the Paseo de Gracia, it has been observed, are among the major contributing features to that street. They are of a special material, not used anyplace else. To examine the walks and to observe a relatively small sub-sidewalk reconstruction of water or electric lines, a regular urban experience, is to realize that the city must keep plenty of those tiles on hand and that the walks are maintained well. The fountains in Rome are almost always clean and are regularly maintained; not so unpaved grass areas, often neglected. The brick sidewalks and crosswalks along Market Street, in San Francisco, have been poorly maintained and are at times replaced with other materials, including asphalt. Newly planted street trees, if uncared for, never achieve the presence that is expected of them. Fountains, if there is no significant commitment to care for them, can become clogged, dirty, empty, inoperative eyesores. As nice as they seem to be in plan, it may be better not to build special features if they will not be cared for.

Physical maintenance is as important as any of the other requirements for great streets. It is more than a matter of keeping things clean and in good repair. It involves the use of materials that are relatively easy to maintain and street elements for which there is some history of caring.

Quality of Construction and Design

In the context of great streets, "quality" of construction and design is difficult to get a handle on. This whole book is about design quality, so the concern is with something more particular. Mostly, it has to do with workmanship and materials and how they are used. There are streets that have all the characteristics we find present on the very best streets and yet do not make the grade. Quality, or rather the lack of quality, is often the reason.

All the best maintenance in the world will not make a wobbly line straight or a skewed line vertical. Nor will it cure a sloppy putty seal, make a muddy color come to life, nor make right a wrong tree. These are matters of materials, workmanship, and design, all with the word "high-quality" before them when it comes to great streets.

There is no such thing as poor-quality or low-quality materials, only problems with how materials are used. Materials that in a given situation will have to take a lot of wear and tear but are not capable of doing so usually have a negative impact. "Thin" materials—such as "brick" paving that is not really made of brick but a one-quarter-inch-thick made-to-look-like-brick substitute—almost always show. Concrete walks or pavers might have been less expensive and better. Anodized aluminum poles or rails or surfaces are not bronze or steel or iron, and if they are used as substitutes that, too, will show poorly. The opportunities for inappropriate uses of materials are endless. It is less a matter of money than of choice.

Workmanship is, presumably, a matter of cost, at least in part. Better workmanship may cost more than less good work. Nonetheless, it, too, shows, particularly when it is pervasive. There is a sense of shabbiness attached to a street where things that are supposed to line up regularly do not, or where there is sloppy painting or bad joinery.

Design is a part of all this, of course, not just workmanship or materials. A simple, thin vertical pipe that holds a streetlight may appear elegant on a drawing but is not likely to remain vertical for long on the street without something at the base, usually something heavy and wider than the pipe, to keep it that way. It helps to understand the history of the design of details, of those on buildings as well as those commonly used in the public way. It is a strong basis for design quality.

Quality is often associated with money, and the implication may be that only communities that can afford them can have great streets. We reject that line of reasoning. Roslyn Place is not a wealthy man's street, nor was it ever. Strøget is not lined with palaces or paved with gold. Here it is appropriate materials and care that are at issue in the making of the best streets, and certainly within the public realm those should be the standard.

CHAPTER TWO

Qualities That Contribute _____

Many of the best streets have trees, but not all of them. Many but not all of the best streets have special public places to sit or stop along the way. Gateways, fountains, obelisks, and streetlights are among the physical, designable characteristics on great streets, but not always. Some physical qualities, then, contribute mightily to making great streets but are not required. On particular streets they can be as compelling and interesting as the necessary qualities, or they can add the salt and pepper, the spice or difference that turns a good street into a great one. Some factors, like accessibility and topography, are ever present. Other variables, most notably density and land uses, though not directly part of street design, are so intimately related to physical place that they cry out for discussion.

Trees _____

Given a limited budget, the most effective expenditure of funds to improve a street would probably be on trees. Assuming trees are appropriate in the first place (not on Strøget, for example) and that someone will take care of them, trees can transform a street more easily than any other physical improvement. Moreover, for many people trees are the most important single characteristic of a good street.[20]

Trees can do many things for a street and city, not the least of which is the provision of oxygen, and of shade for comfort. Green is a psychologically restful, agreeable color. Trees move and modulate the light. In terms of helping streets to work functionally, when planted in lines along a curb or even *in* the cartway they can effectively separate pedestrians from machines, machines from machines, and people from people. The trunks and branches create a screen, sometimes like a row of columns that gives a transparent but distinct edge. Between pedestrian and auto paths they can be a safety barrier for the former. Put a line of trees one lane *into* a street, as has been done on many European streets, to make a parking lane for example, and that lane becomes a part of the pedestrian realm while still functioning as a place to park cars. Even a few trees along the curb of a busy traffic street can have an impact if they are close enough together.

Which trees to use, their placement, their planting, and their maintenance are all important matters. Fortunately, studies abound on the physical nature, growing characteristics, and climatic and soil needs of individual trees. The best studies seem to be locally oriented.[21] Continued observation of trees on

Trees along Viale Manlio Gelsomini, Rome

the best streets allows for the strong conclusion that deciduous trees are more often appropriate than evergreens. Deciduous trees permit sunlight to reach the street in winter when it is either most needed or least a problem. Their leaf patterns are almost always less dense than those of nondeciduous trees and the leaves move more, subject to even slight wind changes; they permit light—mottled, moving light—to penetrate to the pedestrian, and this quality is characteristic of the best streets. Exceptions are easily found and enjoyed, the pines of the Viale delle Terme di Caracalla, in Rome, and the palms of Palm Beach Boulevard, in Palm Beach, Florida, for example, but overwhelmingly one finds deciduous trees on great streets.[22]

To be effective, street trees need to be reasonably close together. If one objective is to create a line of columns that separates visually and psychologically one pathway from another, and if a further objective is to provide a canopy of branches and leaves to walk under, then the trees have to be planted close enough to do that. The close spacing may be more critical to creating a line that separates, because a canopy can often be achieved under a variety of spacings. Walking along a line of trees, it is desirable to be able to see between them, particularly between the first one or two, directly ahead, but also to be aware that one is indeed walking along a line, that the next tree and the following ones form a distinct boundary, a plane. In practice, the most effective tree spacing is from 15 to 25 feet (4.5 to 7.6 meters) apart. On streets where the spacing reaches 30 feet (9 meters) or more, such as the Cours Mirabeau, in Aix-en-Provence, or Mills College, in Oakland, there are likely to be four rows of trees, or two to a side. The trees along Monument Avenue, in Richmond, reach 36 feet apart but there are four rows. It is possible to find all kinds of reasons to plant them further than 25 feet apart—their health, a need to avoid having their branches overlap, the required distances between light poles and even parking meters—but they don't seem to hold up in practice when spacing along the best streets is measured.[23] Branches of trees along the Ramblas and Avenue Montaigne and the Ringstrasse, to name but three of many, overlap, and these trees have been around for a long time. The plane trees along the Viale Manlio Gelsomini, in Rome, may be that street's only saving grace, and the spacing is often 15 to 18 feet. If there is a rule of thumb to be learned from the best streets, it would be that closer is better.

We come across other admonitions in regard to street trees, notably to avoid street corners by 40 or 50 feet (12 to 15 meters), for reasons of sight lines and therefore of auto safety. Nonetheless, tree planting along the best streets either preceded or has otherwise managed to avoid such dictums; it comes as close as possible to street corners. In fact, one reason why street trees are often not effective is a combination of imposed spacing and corner distance rules. Assuming a 400-foot block (twice that of a north-south block in New York), a 50-foot corner distance requirement, and a 50-foot spacing standard, there will be seven trees along a block and then a 150-foot gap for the intersection; not very many trees. A 200-foot block would have only three trees.

Making Great Streets

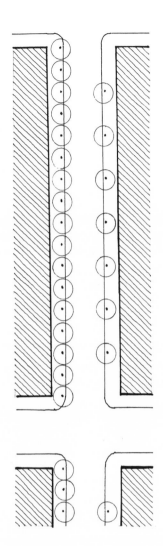

25-foot versus 50-foot tree spacing, the former starting at the corners, the latter removed from the corners

The same spacing requirements help to explain why trees along center-of-street traffic medians are seldom effective. First there are the spacing requirements and then even greater distances required at intersections to allow for left turn lanes. The results are even fewer trees and larger gaps.

The spacing of trees along a street, once started, should not be stopped, not for driveways and not for buildings along the way. If the emphasis is to be on the design of the *street* as opposed to items along the way and if it is the street environment that is the object of design and building, then that end will not be achieved by responding to every "special circumstance." The argument usually involves not wanting trees to block the entrance to a major public or private building, or wanting to create a special place in front of a public building, or to omit a tree in favor of a bus stop or something similar. That doesn't work. It takes away from the street. There is a block along the Via Cola di Rienzo, in Rome, where the trees have been omitted in front of a public market, and that block is nowhere near as pleasant an area as the rest of the street. Along the Ramblas, in Barcelona, trees have been omitted for a distance near the lower end, in front of the Theatre Principio, presumably to give presence to the theater, and there are elaborate five-luminaire streetlights instead. Trees would have been better, or both trees and lights.

Street trees, once established, are able to take considerable abuse. But on the best streets, where the trees make a major difference, they appear to be cared for. There seems to be, on those streets, a long-continuing program for maintenance, one based on an understanding of their importance. One assumes that they were planted well in the first place.

Street trees are a high-priority item on which to spend funds that could have a major environmental impact. Absent a commitment to do them right and to maintain them well later, the monies might just as well not be spent. Done well and maintained well, street trees are grand.

Beginnings and Endings _____

Every street starts and ends somewhere and those locations are usually not too hard to fix. Perhaps in some perverse way it is the obviousness of the observation that keeps this from being an always present requirement for great streets. And yet, though the entry to Roslyn Place is marked ever so subtly by two wrought iron gateposts, they are insignificant to that street's special character. It does not seem reasonable that every great street has to have something special, a physical thing, to mark its beginning or end, or that the start or finish should be crucial to making it what it is. Nonetheless, most great streets have notable starts and stops, not always fine, but notable. It could be argued that, since they have to start and stop somewhere, these points should be well designed.

Qualities That Contribute

Special physical qualities that denote ends are helpful. They say, in effect, that one has arrived, or left, or they give boundaries. They are places to meet, or reference points: "I'll meet you at the Rond-Point entrance to the Avenue Montaigne," or "I live one block east of the Stonewall Jackson statue on Monument Avenue."

The most notably positive street beginnings or endings include the piazza at either end of the Via dei Giubbonari (one funnels you in from a main cross street and the other is an open air public market), the City Hall square at one end of Strøget, and the Plaça de Catalunya that starts both the Ramblas and the Paseo de Gracia. All of them are main destinations as well as starting points. They are served by the streets and serve them as well. Though not a strong visual start for the Ramblas, the Plaça de Catalunya is easily entered from the street, and the Columbus column at the water end of the street marks it well. The two endings of the Via dei Giubbonari, in part because of their shapes, in part because of the market activity, are enticing. It is hard to walk by the street once you see it, and hard not to enter the market once seen. The Kongens Nytorv, at one end of Strøget, is less compelling; it is a bit hard to know where you are there, and from it the street is not all that obvious. The statue of the king at one end of the Cours Mirabeau and the statues at either end of Monument Avenue do their jobs clearly, without overstatement. They simply mark the ends of the streets. The gateways at the other end of the Cours Mirabeau are far more positive than the large, disorienting, ill-defined fountain at the Place Général de Gaulle circle that marks the start of that great street. The Bernini-inspired fountain that starts Boulevard Saint-Michel is an unmistakable presence, and does its job of announcing the street and place, but it is always in shade and has a coldness to it; the water has no sparkle. The Place Edmond Rostand at the entrance to the Luxembourg Gardens is far more inviting, as either a beginning or ending, to pass between the intensely urban street and the magnificently urbane park. For drama and integration of surrounding streets (not just the Champs-Elysées), the Arc de Triomphe and the Place de l'Etoile need to be noted. Perhaps the best entryway to any street anywhere is the one to the Via del Corso framed by the twin churches in the Piazza del Popolo. Looking the other way, the obelisk in the piazza clearly focuses the street's ending. The much less well done ending at the Piazza Venezia has been observed earlier. Fine streets made of trees alone seem to need major markings less than others; the Viale delle Terme di Caracalla is one, and the Mills College entry street is another. So, too, the residentially scaled streets of Bath do nicely without announcements of starts or endings. The Piazza di Porta Ravegnana, in Bologna, and the two remaining towers there constitute a major focal beginning to each of the five streets that radiate from it. In a different way, seemingly by chance but almost certainly by design, that focal point is as ever-present, although not as self-servingly powerful, as the Etoile.

There is every reason why the beginnings and endings of streets should be well marked, as part of the street, to introduce us to them and to take us

Column that starts, or ends, the Ramblas

Making Great Streets

elsewhere. Entrances can always be open and inviting. Experience of fine streets indicates that entries and exits are not always well done or memorable in themselves. That same experience suggests that when they *are* well done they contribute in significant ways to great streets, though they may not detract all that much when they are less than they might be.

Many Buildings Rather Than Few; Diversity _____

Generally, more buildings along a given length of street contribute more than do fewer buildings. At the very least, there will be one vertical line between buildings where one ends and the other begins, and that single line adds interest. The lines are also reference points, like markings on a ruler, that give a sense of scale. The more buildings, the more vertical lines. Diversity, or at least the greater likelihood of diversity, also comes with more rather than fewer buildings.

Henry James, understanding size and scale, writes of one of the largest palazzi on the Grand Canal that its "main reproach, more even than the coarseness of its forms, is its swaggering size, its want of consideration for the general picture, which the early examples so reverently respect."[24] He then goes on to speak of the economic vulnerability of such enterprises.

There are different kinds of diversity, including physical and social, and we are interested in both as well as in how the first might impact on the second. The relationship between more buildings and the likelihood of greater diversity should be no mystery. With more buildings there are likely to be more architects, and they will not all design alike. There are more contributors to the street, more and different participants, all of whom add interest. More buildings are likely to mean more building owners, each with an economic stake in and responsibility for the street. They will do things differently in the first place and maintain and modify them differently as time passes. All of the best streets that have been studied exhibit many buildings and what appear to be many owners. A small street like Roslyn Place, developed at one time and apparently by one developer-owner, has 10 buildings and 18 owners. That diverse ownership shows in windows, in maintenance, in landscape, in color changes, in minor changes to buildings over time. Time is no small factor. With more buildings and owners, change is more likely to come incrementally rather than all at once, and that, too, adds visual interest as well as a sense of continuity. Do more buildings and owners mean more socioeconomic diversity? Perhaps. We would like to think so; at least there is a likelihood of that.

Having more rather than fewer buildings may or may not result in greater diversity of uses and activities. The different buildings can, however, be designed for a mix of uses and destinations that attract mixes of people from all over a city or neighborhood, which therefore helps build community: movies, different-sized stores, libraries. Yes, all of those uses can be designed into one single building—into a shopping center, for example, or a Trump Tower on Fifth Avenue or a Citibank on Lexington Avenue in New York—but those buildings are not truly public; people can be and are regularly excluded, and even when such buildings are on a public street, they lack the interest and diversity that comes with a variety of owners, buildings, stores, and designers. None of them can match the great streets.

Special Design Features: Details _____

Details contribute mightily to the best streets: gates, fountains, benches, kiosks, paving, lights, signs, and canopies can all be important, at times crucially so. At the same time, some contribute less than might be thought. The most important of them deserve special attention.

Paseo de Gracia light

Streetlight on Orange Grove Boulevard, Pasadena

Making Great Streets

Barcelona street light

The *streetlights* on Orange Grove Boulevard, in Pasadena, California, contribute in a major way to the quality of that street. White glass globes, set on simple dark olive-green poles, about 9 feet tall, march along the street, the white globes in front of and in strong contrast to the deep green leaves of the magnolia trees that alternate with palms. Those simple white balls, white, not translucent during the day, form two lines along the street edge, diminishing with the distance, taking the eyes with them. Their whiteness seems to attract the sun. Three of the four streetlight designs along the Paseo de Gracia are important to it: Gaudí's, because of its ever-present frivolous grandness; the ornate five-luminaire corner lights; and the single lights that proceed above head level, between the trees, along the street. The latter are especially important at night, when they do the same thing as those on Orange Grove Boulevard do during the day. The Champs-Elysées has an elegant, single-light fixture along its length, as well as lower lights for walkers along its parklike section. There are high, ornate lights along the Kurfürstendamm in Berlin. For many streets, simple overhead lights in the center of the street, hung from wires attached to the buildings, functionally light the street at the same time as they mark the center, a receding line for the eye to follow, day or night. Lights along the Via del Corso and Via Cola di Rienzo in Rome are effective older examples of this, while downtown San Jose, California, offers a recent successful experiment.

Because of their regularity and location, streetlights form lines, usually of receding poles marked with a fixture on top, that the eyes grasp and follow. They emphasize the linearity of the street. The best of them are not too high, under 20 feet. The seemingly universal choice of street engineers, one or another version of a so-called cobra light, is usually much higher and not terribly pleasant to look at; if it is necessary, it can stand apart and so serve the autos, but it is best not relied upon for where people walk. The best streetlights are well designed in and of themselves and, simple or ornate, they give enjoyment. Though one would expect light spacing to be regular, more so, for example, than the spacing of trees, that is often not the case, as on such streets as the Cours Mirabeau and the Paseo de Gracia. It is noticeable, too, that translucent glass globes, when set atop a pole, are usually less effective than white glass globes. The former, during the day, disappear.

Haussmann, it seems, understood about streetlights:

A gaslamp that is placed too high up will project light further but will not give adequate light to the immediate area around it. Obviously, that was not our goal. The higher a lamp, the greater the unlighted area at its base. By reducing the height of street lamps and the distance between them, and decreasing the intensity of the flame in each lamp so as not to use more gas, we were able to light the city's streets better. Extremely bright lights are useless; they blind people more than they light their way.[25]

Qualities That Contribute

Street designers give a great deal of attention to special *paving* and to *paving patterns*. Special paving can cost a lot of money; in very few instances does it make a significant difference. The Gaudí-designed hexagonal blue-gray tiled walkway on the Paseo de Gracia is a wonderful exception. So are the hexagonal asphalt pavers along Central Park on Fifth Avenue in New York, the blue cobblestones in San Juan, Puerto Rico, and other individual examples that easily come to mind. Generally, though, one wonders how often the results of such efforts are worth the expense, particularly if there is not likely to be a commitment to regular maintenance and an understanding that replacements of the special paving will have to be purchased and stored. The brick sidewalks and intersection crosswalks on San Francisco's Market Street are regularly abused, and often not replaced. The granite inserts that make up the gutters are paved over in places. Only the granite curbs seem to hold up. Better to use more normal, understood paving materials that can be done well and that are more likely to be cared for.

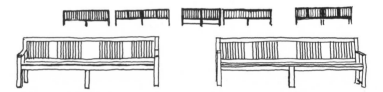

Benches help people stay on the street; they invite our presence by permitting rest, conversation, waiting for a friend, passing the time. They help to make community. They are less expected on residential streets and less present there than on commercial streets. A remarkable number of the very best streets have benches: Strøget, Paseo de Gracia, Cours Mirabeau, Avenue Montaigne, Boulevard Saint-Michel, the Ramblas, and the Grand Canal near the Piazza San Marco. Those same streets have other places for people to sit as well, notably at tables of streetside cafes.

What of undesirables? The essence of the complaint against public sitting places is that they attract beggars, the homeless, etc. That may, in fact, be the case. Public problems can be, may be, should be publicly noticeable— though this argument will hardly convince shopkeepers and others to have benches or not to take them away. Nor will the argument that street design cannot be expected to solve or deny the existence of major social problems, hopefully transient ones. But there are ways to solve that problem, not the least of which is nonviolent yet determined public enforcement that permits everyone to have an unmolested chance at a sitting place. Societies enforce other rules, such as for aberrant driving and parking behavior, often at great expense. Places to sit, in the meantime, help to make fine streets.

The small fountains along the Cours Mirabeau, the special circular seating at corners along the Paseo de Gracia, the drinking fountain and the bird stands on the Ramblas, the statues along Monument Avenue—all of these contribute to these streets. They can be joyful, magic-making things to look at. Signs and awning canopies can be too. The best of the signs are the truly artfully conceived and executed store logos, like the old umbrella announcement along the Ramblas, which is hard not to look at. Such signs are public art in the best sense. Overhead awnings do something else; they create intimate spaces along streets, shady when it is sunny, protected and comfortable when it is not.

Understandably, people become excited about design features on streets that are special, existing ones they have seen and that are forever remembered, or design ideas that they just know will make a particular street great.[26] But it is best not to depend on them. Alone, great fountains, or gates, or paving, or lights, are not enough. Details are the special seasonings of a great street.

Places _____

Somewhere along the path of a fine street, particularly if it is long, there is likely to be a break. More than just intersections, breaks are small plazas or parks, widenings, or open spaces. They are most important on narrow streets and long streets and streets that bend and turn. On those streets particularly they provide stopping places, pauses, reference points along the path.

Strøget: four distinct open spaces along the route

There are four such spaces along Strøget, not quite equally spaced. Each is different from the next, in shape and in activities, but each provides places to sit, to eat, to meet, and to talk. In that sense they are community-building. Højbro Plads, funnel-shaped and very similar in both size and shape to an entrance to the Via dei Giubbonari, is not very large, but it could easily be one of the major meeting places of Copenhagen. People vie for the seats, waiting for one to be free; they buy food, fruit, some vegetables. They talk, they watch and listen to people perform, they see that their kids don't stray too far, they have better views of not-too-distant spires than from the street. The public toilet under the Plads is clean, welcoming, functional, even elegant in execution, an important public service that might even be an attraction to the space and street. The Largo dei Librari along the Via dei Giubbonari, the Piazzetta di San Simeone along the Via dei Coronari in Rome, small open spaces along the Grand Canal at its major bridges and at the Piazza San Marco, the two central statues along Monument Avenue in Richmond, and the redesigned gore corners along Market Street in San Francisco, with places to sit, are all examples of spaces that are important contributions to their streets.

One cannot forget that a major purpose of streets is to enable one to get from one place to another, not only to a location on the street but to and from areas beyond it. That is possible on all but one of our great streets, Roslyn Place, which is a cul-de-sac. Even the entry street of Mills College, in Oakland, is the main distributor of movement to other campus locations. Two of the streets, the Via dei Giubbonari and Strøget, are only for people (though the former permits vehicles), but they certainly take people beyond the areas through which they pass and may be sought out as such. What sets the great streets apart is that they take people along their ways, from one part of the city to another, whether on foot or in a vehicle, with grace and at a reasonable pace. True, an Italian in a car speeds whenever there is a chance, even on the Viale delle Terme di Caracalla. In an automobile, it may be possible to speed on the Paseo de Gracia, and some do. It is not the kind of street where one would want to cross against the traffic lights, but those lights seem oriented as much to pedestrians as to drivers. For all of them, whether on foot or in a car, it is more pleasant to move along with delibera-tion, taking in what is at hand for the eyes and imagination. Even where speed is possible there are buffers to protect those who move more slowly. The streets where autos are most welcome—Paseo de Gracia, Cours Mira-beau, Monument Avenue, Avenue Montaigne, Boulevard Saint-Michel—are also those that one might seek out to enjoy in an automobile, to travel slowly, taking in the sights. On buses these are streets where one most en-joys the passing scenes.

There is another kind of street accessibility to consider: people must be able to get to the street with ease. In part it is a matter of location, particularly for major city-making or community-making streets. Notably, it is not diffi-cult, is even easy, to find and get to the best streets, within the city as a whole or in their more local context. Besides being places one can walk to, great streets seem to be accessible by public transit, whether crossing them or along them or under them. Accessibility is also a matter of public access at places along the street, by intersecting or crossing streets or public ways. Streets with one entry for every 300 feet (90 meters) are easy to find, and some of the best streets approach that figure (Monument Avenue with one entry for every 275 feet or Avenue Montaigne with one for every 255 feet, for example), but there are more entries on the busiest streets.[27] The Grand Canal might look the same from the air without its intersecting walks and canals, which occur approximately every 75 feet of its length, but it would be a very different street: it would not be a part of the community. For contrast, consider that in Irvine, California, there is not likely to be more than one public entering street for every 660 feet along a major street in the business district.

Still another type of access to be considered is for handicapped people. None of the identified great streets were designed with handicapped people in mind. And yet it is surprising that many of them accommodate wheelchairs with ease; the Via dei Giubbonari, Strøget, the Ramblas all do. Many of the best streets have places to rest. Handicapped people regularly use the boats along the Grand Canal. There is a regularity about most of the best streets that one imagines to be relatively decipherable for the visually handicapped. Access for the handicapped, in a most elemental sense, is not too hard to achieve. Witness the ramps that have been added to so many streets around the world.

Density Helps

The subject of residential density and activities—the consequence of what urban planners call land uses—have been largely avoided thus far, this despite admonitions that it is people and activities more than what is physical and buildable that make the best streets, an argument that we can accept. What must be acknowledged, however, is that in physical design terms one doesn't design or build density or land uses. One can design *for* a certain number of people for a given unit of land, or *at* a density of such and such, and those are physical relationships, but they are more a matter of urban policy made by urban policy makers, though designers may influence them. Similarly with activities and land uses, designers may influence buying and selling, or playing, or working, or interacting, or shopping, but they don't design them. The determination having been made that one space shall have a theater, another sell cheese, and another be for people working at desks, a designer can design those spaces as well as spaces that can accommodate multiple uses; but the initial determinations are more matters of policy, often enacted into laws, that designer-builders will respond to, and not necessarily their basic task. Conversely, land use policy will certainly result in physical building, as it is intended to, but it is not physical in and of itself.

Whether or not they are directly designable and buildable, density and land use matters are important to streets. The best streets are wonderful places to be even if there aren't many or even any people on them. Roslyn Place is comfortable, thought-provoking, pleasant to the eyes on a mid-Saturday afternoon in the summer. Strøget is a fine walking environment late at night. The Grand Canal may be as pleasant a street to be on very early in the morning, with few boats or people and only Turner-like visions, as it is at midday. People, though, are present even at those special times, if only in the mind's eye. Part of these streets' special character when no one is on them may be the contrast with how we normally experience them, that is, with people.[28] Void of human activity, streets soon cry out for people, they need people at the same time as they are for them, they are activated by people at the same time as they contribute to making a community for them. And that is achieved in considerable measure by having many people live along them or nearby—a matter of density.

Streets with many people living along them or near them are more likely to have people on them than those that do not. It is a matter of numbers and ease of access. Time and again in the 1980s and early 1990s, community groups responsible for planning or replenishing their central areas have called for streets, particularly main streets, to be what they call "24-hour" streets, areas populated and with a human presence all the time. It is density that achieves that objective. Elsewhere it has been observed that a minimum net residential density of 15 dwelling units per acre can achieve active urban communities, and that 50 dwellings per net acre are possible without going above four stories or requiring overly wide streets.[29] Mixed with other uses, particularly in central areas, the densities might be lower, though not on an individual building site. It is difficult for streets to help make community if there are not people to get to them easily: nearby density.

Diversity

Strøget may no longer have many people living along it, but as the main shopping and commercial street of Copenhagen it is anything but a vacant area and housing is not far away. It is an area that is physically and economically diverse. Diverse uses enliven the area and the street, bring different people for different purposes, help to keep it going. The Via dei Giubbonari, in addition to its stores and apartments, has a school, offices, headquarters of a political party, a movie house, two churches, and restaurants on a street that is not very long. The Paseo de Gracia, Boulevard Saint-Michel, the Ramblas, the Grand Canal, and the Cours Mirabeau have diverse uses and are situated in areas of variety as well. Avenue Montaigne and Monument Avenue may be the most homogeneous of the great streets. On most of these streets, there exist many different kinds of buildings designed for their uses— cinemas, theaters, or schools—or for earlier uses no longer present but adapted to present occupants—movie houses that became restaurants or stores—all of which add to interest and activity. Variety, activity, liveliness of physical place are likely effects of diversity of uses.

Length

Roslyn Place is about 250 feet long (75 meters), the Via dei Giubbonari about 900 feet (275 meters), the Paseo de Gracia about 1 mile (1.6 kilometers), and the Grand Canal about 2 miles. Great streets, it seems, come in all lengths. Why not? Yet at some point it can become difficult to sustain visual interest, diversity, eye- and thought-provoking images. Enough can become enough, or too much. If something special continues long enough it may no longer be special. The gentle turns and curves of the Grand Canal and the ever-changing buildings and light maintain interest, but even they have a limited power to attract: somewhere between the Rialto Bridge and the railway station one may be excused for wondering what is in his or her daily newspaper. Though we cannot specify just how long is too long, we can hypothesize that at some points along a long street some changes are necessary if interest is to be sustained. They may consist in some special focal point like the statues along Monument Avenue, or a special building like the theater on the Ramblas, or a park like that along the Ringstrasse in Vienna, or perhaps a change in the street section.

Slope

More often than not, the best streets have noticeable changes in elevation, albeit none very steep. The Via dei Giubbonari drops from either end toward the center, so there seems to be a middle view, if not a distant one, for much of its length, and it is possible to see where the street is going. Walking toward the sea on the Ramblas there is a bit of a view, not of the water but of the street ahead. Returning, the view (mildly uphill) is foreshortened and there is a not unpleasant sense of more people than might actually be there, not unlike photos taken through a foreshortening lens of about 90 millimeters. Topography and slope help by increasing views and adding drama. In the extreme—San Francisco for example—hilly streets that offer wonderful views might even take one's mind from the reality that the street itself is less than it could be. There would seem to be no reason why great streets could not have much greater elevation changes than those in this book. Certainly such streets must exist. The limit would be slopes so steep as to be difficult or uncomfortable for major population groups—the elderly, handicapped, mothers with young children. Otherwise, slope helps.

Parking

The boats on the Grand Canal keep moving. Pickup and delivery craft stop for short periods: an occasional motorboat can be found in front of a palace, groups of gondolas can be found in some places along the way, noticeably at *traghetto* stops, and there are taxi stations that seem always to have water taxis tied up; but compared to the amount of traffic on the canal and the number of possible stopping places along it, these are exceptions. There is little parking along the Grand Canal. None of the other great streets can be characterized as having an abundance of parking places, on street or off.

Automobile parking is a pervasive issue. Prepare a plan for an individual street or neighborhood, or for a central area, and parking is certain to be a major subject—a bone of contention—more time and energy consuming than housing. It has to do with accessibility. People with automobiles would like to park as close as possible to their destinations—directly in front is best. Merchants want them to. Parking standards and programs abound. So do guidelines and case studies for how best to landscape at-grade off-street parking lots, or where to locate and how to design and sometimes hide garages.

Qualities That Contribute

These standards can impact streets mightily and have done so, particularly in the United States. For example, if you put all of the parking in lots or structures behind the stores, then those stores will reorient to the rear, deadening the street. Pasadena's Colorado Boulevard is a prime example. Large ground-level lots along a street leave gaps in street definition and activity. Garages on the street have a hard time fitting in, but can be made to do so, although they may be too expensive on a really busy street. Fail to provide the parking, we are told, and people will go elsewhere, to where parking is plentiful. Maybe so, and maybe not. We will not resolve the issue here, nor make the attempt.

On-street auto parking is permitted and provided for along many of the best streets, far more than where there is none, but almost certainly in amounts that are far below demand or what any contemporary standard would require. At best, drivers seem to have a long shot at finding a space in the block they are destined for; they take the chance, usually lose, then look elsewhere nearby for a place to park. That may be enough: a chance. The boulevard access streets are among the best in terms of the ways in which cars are handled, not in the numbers of cars accommodated. Avenue Montaigne and the Paseo de Gracia are examples; parking on those streets is on relatively confined, slow-moving access streets that, by virtue of trees and pace, are part of the pedestrian realm. Driveways off of the best streets, or garage entrances for access to parking or for service, are rare, even on a fine residential street such as Monument Avenue. Though present on more streets than not, auto parking in great amounts, to any contemporary standard, is not a characteristic of great streets. They seem to do well without "enough."

Contrast

Contrast in design is what sets one street apart from another, and ultimately what makes one great and another less so. Contrast in shape or length or size, or to the pattern of surrounding streets, is another matter. For many streets one or another of these qualities sets them apart from other streets; the Champs-Elysées is wider and longer than any other street in Paris; Regent Street in London is different in shape and regularity from the streets of Soho or Mayfair; the Ramblas stands visibly apart from the narrow, short streets to either side; Roslyn Place is shorter and narrower than most streets in Shadyside or in Pittsburgh as a whole; the five streets of Bologna that focus on the two towers at Piazza di Porta Ravegnana form in themselves a distinct pattern that sets them apart from others. For some of these streets it might not be too difficult to pick out the most special one or two from an otherwise unmarked map. But that is not always the case. Strøget or the Avenue Montaigne are not all that different in size or shape from other nearby streets. The Via dei Giubbonari, though more regular and longer than most of those in its immediate vicinity, might be difficult to single out from a map. Roslyn Place might be so short as to go unnoticed.

In the end, shape or size or regularity within an urban physical context may set one street apart from others, may make it more noticeable, may give it a head start toward being special, but that is not likely to be enough and may not be a critical factor in determining a great street. It is the design of the street itself that makes the difference.

Time _____

Roslyn Place is a twentieth-century street that, with the exception of one building, was conceived and carried out in one fell swoop, not unlike the larger-scaled process of United States suburban residential development of the last half of the twentieth century. The Via dei Giubbonari has existed in one form or another for 2,000 years; it has evolved, and those many years alone suggest that it will continue to change. Between these extremes of age and evolution, there are many variations of old or new streets and rapidly or slowly developed ones. If one criterion for being outstanding is that a street stand a test of time, be long continuing, then the likelihood is that the examples for study will be older rather than newer.

Assertions are made that time is needed to make a great street, presumably to achieve diversity and change and a sense of history that comes with years—a patina, not a grime—and presumably it is the buildings more than the public way itself that are at point. That is not necessarily the case. There are many fine streets along which the buildings were developed in a relatively short time span, many along the French streets of the nineteenth century, the Boulevard Saint-Michel and Cours Mirabeau among them. On others, like Monument Avenue or the Paseo de Gracia, the buildings took longer, about 100 years, and on Strøget the time period is longer still.

For public rights-of-way, the story seems different, at least in part. The basic physical nature of most of them was established in a short period, the consequence of a decision to design and build, or rebuild, a particular street. There are notable exceptions, like Strøget or the Via dei Giubbonari or the Kurfürstendamm in Berlin, but Monument Avenue seems a more typical case. The basic design having been set, these streets are regularly amended, tinkered with, improved over time. Major changes to the Champs-Elysées, we are led to believe, are forthcoming, but presumably they will not affect the main line of trees, or the building line. The present central trees of the Kurfürstendamm are relatively new, but there have been other planting designs over the years.[30] Lighting systems seem to be regular additions to streets, often without taking down the old ones.[31] There is no rule that says that the changes will make or keep a street fine or return one to its former status. As yet they have not done so on Market Street.

Qualities That Contribute

To the extent that incremental building and change do bring the diversity and sense of history that can give body and substance to a street, it may be argued that smaller, rather than larger, building parcels help. Diversity is likely to be greater initially as well as over time, as building decisions can be made incrementally.

If it is history and age that we want to see on a street, then there is nothing like time to gain them, remembering that many less than lovely streets have also been built over time. For the futurists and the impatient, however, it is encouraging to know that great streets can be built now.

Roslyn Place

CHAPTER THREE

Conclusion: Great Streets and City Planning _____

The twentieth century has seen the development and widespread acceptance of two major city design manifestos; that of the new town or garden city movement, and the Charter of Athens.[32] Both were in large measure responses to the building excesses and resultant foul living conditions of the nineteenth-century industrial city. Change was in order and dramatic changes were proposed. Both manifestos, reflections perhaps of not so different utopian ideals, concentrated on new building, and both ultimately eschewed streets as they had been known as central and positive to urban living. Ultimately the new town– and garden city–inspired communities became the models for the moderate- and low-density suburban development that emphasized central green areas rather than streets as the means of achieving face-to-face communication, and buildings well set back and, if possible, divorced from streets. The superblock idea, not inherently anti-street, became that way as it became part and parcel of both design movements.[33] Both, too, called for a separation of land uses, rather than a healthy integration, and both were to achieve their ends via massive public initiatives and centralized ownership and design of land.

The Charter of Athens could find realization on either new sites, like Chandigarh or Brasília, or in the older central cities. In the latter, there would have to be clearance of large unhealthy urban environments in order to rebuild at a scale necessary to have an impact. Here, the rejection of streets as places for people and for the making and expression of community was even stronger, in favor of efficiency, technology, and speed, and, to give credit, of health as well, as the prime determinants of street design.[34] Building orientation to streets was seen as a fundamental wrong. The most memorable images of what those developments might look like are perspectives taken from a viewpoint high in the air with the uniform height of tall, tall buildings as the horizon line, or drawings of two people sitting at a table somehow overlooking a large, presumably public space with no one in it. This could not be said of the early garden cities, notably in communities like Welwyn Garden City, where houses did indeed face narrow streets, with results not unlike Roslyn Place.

As well-intentioned and socially responsive as those manifestos were, their results, abundantly visible by the 1960s, rarely encourage or celebrate public life. They seem to be more consistent with separation and introspection—buildings and people alone, with space on all sides—than with encountering and dealing with people regularly. They have been more consistent with vehicle movement than with people movement. Fewer things that people need or want are close at hand within walking distance. They seem to have forgotten that communities are not made in automobiles, nor are people directly encountered.

Better models than these two were in order: ones not so dependent on central power and ownership and design, ones that saw incremental physical change and conservation as more desirable than massive clearance of what existed, ones that were based on not only an acceptance but also a desire for and love of urban life, of encountering people in healthy environments. They were forthcoming, not least in Jane Jacobs's book of the 1960s, *The Death and Life of Great American Cities,* that challenged the city-building practices of the times.[35] Other notable critiques and alternatives have followed.[36] Kevin Lynch's *Theory of Good City Form* set out values that a good city should strive to achieve as well as Lynch's own utopian model, with remarkably comprehensive appendixes that catalogue other theories and models.[37] In 1987, the late Donald Appleyard and I put our thoughts into writing, spurred and aided by students, in what we called "Toward a New Urban Design Manifesto."[38] Responding to social values and objectives of urban life such as comfort, identity and control, access to opportunity, imagination and joy, authenticity and meaning, community and public life, and urban self-reliance, we called, in rather general terms, for six physical qualities: livability; a minimum density; an integration of uses; buildings that defined space rather than being set in space; many rather than fewer buildings; and public streets. The present inquiry has been directed toward spelling out in greater detail what is required to achieve one of the fundamental parts of good cities; good, no, great streets.

There remains considerable tenuousness, iffiness, in the determination of what makes great streets, and that will continue. Places to walk, physical comfort, definition, qualities that engage the eyes, complementarity, and good maintenance are physical characteristics of all great streets, but far from all streets that have them are great. More is required: what I have been calling magic. In some respects, the problem, if it can be called that, starts with the multiple social purposes of streets. It is useful to review them.

Beyond functional purposes of permitting people to get from one place to another and to gain access to property, streets—most assuredly the best streets—can and should help to do other things: bring people together, help build community, cause people to act and interact, to achieve together what they might not alone. As such, streets should encourage socialization and participation of people in the community. They serve as locations of public expression. They should be physically comfortable and safe. The best streets create and leave strong, lasting, positive impressions; they catch the eyes and the imagination. They are joyful places to be, and given a chance one wants to return to them. Streets are places for activity, including relaxation. The best streets continue, are long-lived.

It may be that the purposes of streets relating to movement and access are afforded greater attention in industrial societies because they seem reasonably clear, easily objectified, measurable. Comfort is increasingly measurable, the other objectives much less so. Participation and socialization often mean different things to different people. Imagination and joy cover many concrete possibilities. Community may be realized by directly working with others or by each person doing his or her part separately. It is not always clear why people go to one street and not to another—the reasons may change, and they may have nothing to do with physical qualities. Physical qualities of streets, it has been observed, may not be the most important contributor to making community. They can help, but their direct contributions are likely to remain murky. Nonetheless, they are important; people spend time and money on making them fine settings for their activities, and it is the physical qualities that designers design.

Considerable progress has been made in establishing operative definitions of some of the qualities that make great streets. More is measurable and definable than we once thought. We continue to know more about definition, transparency, spacing (of trees, for example), human scale, and what makes new buildings fit in with others in specific environments. Much, however, remains uncertain, and so it is not easy to know when a quality has been achieved in the best way, or when, for example, buildings are so tall as to be oppressive. In the realm of street design, it may not be all that critical to know the answers to some of these questions with precision. Understanding what the most critical factors are, and knowing what has been tried and has worked or failed in a variety of situations, may be enough. Street design, like any other creative act, always involves leapmanship, a point where it is necessary to jump from the known to something else that is desired, without knowing for sure where one will land.

There is magic on great streets, and presumably in their making. It is more than putting all of the required qualities on a street, and it is more than having a few or many of the physical, desirable things that contribute to them. Sorcery and charm, imagination and inspiration are involved, and may be the most crucial ingredients. But not without social purpose. The making of great streets is not an exercise in design for design's sake, to satisfy alone someone's concept of beauty. The magic may not be all that exciting or dramatic at the time of design. To use a nonstreet example, it seems that Thomas Jefferson was clear in his social and educational objectives for the University of Virginia: community, teachers and students living together while respecting each other's privacy, the centrality of knowledge as expressed in the library, the importance of land and gardens and of views as parts of a full life. He put them together in a straightforward, seemingly simple way, not without knowledge of physical models gained from study and experience. The result is, in the end, magic. One can imagine that the best streets were done that way, and will continue to be. Models, a knowledge of what has been done in the past, can help bring the magic into being.

Jefferson used and adapted models for his university. Too often, however, models aren't referenced or used. Finding them—what they look like, their dimensions, their contexts, their relationships to each other—has been difficult. That is a major purpose of this book: to offer knowledge about the best streets so that the creativeness, the magic, may come to be for new streets.

Design counts! Great streets do not just happen. Overwhelmingly, the best streets derive from a conscious act of conception and creation of the street as a whole. The hands of decision makers, sometimes of specific designers, are visible. In cases where the initial layout and properties of the street evolved, such as at Strøget or the Ramblas, there is likely to have been a major concerted design effort at some point in time to make the street what it has become. By contrast, some fine streets have evolved to what they are without planning, the Via dei Giubbonari most notably, and there seems little in the way of program or special policy to maintain it. Similarly, compelling streets in medieval cities are plentiful, and they are all of one type. The objective of design may well have been not a great street, but rather a street that simply does its job. And there are as many or more bad streets that have been designed. But the best streets, by and large, get designed and then are cared for, continuously.

Technology, some say, makes cities as we have known them unnecessary. Advances in communication and new methods of production make it less necessary for people to live in close proximity to each other. Today's cities are leftovers from methods of production and achieving security that are no longer necessary and can disappear. There is evidence as well that many people, particularly in North America, given a choice, would not prefer cities—but rather what has become known as a suburban lifestyle or a low-density, nonurban lifestyle. Nonetheless, even assuming that they were unnecessary, cities would still be desirable for many people. We can build and live in cities because we want to, not because we have to but because they offer the prospect of a fulfilling gregarious life. Urban streets have been and can be major contributors to that kind of life.

Continually I return to an awareness of the large proportion of urban developed land that is devoted to streets and to the understanding that the purpose of streets is much more than to get from one place to another. Streets more than anything else are what make the public realm. They are the property of the public or are under direct public control. The opportunity to design them in ways that meet public objectives, including the making of community itself, is as exciting as it is challenging. If we do right by our streets we can in large measure do right by the city as a whole—and, therefore and most importantly, by its inhabitants.

The best new streets need not be the same as the old, but as models the old have much to teach. Delightful, purposeful streets and cities will surely follow.

The Rambles.

Street	Date/Time	Effective Walk Width	Number of People	People per Minute per Meter	Notes
Barcelona shopping street, south of Plaça de Catalunya on east side	May 1990 8:25–8:30 P.M. Monday	5.5 m.	240	8.7	Most walking fast; some strolling and window shopping but no stopping.
	6:15–6:20 P.M. Monday		358	13.0	Many speeds; some stopping at windows. A sense of crowding; some spillover into street; could not run.
	6:30–6:35 P.M. Monday		347	12.6	Same as above; hard to count when people come in surges.
Via Cola di Rienzo, Rome	May 1986 4:31–4:41 P.M. Saturday, south side	4.5 m.	238	5.2	370 autos and cycles in 10 minutes. Pedestrian counts much higher than these in February-March-April 1991 on Saturday nights at 7:00 P.M. Crowded so that fast walking not possible.
	4:43–4:53 P.M. Saturday, north side		469	10.4	
	5:27–5:32 P.M. Monday, south side		124	5.5	
	5:16–5:26 P.M. Monday, north side		383	8.5	
	5:43–5:48 P.M. Monday, south side		157	6.9	
	5:36–5:41 P.M. Monday, north side		249	11.1	
Via del Corso, Rome at Via Frattina, east side	June 1990 11:25–11:30 A.M. weekday	3.0 m.	202	13.5	Not possible to stay in walk; people walk in street; many different paces but not fast.
at Via Vittoria	11:39–11:44 A.M. weekday	5.5 m.	253	9.2	Walk not wide enough; people came in spurts; much window shopping; people walk around parked cars, further into street; perhaps 80% fewer walk on sunny side; many paces.
south of Via Condotti	5:30–5:35 P.M. Saturday	11 m.	650	11.8	No cars; surges where it's hard to count; leisure walking; fast pace possible near blank wall.
	6:20–6:25 P.M. Saturday	11 m.	678	12.3	
north of Via Condotti	5:40–5:45 P.M. Saturday	11 m.	707	12.9	Some cars, taxis, motorbikes; hard to count during rushes; leisurely and some fast walking.
	6:12–6:17 P.M. Saturday	11 m.	765	13.9	
	26 April 1986 6:32–6:37 P.M. Saturday	11 m.	830	15.1	Could have missed some people; possible to walk fast.
	12:00–12:10 P.M. Saturday	11 m.	537	4.9	Not busy.

Location	Date/Time	Width	Count	Rate	Description
Via dei Giubbonari, Rome	June 1990 8:00–8:05 P.M. Friday	6.7 m.	220	6.6	Some cars and motorbikes; most people walking fast, in one direction. No sense of crowding, maybe because of directional flow. Hard to walk fast against flow.
	26 April 1986 5:59–6:09 P.M. Saturday	5 m.	840	16.8	Crowded; must walk slowly; people in the way.
	April 1986 midday, 10 minutes	5 m.	377	7.5	Leisurely walking; can walk at any speed.
Maiden Lane, San Francisco, east of Union Square	23 December 1988 12:22–12:32 P.M.	11.2 m.	252	2.3	Most people on walks; never felt crowded; speed between slow stroll and purposeful walk.
	21 January 1989 1:25–1:35 P.M.	11.2 m.	140	1.2	Empty at times.
Market Street, San Francisco, at Powell Street	23 December 1988 1:00–1:10 P.M.	11.9 m.	1110	9.3	Purposeful walking; surges with traffic lights; only at peak of a light was walk too crowded for normal pace.
	21 January 1989 12:50–1:00 P.M.	11.9 m.	390	3.3	Never crowded.
Paseo de Gracia, Barcelona	May 1990 12:30–12:35 P.M. Monday	4.3 m.	188	8.8	Fast, purposeful walking, some strolling; waves due to traffic lights; generally uncrowded.
Post Street, San Francisco across from Gumps, at #251	21 December 1988 2:02–2:12 P.M.	5.2 m.	237	4.5	Purposeful walking; people in small groups; free movement.
	21 January 1989 1:25–1:35 P.M.	5.2 m.	126	2.4	Generally purposeful walking, people seem to have destination in mind.
at Gumps, #250	21 December 1988 2:18–2:28 P.M.	4.5 m.	417	9.3	Very crowded, often too crowded to move; police barriers in front of display windows.
at #555	21 December 1988 1:40–1:50 P.M. Thursday	4.8 m.	56	1.2	Purposeful walkers, mostly eastbound; not crowded.
Princess Street, Edinburgh	May 1990 2:15–2:20 P.M.	5.5 m.	310	11.3	Brisk walking pace; no dawdling; slight sense of crowding.
Ramblas, Barcelona	May 1990 5:15–5:20 P.M. Sunday	14 m.	240	3.4	Walking at all speeds; no sense of crowding, but a nice sense of people.
at Theatre Caputxins	5:00–5:05 P.M. Monday	7.3 m.	252	6.9	All paces; running would be hard; sense of many people but not of a rush or a jam.
	5:30–5:35 P.M.	7.3 m.	327	8.9	Some big surges; more crowded; pace a bit faster but not a big difference.
Regent Street, London north of Oxford Street	May 1990 11:15–11:20 A.M. Monday	5.5 m.	56	2.0	Any speed possible; most walking fast.
at Great Marlborough	11:45–11:50 A.M.	4.6 m.	190	8.3	Most walking fast; any speed possible; sense of many people, but not of congestion.
Strøget, Copenhagen at first intersection from east end	July 1990 12:25–12:30 P.M.	10 m.	653	13.1	Many strolling; some fast; big surges because of traffic light; many baby carriages; hard to walk fast continuously; blocked at times.
at Nikolaj Plads, Illums Department Store	12:45–12:50 P.M.	11 m.	792	14.4	Mostly strolling; some fast; some surges; a sense of crowded street but not unpleasantly so; people don't get in each other's way.

Notes _____

An Introduction to Great Streets

1. *Webster's New Collegiate Dictionary* (Springfield: G. and C. Merriam Co., 1974).

2. Marshall Berman, *All That Is Solid Melts into Air* (New York: Viking Penguin, 1988), 194, 215, 229.

3. Ibid., 193, and the whole chapter "Modernism in the Streets."

4. Carl E. Schorske, *Fin-de-Siècle Vienna: Politics and Culture* (New York: Vintage Books, 1981).

5. Response by Dolf Schnebli to a questionnaire in 1985.

Part One: Great Streets

1. William Roger Greeley, "Some Definitions: Names of Streets, Ways, etc.," *City Planning* 3, no. 2 (April 1927), 108.

2. *Webster's New Collegiate Dictionary* (Springfield: G. and C. Merriam Co., 1974).

3. François Loyer, *Paris Nineteenth Century: Architecture and Urbanism*, trans. Charles L. Clark (New York: Abbeville Press, 1988), 121.

4. Ibid., 113.

5. This large extension of Barcelona was laid out by Ildefons Cerda in 1859. Much of Madrid exhibits the same pattern. See David Mackay, *Modern Architecture in Barcelona (1854–1939)* (Sheffield: Anglo Catalan Society, 1985).

6. Jacques Hillairet, *Dictionnaire historique des rues de Paris*, vol. 2 (Paris: Editions de Minuit, 1963), 139.

7. The traffic engineer's usual answer to this question is, "They don't work."

8. For a discussion of Boulevard Sébastopol as well as many others, and of the buildings along them, see Loyer, *Paris Nineteenth Century*, 113–124, 233–237, 263–265.

9. Bernard Berenson, *The Passionate Sightseer* (London: Thames and Hudson, 1960, 1988), 54.

10. Stanley Milgrim, "Psychological Maps of Paris," in *Environmental Psychology: People and Their Physical Settings*, 2d ed., ed. Harold M. Proshansky et al. (New York: Holt, Rinehart and Winston, 1976), 104–124. In surveys by the author of pedestrians in San Francisco, more than any other street they note the Champs-Elysées as an example of a great world street.

11. See, for example, Alan Riding, "Patching Up a Boulevard's Broken Dream," *New York Times*, 17 January 1990, or "A Plan to Spruce Up the Champs-Elysées," *San Francisco Chronicle*, 11 January 1990.

12. Johann Wolfgang von Goethe, *Italian Journey*, trans. W. H. Auden and Elizabeth Mayer (San Francisco: North Point Press, 1982).

13. Of the retail and service stores listed in *Stradale: elenco guida del lavoro*, 1988/89, not including office uses, some 125 of 220 were clothing stores.

14. Loosely reported from long talks with Jack Kent, a native San Franciscan.

15. See, for example, Robert O'Brien, *This Is San Francisco* (New York: McGraw-Hill, 1948); William Bronson, *The Earth Shook, the Sky Burned* (Garden City: Doubleday, 1959); Lucius Beebe and Charles Clegg, *San Francisco's Golden Era* (Berkeley: Howell-North, 1960); Harold Gilliam, *The Face of San Francisco* (Garden City: Doubleday, 1960); Paul C. Johnson and Richard Reinhardt, *San Francisco: As It Was* (Garden City: Doubleday, 1979).

16. Laurie Olin, the noted landscape architect, put it this way in a discussion of the Ramblas with the author, and it is most apt.

17. Samuel Packard, "The Porticoes of Bologna," *Landscape* 27, no. 1 (1983), 19–29.

18. Discussions with Giuseppe Campos Venuti, the city planner of Bologna for many years and its leading light in post–World War II planning and development, provided much insight into his city.

Part Three: Street and City Patterns: Settings for Streets and People

1. See, for example, John Reps, *Cities of the American West* (Princeton: Princeton University Press, 1979).

2. For example, the 1980 Mission Bay Plan for an area of San Francisco's central waterfront is for an area covering 315 acres, or almost half a square mile. Much of Venice would fit into such an area. In Venice, in February 1991, a conference, "Cities on Water," was focused almost entirely on major projects the world over, many of them larger than the Mission Bay Plan.

3. For cities like Venice and Ahmedabad, it is not possible (at least for me and my colleagues) to draw some of the public ways as narrow as they really are and still have them read at a scale of 1 inch to 1,000 feet. So we used the smallest pen nibs we could find, understanding that this thinnest line is but a convention.

4. Mayor Larry Agran in a meeting with the author.

5. Anne Vernez Moudon, *Built for Change* (Cambridge: MIT Press, 1986).

6. At the time of the opening of the theater complex at the Barbican, an apt British Underground advertisement for the new season noted that it was a wonderful place and would be a wonderful season, "if you can find the entrance."

Part Four: Making Great Streets

1. Marshall Berman, *All That Is Solid Melts into Air* (New York: Viking Penguin, 1982), 196.

2. See John J. Fruin, *Pedestrian Planning and Design* (New York: Metropolitan Association of Urban Designers and Environmental Planners, Inc., 1971). "Level of service" descriptions, a phrase reminiscent of vehicle roadway levels of service used by traffic planners, are significantly different from field observations such as were carried out as part of these studies and are reported in the text.

3. The pedestrian data comes from field counts by the author (except for San Francisco counts by Kent E. Watson) as part of field studies of streets for this book. More complete information is given in the appendix.

4. See, for example, Donald Appleyard, *Livable Streets* (Berkeley: University of California Press, 1981), 248–251; Brenda Eubank-Ahrens, "A Closer Look at the Users of Woonerven," in *Public Streets for Public Use*, ed. Anne Vernez Moudon (New York: Van Nostrand Reinhold, 1987), 63–79; W. Homberger et al., *Residential Street Design and Traffic Control* (Englewood Cliffs: Prentice Hall, 1989), 49–78.

5. Edward Arens and Peter Bosselmann, "Wind, Sun and Temperature—Predicting the Thermal Comfort of People in Outdoor Spaces," *Building and Environment* 24, no. 4 (1989), 315–320; Peter Bosselmann et al., *Sun, Wind and Comfort* (Berkeley: Institute of Urban and Regional Development, University of California, Berkeley, 1984); and Peter Bosselmann, "Experiencing Downtown Streets in San Francisco," in Moudon, ed., *Public Streets for Public Use*, 203–220.

6. See, for example, W. H. Whyte, *The Social Life of Small Urban Spaces* (Washington, D.C.: Conservation Foundation, 1980). This finding has also been made repeatedly in studies on comfort by students in an environmental design research course at the University of California, Berkeley.

7. In June 1984, the voters of San Francisco adopted Proposition K, to provide year-round sunshine protection in parks and squares under the supervision of the Recreation and Parks Department. Section 146 of the San Francisco zoning ordinance addresses sunlight access to public sidewalks in the downtown, and Section 148 addresses wind.

8. Hans Blumenfeld, *The Modern Metropolis: Its Origins, Growth, Characteristics, and Planning*, ed. Paul D. Spreiregan (Cambridge: MIT Press, 1967).

9. Leon Battista Alberti, *Ten Books on Architecture*, trans. C. Bartoli and J. Leoni (New York: Transatlantic Arts, 1966); Andrea Palladio, *Four Books of Architecture* (New York: Dover Publications, 1965).

10. François Loyer, *Paris Nineteenth Century: Architecture and Urbanism*, trans. Charles L. Clark (New York: Abbeville Press, 1988), 121.

11. Blumenfeld, *The Modern Metropolis*, 216–234.

12. Ibid., 219.

13. James J. Gibson, *The Perception of the Visual World* (Boston: Houghton Mifflin, 1950).

14. See, for example, Richard Hedman with Andrew Jaszewski, *Fundamentals of Urban Design* (Washington, D.C.: Planners Press, American Planning Association, 1984).

15. In December 1990, Peter Bosselmann and I observed, photographed, and measured a number of streets in San Francisco in an effort to get more closely at this question of what it may take in building height relative to street width to achieve street definition. Before going into the field we had previously chosen a number of streets likely to have different cross-sectional characteristics: narrow streets or even alleys with moderate-sized buildings; typical San Francisco streets with low, moderate, and tall buildings; a variety of wider streets with a range of building heights; and some streets we remembered as very wide with low and moderately scaled buildings. We tried to choose streets without trees (or any significant plantings) and we wanted streets that were as level as possible. Some streets, in fact, had some slope; San Francisco is San Francisco after all. In all we visited 13 streets, and Market Street, with different characteristics depending on location, was measured at three places. The day was sunny and cool.

For each street at each location we first discussed whether or not there was a sense of definition. If there was strong definition we discussed how much lower buildings could be and still have a sense of definition. At each location we measured (by pacing) the width of the street as a whole and the distance to the far building wall from where we were standing (usually in the middle of a sidewalk, sometimes at a curb). We then took three to four photographs: directly up the street; at a slightly skewed angle toward a far point along the street; at a 30-degree angle (from straight ahead) to a point on the far side of the street; and perpendicular to the street. When it seemed relevant, particularly if there was a slope to the street, we did the same in the opposite direction. The photographs and measurements could then be related to the initial observations and tentative conclusions about the presence or absence of definition.

16. This phenomenon is discussed in Gibson, *The Perception of the Visual World*.

17. Ibid., 40, 155.

18. It may be, then, that streets with north-south orientation are in a better position to take advantage of light movements over a day, but on examination there is no apparent correlation between compass direction and great streets.

19. In a survey of approximately 100 people on San Francisco streets in 1989–1990, at four different locations, "cleanliness and good maintenance," and "smoothness and absence of potholes," were physical characteristics given second and third most often as most desirable to have on the best streets. Trees were the most frequently mentioned characteristic.

20. See note 19.

21. For example, *Street Tree Selection*, a study done for Howard Hughes Properties by the SWA group with Hanna/Olin Ltd. and Campbell and Campbell in 1988 for Playa Vista, Los Angeles; or *Green Streets*, prepared by the Urban Trees Design Group for the City of Oakland, California, 1981.

22. Though I am not an advocate of one tree or another, it seems to be the case that one or another variety of the London plane tree (*Platanus acerifolia*) is what is most found on streets.

23. The Oakland study, for example, goes to great imaginative lengths to rationalize why trees on major streets should be 44 feet or 66 feet apart based on the spacing of parking meters.

24. Henry James, "The Grand Canal," in Richard Harding Davis et al., *The Great Streets of the World* (London: McIlvaine and Co., 1892), 164–165.

25. Loyer, *Paris Nineteenth Century*, 312.

26. See, for example, my own notion of how to enliven Market Street in San Francisco, an idea inspired by statues in Rome: Allan B. Jacobs, "Gianicolo Busts," *Places* 5, no. 1 (1988), 57–59.

27. In these calculations an entry point is any public intersection, including those at the ends or beginnings of the streets.

28. Tom Aidala, in his letter-essay to the author commenting on what makes a great street, says: "Streets are great at some times of a day and not at others. For myself, any busy, well defined street that I experience under one set of circumstances—say, daytime—becomes when deserted, 3 AM to 4 AM, great. . . . I find those streets in those circumstances great because the experience of being alone where normally thousands move, of being so silent where normally chaos whirls about me, makes the experience great and so anything that is part of the experience, say the street, is great also."

29. Allan Jacobs and Donald Appleyard, "Toward a New Urban Design Manifesto," *Journal of the American Planning Association* 53, no. 1 (Winter 1987), 112–120.

30. J. Metzger and V. Dunker, *Der Kurfürstendamm* (Berlin: Konoplea, 1986).

31. For example, on the Ramblas, where thankfully the older lights also remain; or cobra head lighting for automobiles that have been added on many streets.

32. Ebenezer Howard, *Garden Cities of Tomorrow* (London: Faber and Faber, 1946; first published 1898); Le Corbusier, *The Athens Charter*, trans. Anthony Eardley (New York: Grossman, 1973; first published 1943, from a conference of 1933).

33. Clarence Stein, *Toward New Towns for America* (Liverpool: University Press of Liverpool, 1951). See particularly Sunnyside Gardens as compared to later designs, such as for Radburn, New Jersey, and Greenbelt, Maryland.

34. See, for example, the chapter on "Traffic" in the Athens Charter.

35. Jane Jacobs, *The Death and Life of Great American Cities* (New York: Random House, 1961).

36. For example, see Richard Sennett, *The Fall of Public Man* (New York: Alfred A. Knopf, 1974).

37. Kevin Lynch, *A Theory of Good City Form* (Cambridge: MIT Press, 1981).

38. Appleyard and Jacobs, "Toward a New Urban Design Manifesto."

Accessibility, 8, 11, 302–303

Access roads, 37, 46, 53, 78

Ahmedabad, 205, 258, 259, 261, 268

Aix-en-Provence, 45–46, 206
  Cours Mirabeau, 45–51, 294, 296, 299, 300, 301, 302, 307

Alberti, Leon Battista, 277

Amsterdam, 115, 184–187, 207, 255, 256, 257, 260, 283
  Achterburgwal, 184–186
  Looiersgracht, 184–185
  Prinsengracht, 185–186
  Reguliersgracht, 185
  Voorburgwal, 185

Ancient streets, 134, 136–137

Appleyard, Donald, 312

Arcades, 5, 115, 123–131, 276

Barcelona, 37, 93, 208–209, 255, 257, 259, 261, 267
  Gothic Quarter, 37, 93, 96, 261
  Paseo de Gracia, 37–44, 51, 208, 257, 273, 285, 289, 291, 296, 299, 300, 302, 306, 307
  Plaça de Catalunya, 37, 93, 273, 279, 280, 296
  Rambla de Catalunya, 146–147
  Ramblas, 37, 93–99, 148, 209, 258, 273, 283, 294, 295, 296, 300, 301, 303, 305, 306, 314, 315

Bari, 210, 255, 259, 267

Bath, England, 115–122, 211, 281, 288

Beginnings and endings, 21, 27, 37, 45, 67, 75, 80, 94, 100, 110, 112, 125, 152, 158, 162, 166, 192, 194, 295–297

Beijing, 113–114

Benches, 42, 48, 79, 146, 166, 168, 190, 195, 198, 300

Berenson, Bernard, 66–67

Berlin, 212–213
  Kurfürstendamm, 7, 158–161, 203, 299, 307
  Unter den Linden, 148–149

Berman, Marshall, 5, 6–7, 10, 272

Bern, 115, 123, 276

Block patterns. *See* City fabric

Blumenfeld, Hans, 278–281

Bologna, 5, 115, 123–131, 214–215, 255, 257, 259, 261, 267, 276
  Piazza di Porta Ravegnana area, 124, 125–131, 214, 296, 306

Boston, 11, 216, 256, 259, 260, 261, 263–266

Boulevards, 35–60, 75–79, 100–106, 110–112, 142–145, 158–161, 174–177, 257, 267

Brasília, 202, 217, 255, 258, 259, 260, 267, 311

Buildings. *See* Complementarity, of buildings; Detailing, architectural; Dimensions; Doorways; Windows

Buses. *See* Public transit; Traffic, vehicular

Cairo, 218, 255, 261, 268

Canaletto, Antonio, 63

Canals, 63–74, 115, 184–187, 257

Canberra, 258

Cellini, Benvenuto, 33

Central commercial streets, 152–165

Ceremonial space, streets as, 5

Chandigarh, 311

Change, historical, 6, 11, 19, 80, 88–89, 122, 129, 261–266, 307–308

Charter of Athens, 311

City Beautiful movement, 36, 92

City fabric, 5, 10–11, 27, 79, 80, 88, 96, 100, 115–131, 202–268

City planning, 35–36, 264–266, 303–304, 311–314. *See also* Regulation

Cleveland Heights
    Fairmount Boulevard, 100, 174–175, 281
    Roxboro and Tutor roads, 180–181, 281

Comfort, 8, 9, 27, 84, 96, 124, 274–276, 281, 293, 312, 313

Commercial uses, 4, 27, 33, 43, 48, 56–59, 77, 80–81, 95, 116, 122, 138, 140, 143, 146, 166, 168, 305. *See also* Central commercial streets

Community, streets as making, 8, 9, 11, 16–17, 107, 115, 122, 129, 144, 158, 182, 272, 297, 302, 313–314. *See also* Meeting places, streets as

Complementarity, of buildings, 42, 48, 56, 71–72, 94, 162, 287–289, 297, 313

Congrès Internationaux d'Architecture Moderne (CIAM), 267, 311

Copenhagen, 219, 255
    Helligåndskirke, 27, 30, 31
    Højbro Plads, 27, 28, 29, 33
    Kongens Nytorv, 27, 296

Strøget, 20–33, 258, 284, 285, 289, 293, 296, 300, 301, 302, 303, 306, 307, 314

Country roads, 107

Criteria of great streets, 8–10, 270–308

Curitiba, Brazil, 9

Definition, sense of, 15, 64, 65–66, 94, 143, 154, 184, 194, 277–281, 313

Density, 19, 96, 122, 182, 303–304

Detailing, architectural, 26, 42, 64, 74, 77, 89, 94, 96, 105, 118, 120, 155, 160, 162, 186, 283–285, 289

Dimensions
    of buildings, 21, 26, 42, 48, 71–72, 77, 80, 94, 103, 140, 146, 148, 150, 154, 160, 162, 166, 170, 173, 184, 186, 198, 281, 288
    of streets, 15, 20, 37, 46, 51–53, 56, 83–84, 110, 136–199, 278, 281, 304

Disneyland, 170–171

Diversity, 105–106, 297–298, 304

Doorways, 26, 27, 43, 94, 154, 166, 170, 286

Edinburgh, 194
    Princes Street, 2, 194–197

Expressways, 88, 256

Flexibility, 168

Florence, 220, 259

Fountains, 45, 46, 48, 50, 56, 296, 300

French street design, 5–6, 35

Garden city movement, 267, 311

Gaudí, Antonio, 41, 42, 289, 291, 299, 300

Gibson, James J., 281–282

Goethe, Johann Wolfgang von, 79

Gogol, Nikolai Vasilievich, 6, 272

Grids, 255, 257–258, 261

Guardi, Francesco, 63

Haussmann, Georges, 36, 277, 299

Herculaneum, 136–137, 259

Hong Kong, 282

Intersections, 37, 48, 53–55, 143–144, 161, 195, 202, 302

Irvine, California, 221–222, 255, 258, 259, 260–261, 266, 267, 268, 302

Jacobs, Jane, 312

James, Henry, 297

Jefferson, Thomas, 313–314

Julius II, pope, 36, 140

Land use, streets as, 6, 265–266, 267

Lindau, Paul, 148

Litchfield, Connecticut, 281

London, 223–224, 258, 260
   Barbican development, 267
   Piccadilly Circus, 2, 162, 258
   Regent Street, 2, 162–165, 258, 306

Los Angeles, 225–226, 255, 258, 259, 261, 267, 268

Loyer, François, 35

Lucca, 227, 255, 259, 267

Lynch, Kevin, 312

Madrid, 228, 255

Maertens, H., 278–281

Main streets (street type), 5, 138–141, 166–173

Maintenance, 92, 129, 142, 174, 289–291. *See also* Trees, maintenance

Medieval European streets, 20–34, 96, 123–131, 138–139

Meeting places, streets as, 4, 27, 33,125. *See also* Community, streets as making

Merritt Parkway, 2

Minneapolis, 100

Monuments, 45, 50, 100, 103, 104, 296

Moudon, Anne Vernez, 265

Mountain View, California
   Castro Street, 168–169

Movement, 4, 63, 74, 282–283. *See also* Sunlight and shadow

Nash, John, 164

New Delhi, 229–230

New Orleans, 115
   St. Charles Avenue, 100, 115

New York, 230–231, 255, 258, 259, 260–261
   Avenue of the Americas, 2, 284
   Broadway, 258
   Fifth Avenue, 2, 198–199, 288, 300
   Park Avenue, 258
   Trump Tower, 2, 298

Oakland, 233, 257, 259
   Mills College for Women, 107–110, 283, 294, 296, 302

Ohio Turnpike, 2

Olin, Laurie, 96

One-sided streets, 194–199

Open space, 4
Orientation, 257–258
Ostia Antica, 136–137

Palladio, Andrea, 277
Palm Beach, Florida
    Palm Beach Boulevard, 294
    Royal Palm Way, 192–193
Parades, 78, 85, 152
Paris, 36, 234–235, 255, 257, 259,
        260, 267, 288
    Arc de Triomphe, 75, 296
    Avenue des Champs-Elysées,
        36, 37, 51, 75–79, 190–191,
        203, 234, 258, 279, 283, 296,
        299, 306, 307
    Avenue Montaigne, 51–55, 283,
        294, 300, 302, 306
    Boulevard Saint-Germain, 59,
        60
    Boulevard Saint-Michel, 2, 56–
        60, 77, 276, 283, 285, 286,
        289, 296, 300, 302, 307
    Boulevard Sébastopol, 56
    La Défense, 290
    Sorbonne, 60
Parking, 17, 33, 37, 78, 79, 155,
        161, 168, 182, 186, 293, 305–
        306
Parks, 143, 195, 198
Pasadena
    Colorado Boulevard, 286, 306
    Orange Grove Boulevard, 100,
        176–177, 299
Paving materials, 19, 32, 41, 89,
        92, 98, 104, 110, 140, 174,
        186, 188, 190, 195, 198, 291,
        300
Pedestrian volume, 273, 316–317
Philadelphia, 100, 236

Phoenix, 255, 258
Pittsburgh
    Roslyn Place, 2, 14–19, 182,
        281, 283, 288, 289, 295, 297,
        302, 303, 306, 307, 310, 311
Plazas, 27, 67, 84, 89, 92, 138,
        143, 154, 274, 301–302
Political space, streets as, 5
Pompeii, 136–137, 237, 259
Porticoes. See Arcades
Portland, Oregon, 238, 258, 261,
        267
Proportions, of streets, 21, 83,
        277–281
Public transit, 19, 32, 37, 53, 56,
        82, 85, 88–89, 92, 144, 152,
        170, 195
Puig i Cadafalch, Josep, 42

Rasmussen, Steen Eiler, 164
Redevelopment, 36, 202, 264–266
Regulation, 17, 129, 150
Residential streets, 15–19, 100–106,
        116–122, 174–187, 281, 286
Richmond, Virginia, 100, 239, 261
    Fan District, 100, 102
    Monument Avenue, 100–106,
        279, 280, 283, 288, 294, 301,
        302, 305, 306, 307
Rio de Janeiro
    Botanical Gardens, 188–189
Rome, 35, 240, 255, 257, 259, 260
    Borgo Pio, 166–167
    Campo dei Fiori, 25, 27, 33
    Piazza Colonna, 80, 84
    Piazza del Popolo, 4, 80, 81, 82–
        83, 84, 154, 255, 257, 296
    Piazza Venezia, 80, 83, 84
    Via Arenula, 4, 32, 33

Rome (*continued*)
    Via Cola di Rienzo, 154–157,
        283–284, 295, 299
    Via Condotti, 80, 81, 84
    Via dei Coronari, 138–139, 301
    Via dei Giubbonari, 10, 20–34,
        203, 273, 275, 279, 281, 289,
        296, 301, 302, 303, 305, 306,
        307, 314
    Via dei Greci, 83, 281
    Via del Corso, 4, 79–84, 203,
        273, 281, 296, 299
    Via di Ripetta, 36, 80
    Via Giulia, 36, 138, 140–141
    Viale delle Terme di Caracalla,
        110–112, 294, 296, 302
    Viale Manlio Gelsomini, 294

Safety, 8–9, 15
St. Petersburg
    Nevsky Prospekt, 4, 5, 10, 272
San Francisco, 115, 241–242, 255,
        256, 257, 258, 259, 260, 261,
        265, 268, 274, 276, 285, 305
    Bank of America Building, 274
    Civic Center Plaza, 92
    Ferry Building, 85, 88, 92
    Golden Gate Avenue, 274
    Hallidie Plaza, 88, 92
    Justin Herman Plaza, 92
    Market Street, 2, 4, 5, 85–92,
        241, 257, 274, 284, 291, 300,
        301, 307
    Mechanics Monument, 92
    Twin Peaks, 88
    Van Ness Avenue, viii
    Zellerbach Building, 85
San Jose, California, 299
San Juan, Puerto Rico, 300
Santa Monica, California, 243,
        255, 258

Sargent, John Singer, 63
Savannah, Georgia, 115, 244, 255,
        256, 257, 261
Scale, 258, 259–266, 268, 278, 313
Schnebli, Dolf, 7
Schorske, Carl, 7
Seoul, 245, 255, 261, 268
Setagaya, Japan
    Yohga Promenade, 178–179
Sidewalks, 41, 43, 46, 56–59, 78–
        79, 89, 161, 168, 174, 198,
        273
Sitte, Camillo, 7
Skyscrapers, 2, 87, 89, 274
Stores. *See* Commercial uses
Streetlights, 41–42, 79, 98, 99, 104,
        138, 144, 146, 148, 155, 160,
        161, 166, 176, 190, 298, 299
Sunlight and shadow, 4, 48, 56,
        57–60, 63, 65, 74, 83, 95, 96,
        150, 274–276, 281, 282–283
Sydney, Paddington area, 136,
        182–183

Tokyo, 248, 256, 261
Topography, natural, 256, 305
Toulouse, 246–247, 267
Traffic, vehicular, 15, 32, 33, 46,
        53–55, 75, 84, 105, 110, 113,
        143, 144, 155, 160–161, 162,
        190, 198, 271, 272–273, 283,
        293, 294–295, 302
Transparency, sense of, in
        buildings, 16, 21, 43, 83, 94,
        118, 140, 143, 285–287, 313
Trees, 15, 48, 57, 79, 89, 95, 96,
        103–104, 148, 158, 160, 195,
        198, 273, 280, 282–283, 293–
        295
    maintenance, 75, 78, 174, 176,
        295

planting patterns, 37, 41, 48, 53, 57, 78, 79, 96, 104, 109–110, 113, 144, 146, 148, 155, 160, 174, 176, 180, 186, 188, 190, 192, 195, 294–295

tree streets, 107–114, 188–193

varieties, 15, 37, 48, 53, 57, 75, 79, 95, 96, 103, 107, 109, 110, 148, 155, 160, 174, 176, 188, 190, 192, 294

Turner, John Mallord William, 63

Venice, 62–74, 202, 249, 255, 259, 260–261, 287

Accademia, 67, 68

Giudecca, 277, 278

Grand Canal, 62–74, 203, 257, 258, 285, 288, 289, 297, 300, 301, 302, 303, 304, 305

Murano, 71

Piazza San Marco, 63, 67, 68, 300, 301

Rialto, 63, 65, 67, 68, 69, 73

Strada Nuova, 71, 172–173

Vicenza, 115, 276

Vienna, 250

Ringstrasse, 7, 142–145, 203, 294, 305

Views, 37, 75, 78, 80, 82–83, 88, 118, 174, 195, 197

Wagner, Otto, 7, 143

Walnut Creek, California, 251, 255, 258

Washington, D.C., 252, 255

Massachusetts Avenue, 100

Water streets. *See* Canals

Whistler, James Abbott McNeill, 63

Wind, 274–276, 281

Windows, 19, 21, 33, 42, 43, 65–66, 77, 83, 84, 89, 118, 154, 198, 284, 285–286

Woods, John, 120

Yokohama

Motomachi, 150–151

Zurich, 253–254, 256, 259, 260, 261

Bahnhofstrasse, 152–153, 203